M000159697

THE OPENING OF
THE AMERICAN MIND

THE OPENING OF THE AMERICAN MIND

TEN YEARS OF

THE UNIVERSITY OF CHICAGO PRESS

CHICAGO AND LONDON

The University of Chicago Press, Chicago 60637
The University of Chicago Press, Ltd., London
© 2020 by The University of Chicago
All rights reserved. No part of this book may be used or
reproduced in any manner whatsoever without written
permission, except in the case of brief quotations in critical
articles and reviews. For more information, contact the
University of Chicago Press, 1427 E. 60th St., Chicago, IL 60637.
Published 2020
Printed in the United States of America

29 28 27 26 25 24 23 22 21 20   1 2 3 4 5

ISBN-13: 978-0-226-73580-1 (cloth)
ISBN-13: 978-0-226-73871-0 (paper)
ISBN-13: 978-0-226-73885-7 (e-book)
DOI: https://doi.org/10.7208/chicago/9780226738857.001.0001

Library of Congress Cataloging-in-Publication Data

Title: The opening of the American mind : ten years of the Point.
Other titles: Point (Chicago, Ill.)
Description: Chicago : The University of Chicago Press, 2020.
Identifiers: LCCN 2020026852 | ISBN 9780226735801 (cloth) | ISBN 9780226738710
(paperback) | ISBN 9780226738857 (ebook)
Subjects: LCSH: Philosophy, American—21st century. | Philosophy, Modern—
21st century.
Classification: LCC B946 .O64 2020 | DDC 191—dc23
LC record available at https://lccn.loc.gov/2020026852

♾ This paper meets the requirements of ANSI/NISO Z39.48-1992
(Permanence of Paper).

Contents

•

TIRED OF WINNING

•

•

THINKING AHEAD

•

Introduction

by Jon Baskin & Anastasia Berg

Written more than thirty years ago on the same University of Chicago campus where we would launch *The Point* in 2009, Allan Bloom's *The Closing of the American Mind: How Higher Education Has Failed Democracy and Impoverished the Souls of Today's Students* set off a raucous and often rancorous debate about the state of higher education. At its heart was the allegation that a new nihilism was gaining ground on America's elite campuses. The culprit was an egalitarian relativism—the new "education of openness"—that persuaded the nation's best college students it was immoral and probably impossible to make meaningful judgments about different cultures, life choices or ideas of the good. As they mouthed the slogans of diversity and tolerance, Bloom believed, his university colleagues were undermining the traditional basis of humanistic education— the "search for a good life." "True openness," as Bloom saw it, was inextricably linked to the "possibility of knowing good and bad." Thus what was advertised as a "great opening" was in fact a "great closing."

Reading *Closing* today, at a time when the "crisis of the humanities" consists less in high-minded debates about the viability of moral philosophy than in a daily drumbeat of apprehension about falling enrollments, the digitization of academic life and the corporate restructuring of the university—all likely to be exacerbated by the public health crisis that swept the country as we were completing this introduction—it can be tempting to dismiss Bloom's concerns as anachronistic. To be sure, there have been threats to higher education in the ensuing years that Bloom did not fully anticipate or even envision—threats that have little to do with relativism or egalitarianism. Yet it would be foolish for us to deny that these threats have been aided and abetted by many of the trends that Bloom was among the earliest and most articulate to discern. Bloom foresaw, more vividly than many of his contemporaries—or ours—the fate awaiting humanities departments that neglected to address the fundamental questions: Is there a God? Is there freedom? Is there punishment for evil deeds? Is there certain knowledge? What is a good society? How should I live? These were the questions that had always attracted the brightest students to the humanities, Bloom observed. What did professors expect to happen when they informed those students that the texts humanists had consulted for answers for millennia were nothing more than vectors of ideology and oppression? Who could blame them for transferring into economics or computer science—as so many now have?

At a time when scholars are habitually asked to account for the "value" of the humanities—whether to our economy, our political life or our attempts at therapeutic self-improvement—there is much to be learned from Bloom's insight that what some pejoratively label the "elitism" of the traditional humanities was in fact their greatest strength. Bloom recognized that if the humanities relinquished their role as the steward of the great conversation, they risked relinquishing much more than that. Like many of the thinkers he asked his students to grapple with, he was highly sensitive to the vulnerability of intellectual life to technocracy, greed, materialism and an immoderate individualism. If the university did not continue to be valued above all for its capacity to introduce America's most privileged students to a robust dialogue—in its full grandeur and even occasionally in its arrogance—about the virtuous life and the just society, he had little doubt about what other masters it might serve.

Bloom's pessimism about the humanities has been vindicated not only by shrinking enrollments but also by the almost complete disappearance of the assumption that the humanities can offer guidance on how to live. Paradoxically, it is this very development that reveals the true folly of Bloom's argument in *Closing*: not his contention that humanities departments should address the fundamental human questions but his conviction that such questions could be addressed *only* within the confines of academia. The founders of *The Point* came to the University of Chicago, to the very same graduate program Bloom once led, in part because we shared his confidence that the humanities could speak to our most urgent personal, philosophical and political concerns. But the impetus behind *The Point* ran counter to Bloom's restrictive account of who was qualified to participate in the conversation of culture. Indeed, our decision to start a magazine—a resolutely nonacademic forum for the exchange of ideas, interpretations and interests—followed from our rejection of any notion that the "souls of today" were dependent for their salvation on higher education.

Bloom, who spent his career teaching at the University of Chicago and Cornell, despaired of any "general reform" in society. He wrote for "a few, the true friends" of philosophy, who also happened to be students at "the twenty or thirty best universities." When he was promoting *Closing*, he spoke repeatedly about the "four years of freedom" enjoyed by these students, a "charmed" period that fell "between the intellectual wasteland" of the student's family life and the "inevitable dreary professional training that awaits him after the baccalaureate." In such statements, rather than in his defense of the great books or his concern about relativism, Bloom reveals the dark side of his elitism. In theory, Bloom stood for the dignity of the different ways of life that were investigated in the great tradition; in practice, he was repulsed by the ways of life that differed markedly from his own. Beyond the university walls, he believed, lay a brown fog within which crowds flowed somnolently from birth to the office to death. At best, his elite students, having been exposed for four years to something higher, could get their listless compatriots to shuffle in the right direction. That the opening of the American mind might involve opening oneself to America—the actual as opposed to some ideal America—in addition to instructing it does not seem ever to have occurred to him.

The Point was not conceived with Bloom's project in mind. But his one-way approach to intellectual "dialogue," if perhaps predictable coming from a cultural conservative, is worth recounting here in part because we believe it describes a broader tendency to which the magazine has always been opposed. Skepticism about the ability of the public to think, whether based in a belief in natural inequality, or in the ideological mystifications of religious faith or consumer capitalism, is a perennial theme across our political spectrum. Among today's leftist and liberal intellectuals, many who reject elitism toward the public in the strongest possible terms in theory seem unable to help recapitulating it in practice. In their insistence on monitoring what counts as acceptable public discourse, on "correcting" their fellow citizens' faulty ideas and on reducing intellectual life to a "war of position" in which they play the role of enlightened vanguard, they betray their own contempt for actually existing democracy. Those who endorse Hillary Clinton's judgment of the "irredeemable" prejudices of large portions of the American public—no matter how politely or privately—can hardly claim to distinguish themselves from Bloom's conviction of that public's irredeemable thoughtlessness. In fact, both attitudes are a manifestation of thoughtlessness—the thoughtlessness regarding one's own inevitable ignorance that is always most tempting to the intellectual. The progressive commentator is unlikely to speak in such reverent terms as Bloom about the university's responsibility to tutor the public, yet they are no less likely to conceive of the office of public intellectual as one of permanent lecturer.

The goal of *The Point*, in contrast to all those who show contempt, purposefully or not, for the nonacademic public, has never been to reform, protect or otherwise project the virtues of the university. For us, "true openness" dictates a converse movement, one that does not culminate with the minds of college students, no matter how closed or coddled. It means leaving the library stacks—and every other enclave of settled opinion—and confronting the pandemonium of the American mind in its multiple manifestations: in contemplation and reading but also at work and at home, in love, in protest and at play. "You think your pain and your heartbreak are unprecedented in the history of the world, but then you read," said

James Baldwin, describing the first half of a movement that we turn to Thoreau to complete: "A truly good book . . . is so true that it teaches me better than to read it. I must soon lay it down and commence living on its hint." The American mind we admire and have encouraged to express itself in our pages is not a mind bred in isolation to rule or instruct its fellow citizens but one driven out into the world by its curiosity. It is a mind that wants to understand, not only the contest of ideas as they have been explicated in great books, but also the drama of social and personal life in which we try to test those ideas against our own experience.

When we ask ourselves what to eat, where to work, how to vote, whom to love or what to worship, we are immediately cast into philosophy. Whether or not we have had our "four years of freedom" at a great university, we will be compelled to make arguments to ourselves in response to these questions, and the answers we arrive at will take the shape of our lives. But these lives take place in a shared world, alongside family, friends and fellow citizens who will arrive at their own answers, often sharply at odds with our own. To acknowledge this is to recognize the fact not of relativism but of pluralism. Pluralism does not release the individual from the responsibility to choose or to judge, because it does not assert that all choices are equal, or that judgments of good and bad are futile. It does demand that we make our choices and judgments with humility, in recognition of the fact that other choices and judgments are both possible and defensible.

Just as there is no escaping the burden of making our own choices, so is there no escaping living with the choices these others make. We do have a choice about *how* to live with them. We can do so grudgingly, tolerating the differences of our fellow citizens out of prudence or fear, or simply because we see no alternative. In such cases, we harbor the secret hope that one day we will bring them all over to our way of thinking. This was Bloom's hope—at least for the portion of the population that he considered up to it—just as it is the hope of all those today who see the job of the public intellectual as one primarily of correction and condemnation. Such a hope is plainly incompatible with the imperatives of true openness, not to mention with the character—insofar as one can be discerned—of the "American mind." For it denies precisely what American intellect has always stood for at its best: the faith that there is no canon capacious enough to encompass the full breadth of our experiences, no principles so authoritative that they can trump our collective testimony.

There is another choice as to how to confront the fact of pluralism—that is, of living with people who hold views that are alien and sometimes repellent to us. In her lectures on the life of the mind, Hannah Arendt, another former professor at the University of Chicago, points out that Socrates, in speaking to Athenians who were shopping in the marketplace, on their way to war or tending to their gardens, intended in the first place not to instruct his fellow citizens but to learn together with them how best to live. For those who looked on—often the future leaders of Athens, the kind of elite youths who would be students at top universities today—what he modeled in these dialogues was not any special knowledge or vocabulary; still less did he sanction the appeal to tradition or convention. What he modeled, rather, was the "soundless solitary dialogue we call 'thinking,'" an activity that "is not a prerogative of the few but an ever-present faculty in everybody." Indeed, according to Arendt, Socrates demonstrated that thinking was only apparently solitary. Thinking would be impossible if it did not involve voices other than one's own, including the voices of those who were not in the academy and had no desire to wall themselves off in it. True openness followed from truly democratic pluralism. Only through dialogue with our fellow citizens—only by continuously opening ourselves to their criticism, instruction and difference—can we credibly claim to maintain an open mind.

•

Whereas *The Closing of the American Mind* was a polemic on behalf of Bloom's idea of true openness, *The Opening of the American Mind* seeks to offer a demonstration of ours. *The Point* was launched on the South Side of Chicago in January 2009, the same month that a brilliant and charismatic former law professor was sworn in as the forty-fourth president of the United States. As graduate students at the time, the founders of the magazine had benefited from being protected, to some extent, from the realities of daily life in America at the tail end of the Bush presidency and the beginning of the financial crisis. But with Obama's election we could sense, in the city and the country, the beginning of a renewed conversation about who we were and what we wanted. However much we valued our reading and our seminar discussions, this was a conversation to which we believed we could contribute, and from which we did not want to be protected.

This book tells the story, through the essays in the magazine that best capture the spirit of their time in thought, of the decade that followed. It is also an argument about how to tell that story. To create a public space that could do justice to the adventure of the American mind—in its full diversity and vitality—meant allowing our writers to go wherever their experience would take them. It meant publishing liberals and conservatives, philosophers and activists, Marxists and Catholics, New Yorkers and Midwesterners. And it meant continuously asking our writers not to relinquish their convictions but to trust that they were strong enough to withstand intelligent questioning and criticism. What emerges is, perhaps surprisingly, not a series of incongruous portraits. Still less is this collection an ode to centrism, compromise or consensus. What emerges, rather, is a prehistory of our present moment, wherein the distinctive individual perspectives combine to bring the disparate and at times disorienting events of the past ten years into focus.

Given the role that Obama's ascendancy played in the genesis of the magazine, it is ironic that the first part of this book, drawn from the early years of *The Point*, is one of the grimmest. Although there are glimmers of Obama-fueled optimism in these early essays, they are predominantly a record of a country lurching into an existential cul-de-sac. In "Predatory Habits," published in 2010 in our second issue, Etay Zwick looks at the financial crisis through the lens of sociologist Thorstein Veblen's distinction between "productive" and "barbarian" societies. In pointing out how the mores of the barbarian financier had come to define an entire way of life—and not only for bankers—Zwick sets the template for the next two essays, which trace analogous developments in American social and political life. In Ben Jeffery's "Hard Feelings," an essay about the French author Michel Houellebecq's brutalist portrayal of the late-capitalist sexual marketplace, the term "depressive realism" is coined to characterize the only form of literature capable of capturing a social reality where "the news might simply be bad." In "No Such Thing?," inspired by the death of Margaret Thatcher, Jonny Thakkar grapples with the paradox that "in raging against Thatcher, our generation is, among other things, raging against the forces that shaped us—but rage as we might, they did still shape us, and they continue to do so."

Only in the final essay of this part do we begin to glimpse the promise of a politics that might respond to, rather than merely reflect, the ambient atmosphere of foreboding. In 1989, the political philosopher Francis Fukuyama delivered his famous "end of history" speech, predicting that with the fall of Soviet socialism there were destined to be no more viable challengers to "economic and political liberalism." In the ensuing years, critics on the left and right ridiculed Fukuyama's thesis, but, as Daniel Luban argues in "Forward with Fukuyama," it was still not clear, in 2015, that a serious ideological alternative to liberal democracy had emerged, either in America or internationally. Yet Luban, writing four years after Occupy Wall Street in the midst of an unprecedented effort, in his adopted city of Chicago, to privatize what had previously been seen as core functions of the liberal state, sees reason to doubt that Fukuyama's framework will prove as durable going forward. "We still lack the vocabulary to describe what is happening around us," Luban concludes, "but perhaps this very lack is a sign that the end of history will not last forever."

It has become fashionable to speak of the post-Occupy period as representing a new beginning for history, but the abstraction can obscure as much as it illuminates. What did it feel and sound like, in that historical moment, for people to begin to chart a new way forward? For the second part of the book, "After Ferguson," we have chosen essays that address that question from the perspective of emergent activist movements around issues of class, gender and especially race. These pieces both reflect and interrogate the claim made by Cornel West that Ferguson signified "the end of the Age of Obama." In "Linked Fate," Melina Abdullah recounts the "groundswell of rage and pain" that overtook her community in the wake of the acquittal of George Zimmerman in the Trayvon Martin shooting, alerting her as a black woman to the "brutality of state systems meant to disrupt our families and criminalize our very existence." As she traces the opening days of the Black Lives Matter movement in Los Angeles, Abdullah anticipates both the visceral personal engagement and the wider communitarian impulse that would characterize the upsurge in left-wing activism during Obama's second term. In "Who Will Pay Reparations on My Soul?" and "After Ferguson," Jesse McCarthy and Brandon Terry combine their personal experiences with historical and philosophical perspectives on the burgeoning movement, asking questions that remain relevant today about its relationship to the civil rights movement and the German experiment with reparations—as well as what it will take to leverage early "gestures of recognition," as Terry puts it, into "concrete victories and the enduring exercise of responsible political power."

Of course, not all the radical movements that had their origins in the second Obama term were progressive, and even as progressives pushed for a more complete equality, a countervailing set of forces began to appear on the political stage, one that wished not to advance the values of liberalism but to break free from them. "Final Fantasy," the third part of *Opening*, includes writing from the immediate aftermath of the Trump election. Following the election, there was a surge of concern in mainstream media for the "strangers in their own land"—to quote the title of the sociologist Arlie Hochschild's popular book on Tea Party conservatives in Louisiana—who had cast their votes for Trump. But much of this writing seemed to regard the developments as occurring at a safe distance from, or even confirming, the pieties of right-thinking liberals. In "Letter on Our President," written by the *Point* editors, we caution against the temptation of dissociation, recommending that we recognize Trump as "a product of forces and feelings with deep roots in both our history and ourselves." In James Duesterberg's "Final Fantasy" and Kathryn Lofton's "Understanding Is Dangerous," the authors likewise challenge liberal common sense, asking us to consider the full reality and promise of alternative political, cultural and spiritual ideals. What would it mean if the people who were most forcefully committed to restarting history were the ones generally considered to be on the wrong side of it?

In the fourth part of the book we ask what help intellectuals can offer—if any!—during a period of such dramatic national discord. Drawing largely from the magazine's issue 16 symposium, "What Are Intellectuals For?," the essays in this part speak to the questions faced by public intellectuals in the Trump era. How do we balance the call to "resist" with our responsibility as thinkers? How can we create a space for genuine dialogue in a media landscape polarized by the dynamics of us versus them? How, in an increasingly politicized culture, do we do justice to the ongoing importance of aesthetic, spiritual and personal values? From Jon Baskin's "Tired of Winning" to Anastasia Berg's "I Am Madame Bovary" to Rachel Wiseman's "Switching Off," the essays in this part strive to articulate some of the deepest commitments we have always tried to uphold at *The Point*: that intellectuals have a responsibility to consider the truth embodied in perspectives other than their own; that we are part of the public we write for, and therefore do not lecture to it; and that our social and political commitments are strengthened, rather than compromised, by the adventure of genuine dialogue.

In our final part, entitled "Thinking Ahead," we've collected the essays from the past two years that most successfully think beyond the calamities of the present. How might we build on the revelations around #MeToo, the renewed attention to reparations that has followed from the Black Lives Matter movement and the increasingly explicit disenchantment with neoliberal economics—aggravated into desperation by the pandemic and the ensuing economic turmoil? How can we conceive of America's role abroad while avoiding the twin pitfalls of cynicism and naivete? And how can we continue to think beyond the present moment when so much of our current experience is framed in the rubric of crisis? These essays are not programmatic; they do not tell us which policies or ideologies to embrace or express any certainty about how the world will look in the aftermath of the 2020 election or of COVID-19. But they do ask us to expand our imaginations in ways we might not have dared back in 2009. They encourage us to liberate ourselves, to quote John Michael Colón's provocative title, from the "dictatorship of the present"— and to ask ourselves, as Nora Caplan-Bricker does, "What comes next?" "These are not the end times," Justin E. H. Smith observes in his dispatch from New York, in the opening days of the quarantine, but we might welcome the possibility of their bringing an end to some things. "Any fashion, sensibility, ideology, set of priorities, worldview or hobby that you acquired prior to March 2020," Smith writes, "you are no longer beholden to it. You can cast it off entirely and no one will care; likely, no one will notice."

Famously, at the end of his end of history speech in 1989, Fukuyama indicated that life in the forthcoming age would be "very boring." His prediction of the cessation of ideological struggle shares a family resemblance with Bloom's concern about democratic relativism, which he worried was causing his students to lose interest in the struggle to live virtuously as opposed to comfortably. Whatever the value of such insights for understanding their own period, the essays in these pages suggest that they are ultimately unsuitable for coming to terms with the events of our own. They offer undeniable evidence not only of the dissatisfaction bred by the perversely unequal distribution of resources and recognition under end-of-history liberal capitalism but also of the obstinacy of our desire to find greater meaning and purpose in our social lives. At the same time, and increasingly as they move closer to the present, they take note of a new set of challenges, characteristic of any age in which passivity gives way to passion. The danger to today's American mind, it seems, is not that it will close itself to judgments of good and bad but that it will close itself to the possibility of meaningful disagreement about those judgments.

In allowing their impressions, experiences and ideas to be set beside one another, the writers in this collection signal their opposition to the prevailing assumption that political commitment is incompatible with a desire for dialogue, self-reflection or self-criticism. They remind us that, just as there are no alternative facts, so are there no alternative worlds. There are only the fantasy worlds in which we isolate ourselves, and the real one we all share, whose story we can only tell together.

I
THE END OF
THE END OF HISTORY

Predatory Habits

HOW WALL STREET
TRANSFORMED WORK IN AMERICA

by Etay Zwick

ISSUE 2 | WINTER 2010

More than a century ago, Thorstein Veblen—American economist, sociologist and social critic—warned that the United States had developed a bizarre and debilitating network of social habits and economic institutions. Ascendant financial practices benefited a limited group at the expense of the greater society; yet paradoxically Americans deemed these practices necessary, even commendable. Far from lambasting the financiers plundering the nation's resources, we lauded them as the finest members of society. Their instincts, wisdom and savoir faire were idealized, their avarice and chicanery promoted under the banners of patriotism and virtue.

Veblen, an inveterate reader of ethnographies, noticed a historical pattern that could illuminate America's peculiar relationship with its economic institutions. Societies everywhere fall between two extremes. First, there are societies in which every person works, and no one is demeaned by his or her toil. In these societies, individuals pride themselves on their workmanship, and they exhibit a natural concern for the welfare of their entire community. As examples of such "productive" societies, Veblen mentions Native Americans, the Ainus of Japan, the Todas of the Nilgiri hills and the bushmen of Australia. Second, there are "barbarian" societies, in which a single dominant class (usually of warriors) seizes the wealth and produce of others through force or fraud—think ancient Vikings, Japanese shoguns and Polynesian tribesmen. Farmers labor for their livelihood and warriors expropriate the fruits of that labor. Exploitative elites take no part in the actual production of wealth; they live off the toil of others. Yet far from being judged criminal or indolent, they are revered by the rest of the community. In barbarian societies, nothing is as manly, as venerated, as envied, as the lives of warriors. Their every trait—their predatory practices, their dress, their sport, their gait, their speech—is held in high esteem by all.

Our world falls into the latter form. There remains a class that pillages, seizes and exploits in broad daylight—and with our envious approval. Who are the barbarian warriors today? According to Veblen, the modern barbarians live on Wall Street. They are the financiers summarily praised for their versatility, intelligence and courage in the face of an increasingly mysterious economy. Today a growing number of Americans feel at risk of economic despair; in a world of unsatisfying professional options and constant financial insecurity, the image of Wall Street life offers a sort of relief. It symbolizes the success possible in the modern world.

But in order to capitalize mortgage securities, expected future earnings and corporate debts, Wall Street elites must first capitalize on our personal insecurities. They make their exploits appear necessary, natural, even laudable. This is quite a feat, since in those moments when we suspend our faith in the financial sector and candidly examine its performance, we generally judge Wall Street's behavior to be avaricious and destabilizing, immoral and imprudent. At the best of times, Wall Street provides white noise amidst entrepreneurs' and workers' attempts to actualize their ambitions and projects. We are still learning what happens at the worst of times.

THE MYTH OF FINANCE

The myth of the financial sector goes something like this: only men and women equipped with the highest intelligence, the will to work death-defying hours and the most advanced technology can be entrusted with the sacred and mysterious task of ensuring the growth of the economy. Using complicated financial instruments, these elites (a) spread the risks involved in different ventures and (b) discipline firms to minimize costs—thus guaranteeing the best investments are extended sufficient credit. According to this myth, Wall Street is the economy's private nutritionist, advising and assisting only the most motivated firms—and these fitter firms will provide jobs and pave the path to national prosperity. If the rest of us do not understand exactly why trading credit derivatives and commodity futures would achieve all this, this is because we are not as smart as the people working on Wall Street. Even Wall Street elites are happy to admit that they do not really know how the system works; such admissions only testify to the immensity of their noble task.

Many economists have tried to disabuse us of this myth. Twenty-five years before the recent financial crisis, Nobel laureate James Tobin demonstrated that a very limited percentage of the capital flow originating on Wall Street goes toward financing "real investments"—that is, investments in improving a firm's production process. When large American corporations invest in new technology, they rely primarily on internal funds, not outside credit. The torrents of capital we see on Wall Street are devoted to a different purpose—speculation, gambling for capital gains. Finance's second founding myth, that the stock market in particular is an "efficient" source for funding business ventures, simply doesn't cohere with the history of American industrial development. When firms have needed to raise outside capital, they have generally issued debt—not stock. The stock market's chief virtue has always been that it allows business elites to cash out of any enterprise by transferring ownership to other elites. Old owners then enjoy their new wealth, while new owners manage the same old corporation. The reality is that business elites promote the stock market far more than the stock market promotes economic growth.

Rather than foster growth, contemporary financial practices have primarily succeeded in exacerbating income inequality and creating singular forms of economic calamity. In the recent crisis, new instruments for expanding financial activity—justified at the time by reckless promises of universal homeownership—prompted a remarkable spiral of poverty, debt and downward mobility in America. The path from homeownership to homelessness, from apparent wealth and security to lack of basic shelter, is completely novel—as is the now steadily growing social group of "middle-class paupers." (An estimated 10 percent of homeless people assisted by social service agencies last year lost their homes through bank foreclosures, according to the study "Foreclosure to Homelessness 2009.") The homeless-through-foreclosure, having been persuaded by cheap credit to aspire to homeownership, were punished for unbefitting ambitions; any future pathway out of debt will be accompanied by new insecurities about the appropriateness of their life aspirations. Also novel in recent years is the extent to which economic "booms" no longer benefit average Americans. During the last economic "expansion" (between 2002 and 2007), fully two-thirds of all income gains flowed to the wealthiest one percent of the population. In 2007, the top fifty hedge and private equity managers averaged $588 million in annual compensation. On the other hand, the median income of ordinary Americans has dropped an average of $2,197 per year since 2000.

We habitually excuse Wall Street's disproportionate earnings out of a sense that it helps American businesses thrive—but even corporations don't quite benefit from Wall Street's "services." Consider the infamous merger between Daimler-Benz and Chrysler. In 1998, Goldman Sachs claimed that this merger would result in a $3 billion revenue gain. Stock prices responded extremely positively to the merger, which won the coveted *Institutional Dealers' Digest* "Deal of the Year" Award. Only two years later, because of incongruities between the European and American parties, Chrysler lost $512 million in annual income, $1 billion in shareholder value in a single quarter, and was forced to lay off 26,000 workers. With the merger acknowledged as a failure, Chrysler was sold off from Daimler-Benz in 2007. Goldman Sachs, which had already made millions in windfall fees from the original merger, then walked away with millions more for advising the equity firm which now swooped in to pillage an ailing Chrysler. Bad advice seems to do little to tarnish Goldman's golden reputation; after all, the firm can always point to its extraordinary profits as proof of talent and success. (Goldman Sachs ought to love the "bad publicity" it attracts nowadays; the headlines that reveal the billions made shorting housing and securities markets only solidify its status as Wall Street's elite firm—capable of turning a profit even in times of economic crisis.)

The evidence suggests that Wall Street has assumed a negative relation to the economic interests of society at large. Many investment bankers are doubtless nice, hardworking people who give a lot of money to charity; nevertheless, they constitute a distinct class with interests diverging from society's as a whole. This past year, unemployment skyrocketed from 6.2 to 10 percent. Meanwhile, Wall Street announced stock market gains of $4.6 trillion between March and October.

One might object: Surely this "diverging interests" portrait has been complicated since the Clintonian New Economy and the democratization of shareholding? After all, aren't so many of us investors and portfolio holders today? In the past decade, new financial services promised to extend affluence to more Americans if we partook in finance's "collective" economic vision. Broker services like E*TRADE enabled non-elite investors to enjoy increasing wealth as the background of their everyday lives. We all bore investment risks together and eventually we would share the resultant wealth. Or so we thought. Remarkably, business elites have managed to corral almost all of the recent winnings for themselves. In 2007, with the mortgage market on the eve of collapse and global economic crisis imminent, Wall Street meted out record bonuses totaling $32.9 billion. Holders of securities lost $74 billion.

THE MEANING OF FINANCIAL INNOVATION

Early on, capitalism encouraged entrepreneurs to invest in new technology, thus unleashing incredible productive potential. Yet as the hunger for profits outpaced technological innovation, the modern barbarian developed new instruments for increasing the value of his assets—without having to produce anything new. Rather than focus his energies on developing more productive ventures, he started to sell the promise of increased future revenue—which he called an "immaterial asset." The first immaterial assets were patents and trademarks; what were formerly strategies for being more productive, the barbarian now learned to package and sell by themselves. The next step was to sell claims to these immaterial assets in the form of yet another immaterial asset: capital stock. This stock represented a promise of revenue based on other promises of revenue. Over time, more and more immaterial assets were created and sold, then listed on balance sheets as corporate bonds, credit derivatives and hybrid securities. Eventually, a corporation started to look less like a producing firm and more like a bunch of immaterial assets and liabilities. Today a corporation's success often depends on how much credit it can raise—that is, on how successfully it can sell the promise of future success.

Salesmanship and future earnings projections have replaced productivity and innovation as the engines of our economy. The barbarian's pursuit of *financial* profit now determines how a corporation employs its labor and technology—that is, whether it is valuable to be productive. Capitalism, once propelled by technological investment (classical capital), is now driven by immaterial technology that increases the value of immaterial assets (financial instruments moving modern capital). Today Goldman Sachs and JP Morgan don't invest in the promise of producing things of *use* or *real value*. They invest in the promise of rising asset prices (or in the case of shorting stocks, the promise of falling asset prices). In their world, value is defined by gain. It used to be the other way around.

Because of the dynamic of constant financial innovation, patterns of economic boom and bust no longer follow the traditional business cycle model in which: (1) a low interest rate (meaning cheaper credit) leads to (2) increased investments and economic growth; followed by (3) a period of overheating and excess capacity; which is then balanced by (4) a restabilizing period and a cooling of inflationary tendencies. The "new business cycle" is determined by financial innovation, not national productivity and consumer demand. Booms are born when a new financial instrument is dreamed up, and busts occur when the conjurer's secret is uncovered and collapses.

The most recent boom and bust (i.e. our current financial crisis) was based on this secret: "The market for subprime mortgages is not determined by the number of newly aspiring homeowners, but by the promise of profits from mortgage-based securities." Irresponsible lending spelled profits for investment banks, so naturally they encouraged irresponsible lending. The story is familiar by now. Banks invented two kinds of risky securities that promised higher yields: collateralized debt obligations (that pay if high-interest mortgages are repaid) and credit-default swaps (that pay if they aren't). Trading these shadow-financial (i.e. unregulated) securities generated enormous profits—both from constant trading fees and from speculation gains. But selling more subprime mortgage securities required selling more subprime mortgages. So investment banks bought mortgage-lending outfits and themselves offered subprime loans (even to individuals who qualified for better loans). As inevitable loan defaults started to pile up, the value of collateralized debts fell, and heavily invested banks couldn't cover the swaps they sold. Wall Street's expert salesmen had sold too many immaterial assets—too many promises of future value. The entire edifice of lending was paralyzed because it had become profitable to lend irresponsibly.

THE BARBARIAN'S ATTITUDE TOWARD WORK

In barbarian societies, the warriors plunder and parade. Their homes adorned with booty from past raids, they brazenly announce their superiority to the rest of their community. Destructive and wasteful, they avoid accusations of spiritual and social infertility by defining what counts as spiritual and social wealth. As Veblen notes, "The obtaining of goods by other methods than seizure comes to be accounted unworthy of man in his best estate." All throughout history, in fact, virtues of manliness track the least productive—and most esteemed—professions, hobbies and social ambitions. Fight, idle, wear ornate clothing, but suffer not touching the earth or assisting one's fellow man.

Of course, only a select few were privileged to live the lives of warriors. Yet these elites so relentlessly honored their definitions of vigor and dignity that even the gentler non-elites accepted them. Veblen tells of a Polynesian chief who preferred to starve rather than suffer the indignity of feeding himself, as well as of a French king silently burnt alive because the servant whose duties included shifting his master's seat away from a fireplace had taken a sick day. This "moral stamina in the observance of good form"—that is, this foolish commitment to predatory decorum—only served to strengthen the elites' hegemony over the community; non-elites idolized the steadfastness, integrity and apparent dignity of the warrior's way of life.

According to Veblen, every human being has both an "instinct for *workmanship*"—a drive to improve in his craft, to work more effectively—and a "propensity for *emulation*"—a drive to distinguish himself from his peers. But depending on which habits and institutions are dominant in a particular society, these two instincts appear in different forms and hierarchical relations. Today, as in all barbarian societies, the desire for esteem has eclipsed the instinct to produce. This is the legacy of modern finance. The history of Wall Street is usually told through some quasi-Darwinist narrative—bankers worked diligently to invent newer mechanisms for borrowing, lending, hedging and insuring, ones that could better survive in an ever-complicating economic world. But to understand the ways in which Wall Street has reshaped American life, one needn't know which packaging of immaterial assets came first—corporate debt, junk bond or mortgage derivative. The proliferation of all these assets is expressive of a more fundamental revolution, one in which America's production processes acquired new directions, its workforce a different character, and its individual workers a new set of governing instincts.

In *White Collar: The American Middle Classes*, sociologist C. Wright Mills details how the rise of modern finance transformed the nature of the American workforce. With greater access to capital, large corporations increasingly crowded out small entrepreneurs. These corporations required masses of white-collar administrators, salesmen and managers to keep up with ever-proliferating bureaucratic tasks. Other social developments also contributed to the thinning of the American blue-collar: labor-intensive work was exported to cheaper labor markets, increased American wealth restructured socioeconomic ambitions and financial mobility favored capital-intensive production.

The overall effect has been radical: today, fewer Americans than ever are aspiring toward the materially productive professions; meanwhile the habits, talents, language and lifestyle of manual laborers have also been displaced by their white-collar corollaries. Perhaps the most troubling feature of the white-collar mindset is that it conceives of work—not just manual work but any kind of work, and especially its own—as irksome, pointless, an interference with life's pleasures. (Contemporary economists even model work as a "disutility," a sacrifice made for the sake of future enjoyments.) Consider the popularity of comedies like *The Office* or *Office Space*. Why are Americans so charmed by characters like Jim Halpert and Peter Gibbons? It's because they get that work doesn't matter anymore, that it cannot offer genuine satisfaction: work is simply something one has to do. Viewers sympathize with Halpert's detachment from paper sales; his attitude toward work feels appropriate, even noble. On the other hand, Dwight Schrute's zeal for office tasks seems bizarre, at times pathological. Halpert's reluctant and instrumental attitude is no less characteristic of the Wall Street analyst slaving at his desk for eighty hours a week. The analyst knows the satisfaction is not in the work itself—what he "gets" from his job is a paycheck and the prestige that comes with it.

A fuller history of modern finance would move beyond merely cataloguing instances of financial innovation and describe the accompanying transformation of our values. It would trace a larger spiritual transformation, in which our definition of what counts as dignified work shifted away from accomplishments and toward status. Veblen attributed to man a basic drive toward productivity— a taste for usefulness and an aversion to futility. But a society's institutions and values can divert this drive. Why would one bother producing things today, when the jobs producing nothing pay better— not only in cash, but also in prestige? Junk bond or credit-default swap traders produce no real product, all the while securing copious money and esteem. A trader can be celebrated as "masterful" or "naturally gifted," praises that used to be reserved for artisans. Meanwhile, we ignore or denigrate the laborer that fixes our car.

In "truly productive" (i.e. non-barbarian) societies, the "instinct for workmanship" and the "propensity for emulation" act in concert—individuals emulate the artifice of their compatriots, mimicking their movements and habits in an attempt to duplicate (and eventually improve upon) overlapping projects. They compete in workmanship, which helps goad innovation and creativity. But in our world, we no longer look to workmanship as the source of profound esteem. We rarely find inherent meaning in the struggle to improve our craft; the experience of natural self-heartening once called "a sense of accomplishment" has been displaced from our horizon (or at least from our workplaces). Instead of evaluating ourselves through our projects, self-esteem comes to depend on successfully selling others an image of our value. Promotions come to those who can sell themselves as the future of a company. And in this salesmanship society, Wall Street elites are the salespersons par excellence. Their very job is to sell an image of themselves as deserving of our praise and trust.

There is, however, a cost to all this repackaging and reselling. "Elite" tastes and habits shift so often that they start looking empty. Values seem largely unanchored, purposes transient and superficial. One senses that the goals of the avaricious aren't really their goals—can they really want those ugly mansions or gaudy cars?—but a way of not confronting their lack of goals, desires, hopes and joys. Who believes that traders are truly happy?

THE BANKER'S LIFESTYLE

There remains, of course, much that is enviable about the work of the trader; we might congratulate him for discovering a satisfying professional life—comfortable, secure, challenging but not incommensurate with his ability. Yet the many memoirs and ethnographies of Wall Street depict the job differently—less as a rewarding post for the gifted and proven, more as a petri dish of insecurities and dis-ease. Financial workers appear to be on perpetual trial membership; no individual can be sure which rules he has to follow or which mores he must embrace to remain a member. Indeed, Wall Street's various cultural practices—its socialization rituals (the recruitment process), life routine (work hours), the structure of aspiration (chronic job-hopping and job insecurity) and self-presentation (as the smartest and savviest)—seem to steadily produce psychically split individuals. The Wall Street worker may look self-assured, comforted by personal displays of status and absorbed in professional projects. But if the memoirs are to be believed, the trader conceals both a secret detachment from his professional persona—a feeling that he either ought to be or actually is quite different from the person his work demands him to be—and a fear of being called out for his faltering commitment to the lifestyle and profession.

Culturally, this means the trader will take on every aspect of the business lifestyle—the clothing, the cars, the eating habits and the attitude toward peers, the market and the rest of the world. Economically, it compels herd mentality on the trading floor. Without a sure grasp of future market behavior, or even of the basic dynamics that the market will exhibit in the future, speculators seek out any sort of assurance of their expertise, resort to whatever conventions they can grab hold of and behave in ways that minimize their insecurity, isolation and confusion. One doesn't want to be marked as lacking the right attributes for "succeeding." In his memoir *Liar's Poker*, Michael Lewis writes:

> Investors do not fear losing money as much as they fear solitude, by which I mean taking risks that others avoid. When they are caught losing money alone, they have no excuse for their mistake, and most investors, like most people, need excuses. They are, strangely enough, happy to stand on the edge of a precipice as long as they are joined by a few thousand others.

Stories by former brokers suggest that cultural admission into the community is more important than familiarity with the mechanisms of the economy. (Today, no one involved in the market understands how it works anyway.)

The result is a chronic insecurity which may be at the root of what some economists call the "Cassandra effect" in modern finance. Like the Greek prophetess, those with the clearest insight into the future, or into the present's deeper truths, can never convince those most in need of being convinced. The few individuals prescient enough (or reasonable enough) to see through the unsustainability of trading practices are ignored by speculators reluctant to stray from the flock. Warnings about the effects of reckless risk-taking are discounted. Cautious or thoughtful traders are traded for their more insecure and faithful counterparts.

Lacking any secure grounding for his inflated status and pay, the speculator compensates with unfaltering public confidence. He feigns knowledge of the manners of the market. He imagines his job calls upon talents precious to society. This self-deception becomes the norm, a requisite for practices otherwise devoid of justification or satisfaction. But Wall Street's elites are, as we have been told, extremely intelligent individuals; they must be aware of the exaggerated esteem afforded to them. The Wall Street worker understands that he is not yesterday's noble captain of industry, but merely a deckhand on a ship rowing between the Scylla of unethical trading and Charybdis of financial ruin. To pass these troubled waters, someone needs to be sacrificed. On occasion, Scylla will capture a few of the crew (Madoff, Stanford), but generally, only clientele have to be handed over. Lewis describes his peculiar relief at being able to slough off financial losses:

> [The client] was shouting and moaning. And that was it. That was all he could do. Shout and moan. That was the beauty of being a middleman, which I did not appreciate until that moment. The customer suffered. I didn't. He wasn't going to kill me. He wasn't even going to sue me. I wasn't going to lose *my* job. On the contrary, I was a minor hero at Salomon for dumping a sixty-thousand-dollar loss into someone else's pocket.

The culture of Wall Street may have evolved since Lewis's time, but not the paradox that drives it. The networks of acknowledgment and praise run counter to the virtues articulated by its spokesmen (virtues that businessmen sometimes even believe in). Psychic relief and parochial esteem depend on performing poorly in the very activity for which one is publicly praised. Bonuses arrive. Devastated clients disappear.

The institutions and habits that distinguish financial elites as ideal economic agents—and transform recessions into opportunities for billion-dollar profits—make anxiety the norm on Wall Street. It is tempting to close one's eyes to the instability that mars Wall Street life. Who cares that the financial elites work in constant fear of downsizing? (Wall Street cut 116,000 jobs in 2001; 98,000 in 2004; 50,000 in 2006; and 150,000 in 2007.) With Wall Street salaries and bonuses, what does it matter if some traders have to stretch out their severance packages in Buenos Aires for a decade or two? When the economy was hemorrhaging jobs, they extracted record profits and continued to destabilize asset market after asset market. Isn't it time that they suffer a few days? The irony of seeing former Bank of America CEO Ken Lewis picking up an unemployment check might be too sweet to pass up (2008 compensation: $20.13 million). Or maybe too ironic to be sweet (another suspicious bailout). But this instinct of *ressentiment* is dangerous—for when the movers and shakers expect perpetual insecurities in their homes, they welcome those insecurities into everyone else's homes as well. Wall Street's anxieties overflow onto Main Street.

WALL STREET AND MAIN STREET

Amidst nature's unreasonable scarcity, Wall Street often seems like a refuge of reason. It promises us prosperity, so long as we submit to its values. In Karen Ho's ethnography of Wall Street, *Liquidated*, she identifies the three qualities of an ideal investor—*smartness*, *assiduousness* and *flexibility*. Wall Street offered us these ideals in its own image, and we have accepted them as gods. "Make everything in this image; everything more efficient," we are told. But how have we fared with this injunction? How have the idols passed down from Wall Street affected work and life on Main Street?

Not only does Wall Street's highly selective recruitment process—restricted primarily to Ivy League graduates and the current students at the top five American business schools—reflect its idolization of ostentatious *smartness*, it instills this value in future financiers. These young elites are bussed en masse to extravagant recruitment parties, where they are fanned with flimsy adulation of their smartness and precocious accomplishments. Wall Street thus trains its employees in the art of performing eliteness at the same time as it protects its image as the destination of America's elites. A Princeton alumna and former financial analyst herself, Ho writes:

> The conflation of elite universities with investment banking and "the perfect lifestyle" is crucial to the recruitment process, reproducing as it does the ambience of Wall Street cocktail parties, where investment bankers "schmooze clients" in lavish, impeccably catered settings. These norms are enacted for and demonstrated to students, and . . . they immediately pick up on the importance of performing "smartness," not to mention how Wall Street business success is premised on pedigree, [and] competitive consumption.

The hiring strategy of financial firms further confirms that they are not selling a product, or even a service requiring skills or experience. What they have to sell is, literally, their salesmen—whose highly publicized "intellect" and "natural talent" secure the trust of clientele despite the poor track record of their expensive advice. Ho quotes one Harvard student's take on Wall Street recruitment:

> The core competency of . . . an investment bank . . . the real value these companies bring to the world and to their shareholders is their unmatched skill at recruiting fresh-faced young students from the Ivy League. . . . Remember that companies that do nothing of value must obscure that fact by hiring the best people to appear dynamic and innovative while doing such meaningless work.

Financial firms aggressively promote the image of Wall Street smarts by hiring, or more precisely, by producing, Ivy League analysts. Smartness pays, for Wall Street at least.

But how do Wall Street's core values affect life on Main Street? The American college, taking its cue from finance, now trains its students primarily in the skill of performing smartness—that is, in appearing able to suavely manage diverse situations and people. This works excellently for the few who can land jobs in finance and consultancy, but it has disastrous consequences for the rest of the college-educated, now unequipped with any stable skill set or reliable knowledge. Today, 62 percent of Americans aged 25 and older have college degrees. They compete for the 22 percent of American jobs that require higher education. The losers are left unemployed or consigned to drudge in the bottom echelons of the service sector.

The second virtue of Wall Street employees, according to Ho's ethnography, is that they are assiduous. Their days are long, fraught with deadlines and taut with anxiety. In *The Theory of the Leisure Class*, Veblen predicted that conspicuous wastefulness and public idleness would increasingly define American life. Though his arguments about uneconomic consumption habits are borne out on Wall Street, work routines are anything but indolent. Wall Street has managed to persuade its financial footmen to sacrifice almost all of their time to the shrine of the "dynamic worker." Perks like the 7 p.m. free dinner and the 9 p.m. car service encourage workers already yoked to their trading screens to stay in the office just a bit longer. But the truth is that they work late for other reasons. The fact that millions of dollars can be won or lost in just a few minutes has reshaped Wall Street's experience of "time," investing every moment of the day with an urgency alternately exhilarating and oppressive.

Yet the consistent affirmation that Wall Street works harder and longer than anyone else makes other work environments appear wasteful by comparison—manned by idle and complacent employees. To insecure Wall Streeters repeating mantras of their own hyper-efficiency, the outside world comes to appear horribly inefficient. Disciplining corporate America through downsizing seems increasingly appropriate, even necessary. American jobs thus inherit Wall Street's instability and compulsiveness, becoming both all-consuming and highly temporary. American workers are no longer card-carrying members of a corporate entity. They are pieces of fat to be trimmed away.

In other words, Wall Street's cardinal virtue is *flexibility*—the imperative it preaches to both its workers and clients. Financial footmen are used to losing their jobs. High turnovers and chronic exposure to being downsized are accepted features of the playing field; even before the financial crisis, one's financial team or even whole division was liable to dismissal depending on the tides of the market. Of course, Wall Street's inflated salaries compensate for this occupational hazard—but others fare less well. American businesses, seeking to prove their flexibility to Wall Street and sustain their shareholders' confidence, learn to shed workers when the market turns. For workers themselves, corporate flexibility has brought about lower-skilled jobs and salaries that reflect their easy substitutability. America's two largest employers—Walmart and the temp agency Manpower—provide model jobs for an economy that idolizes the flexible.

Stability, once a virtue of both the reliable laborer and the well-tested firm, now portends obsolescence, an inability to innovate. Flexibility is the new cultural imperative—and job insecurity the new background to everyday life. In the twentieth century, finance introduced an era of white-collar employment; now it ushers in an era of temporary work—a post-career era. Even full-time jobs no longer provide financial security, and the aspiration of a long-term career (with any company at all, even resigning oneself to "less fulfilling" jobs) appears increasingly whimsical.

Today, the average American will hold more than ten different jobs over the course of his lifetime. Deprived of what Richard Sennett called the "gift of organized time," he can no longer set goals for long-term personal development. His life feels less like a narrative that he is slowly articulating than a series of discontinuous episodes largely determined by forces beyond his control. At the very least, living a good life would seem to require: (1) the ability to deepen and develop one's personal relationships and (2) a sense of ownership over one's existence. In the post-career era, there is little prospect for either. The average American can only play out the temporary roles the world has chosen for him—roles that feel shallow, fleeting and not his own.

NAMING THE BARBARIANS

Pick up the *New York Times* today, and you're likely to read yet another article about finance's infidelity with the general public, another violation of the (invisible) norms of propriety. It is only with immense discipline, a well-stocked inventory of financial jargon and a readiness for self-deception that one can actually distinguish these "violations" from business-as-usual. Yet despite ubiquitous references to Wall Street offenses, maybe even because of them, Americans don't seem deeply troubled, or even all that perplexed, that this abusive sector remains largely undisturbed. Most of us can dutifully recite the scandals and statistics, but few dare to imagine life without Wall Street. For all the talk of a rapidly evolving economic environment, we treat one feature of this environment as permanent: the existence of a class of individuals who make millions by making nothing. We're no longer surprised to see business elites divine exorbitant bonuses, paid for through record unemployment levels and unprecedented government support. This trick is getting old.

Though Wall Street consistently updates its instruments and practices, one governing rule has remained since Veblen's time: financial propriety has nothing to do with social and economic growth. Certain rules must be followed, but the construction of those rules is absolutely distinct from considerations of general social welfare. Rather, regulations and rules are defined according to the culture's metric of success, of value, of esteem—and that metric is money. All financial practices that increase the wealth of the sector are not merely permitted, they are required. No profitable innovation can be ignored. Destabilizing the global economy is fine. Undermining one's firm, or jeopardizing the system of trading and speculating, is not.

Finance today is not geared toward getting entrepreneurs the credit they need to actualize their good ideas. It is riddled with archaic social forms that perpetuate barbaric status anxieties. The appeal of the Wall Street lifestyle—money, clean working conditions, (paradoxical) status as stewards of prosperity—has blighted the rest of society with its message that the best kind of work is devoid of social utility, knowledge and permanence. Nonetheless, we continue, even in the wake of economic crisis, to accept the barbarians' rules for social and economic life. The discussion in government today revolves around minor matters of transparency and enforcement. The barbarian does not abide by rules; indeed, it is a point of pride that he knows his way around them. No matter what regulations are passed, the barbarian will figure out a way to make money from them.

Ironically, as anxiety-stricken status seekers, bankers are more vulnerable to social censure than to rules. In the past, barbarians have lost power when new moral voices rejected their predatory habits—as Nordic scholar Gwyn Jones argued, Viking practices were weakened when "under the influence of Christianity, an increasing disquietude was felt about the ownership and sale of men." Rather than challenge bankers to develop new weaponry, we should debunk the myths that justify their predatory habits. Bankers, those chronic scavengers of affirmation, are among the least equipped to contend with public dishonor. Today, the stock market continues to climb without offering relief to national unemployment. We are assured, as always, that jobs are a "lagging indicator." But what kind of jobs will they be when they finally come—and will they restore a sense of ownership to our lives? The answer may depend on whether we have the courage to insist that Wall Street's recovery only impedes our own.

Hard Feelings

THE NOVELS OF
MICHEL HOUELLEBECQ

by Ben Jeffery

ISSUE 2 | WINTER 2010

Michel Houellebecq has published four novels, all of them bitter and miserable. Their pessimism isn't the only thing to them, or necessarily the most important thing, but it is probably the first that you'll notice. *Extension du domaine de la lutte* (1994), *Les Particules élémentaires* (1998), *Plateforme* (2001) and *La Possibilité d'une île* (2005)—published in America as *Whatever, The Elementary Particles, Platform* and *The Possibility of an Island*—are callow, cynical and sex-obsessed, openly racist and misogynistic in turn, rife with B-grade porn writing, full of contempt for art and intellectuals, and operate on a kind of low masculine anger at the indignities of being beta-chimp. They are nonetheless serious, and owe their reputation to artistic achievement as much as any naughty thrill they elicit. Translated into more than 25 different languages, Houellebecq has won the lucrative Dublin IMPAC award and the Prix Novembre for *The Elementary Particles*, the Grand prix national des lettres and the Prix Flore for *Whatever* and sustained critical and popular attention during a decade and a half in which the number of writers to emerge from Europe with any sense of significance is next to zero. This comparatively huge success is worth some attention: Houellebecq's books are not historical romances or ripping thrillers, they are modern, nakedly philosophical novels, embodying—I should like to say—one of the more significant efforts by any contemporary writer to understand and communicate the tensions of our times, a great many of which are plainly hostile to the production of engaged literature.

Over 45 years ago Susan Sontag wrote that redundancy—an experience of joblessness or irrelevance—was the chief affliction of modern life, a verdict that has yet to fall out of date. Insignificance and redundancy make special problems for a writer. Speaking generally, what a novelist aims to do is to convey or impose meaning, and meaning is what redundancy undermines—precisely why irrelevance is one of the natural and insoluble terrors of writing. If you were looking for a neat expression for the awful sense of uselessness that anyone with a commitment to the written word must feel from time to time, then Philip Larkin's phrase would be hard to better: "Books are a load of crap." "Depressive realism" (a clinical term) becomes an occupational hazard for the author and reader. It talks like this: you hide from life; you make it up; your claims to deeper meaning are a charade; you lie; you are stupid. Take it as a given that something in the nature of the modern world—its superabundance, perhaps; the overload of information and of competing leisure options—makes it especially difficult now to write pertinent fiction. Literature is anyway a deeply confused business, based on a kind of basic fraudulence. And asking what it is *for* is like asking what life is for (which is to say: have your pick of answer, good luck finding any proof). Consequently, depressive realism is impossible to inoculate oneself against. It is horrible and hard, and entirely *un*-abstract in its horribleness. David Foster Wallace, an author who provided some of the most sensitive articulations of the impulse to communicate through fiction, wrote at length about the perils of living by the word. "I get scared and sad too," he once said rather simply. "I think maybe it's part of the natural price of wanting to do this kind of work." Last year, after a catastrophic attempt to quit his antidepressants, Wallace committed suicide at the age of 46. Without wanting to be morbid merely for the sake of it, it is hard to see the silver lining to that particular storm cloud—hard to see Wallace's death as anything except evidence, if we needed it, that all our efforts to impose meaning on life—to protect ourselves, to cope—are really just made of paper.

I sound this sour note for two reasons. *The Point* has taken it as an informal mission to provide a space for discussion about the modern novel, about the various challenges it faces and about what we can hope for (or expect) from the genre in the present day. This is an admirable sort of conversation to want, but we should be careful while having it to separate circumstantial problems from constitutive ones. It is perfectly fair—and what's more, manifestly accurate—to say that social and cultural conditions are presently antithetical in lots of ways to creating literature that resonates with the times. A familiar way of putting it is to evoke a nefarious alliance of massively multiplied information sources and stimuli with a clustered and distracting mass culture, and the corresponding shrinkage of the average person's attention span and willingness to isolate himself with a book. The novelist is caught in a double bind: in order to properly capture the feel of a kinetic, overloaded modern world she must pack more, and more varied, material into her work, but does so for an audience that has less and less inclination to engage with it. Alternatively, the novelist simplifies and straightens her work in order to win readers, but at the expense of representing the world as she truly perceives it to be (i.e. "selling out"). There is a concern that the novel is simply unable, structurally, to harmonize with an era where the written word has been so heavily marginalized by sound and image. Or maybe the form is exhausted—there being only so many different ways to stick words together into a coherent whole, and only so many styles to adopt and tones to take, etc., might the last three hundred years of cultural activity not have burnt up our artistic resources? These worries are valid enough, but in fact there has never been a moment where the novel really was a pure and uncomplicatedly meaningful thing. It has always been a struggle against the elements.

A second reason for caution would be that it is wrong to expect literature to be therapeutic or life-affirming *qua* literature. In reaction to all the conditions making it uniquely difficult to produce literature for the 21st century it is an easy and often-made mistake to extol the reading of Serious Novels as a type of nourishing, meditative activity—a richer and more fulfilling food contra the junk diet served up by mass culture. This is a bad tack—in principle—because it is egocentric. It tacitly equates good art with what is good for one's health, and thereby reduces it to something that provides a service for well-being. That might sound like elitism (real art is x-and-y, whether you like it or not), but it isn't, really. A novel would have value simply for being truthful, and the truth is under no obligation to be pleasant. Given the dreadful psychic mess that fiction is founded on (the mess that gives depression its grip), to make helpfulness a criterion of literature is to make guarantees one cannot fulfill. As enriching and comforting as they can undoubtedly be, stories are primarily expressive. *What* they express needn't be healthy or positive so long as it is truthful—and the news might simply be bad.

At the beginning of his first book, not a novel but an extended essay on the life and work of H. P. Lovecraft, Houellebecq set out his premises: "No matter what might be said, access to the artistic universe is more or less entirely the preserve of those who are a little *fed up* with the world." Or more than a little:

> Life is painful and disappointing. It is useless, therefore, to write new realistic novels. We generally know where we stand in relation to reality and don't care to know any more. Humanity, such as it is, inspires only an attenuated curiosity in us. All these prodigiously refined "notations," "situations," anecdotes . . . All they do, once a book has been set aside, is reinforce the slight revulsion that is already nourished by any one of our "real life" days.

Certainly these opening notes—those scare quotes around the words "real life"—do not promise a wonderfully appetizing read. But in fact Houellebecq's debut is a delight. *H. P. Lovecraft: Against the World, Against Life* is witty, sympathetic, beautifully written and accomplishes the nicest thing a piece of criticism can: it makes you want to read what you are reading about. Lovecraft, a recluse whose single happy adult relationship was wrecked by his inability to find a salary and who wrote horror stories (so Houellebecq argues) powered on virulent racial hatred, also exemplifies in his life and work one of the engines of Houellebecq's own fiction: the refusal, or the failure, to develop into an adult. However, the claim that it is "useless . . . to write new realistic novels" is something Houellebecq quickly retreated from. Without exception, his novels are concerned with the revulsion and hardship of quote-unquote real life.

But what value has "realism" like that? It's pretty easy, you might think, to adopt a manful tone of voice and say that what matters in Art is not well-being but Truth, even if the truth is brutal and distressing. But if a piece of art is not only truthful but depressing and no good for you in its truthfulness, doesn't that sound like an excellent reason to avoid it? I don't mean to be coy if I say that I'm not sure how to answer that question. Right enough, Houellebecq's characters are defined by isolation and unhappiness, and they take these to be essential rather than accidental parts of human existence. Their social relations are those of failure, determined by what they cannot relate to in others—"It is in failure, and through failure, that the subject constitutes itself," as one puts it, and another: "It is in our relations with other people that we gain a sense of ourselves; it's that, pretty much, that makes relations with other people unbearable"— all of which falls perilously close to navel-gazing. Whether in first or third person, the Houellebecq hero (always male) typically takes the form of a soft-bodied, aging cynic, who yearns exclusively for sex with young women and then spirals off into brooding monologues about the impossibility of living when it eludes him. The quantity of invective is high, particularly in *The Possibility of an Island*, easily the nastiest of the four titles. Its hero, a rich and famous comedian named Daniel, embarks on one love affair with a woman that ends after they both agree that it would be futile to pretend that he could go on wanting her deteriorating body, and then another with a 22-year-old nymphomaniac with whom he falls deeply in love, while admitting that "like all very pretty young girls she was basically only good for fucking, and it would have been stupid to employ her for anything else, to see her as anything other than a luxury animal, pampered and spoiled, protected from all cares as from any difficult or painful task so as to be better able to devote herself to her exclusively sexual service." Eventually she dumps him before running off to an orgy. Elsewhere, Daniel notes that "the dream of all men is to meet little sluts who are innocent but ready for all forms of depravity—which is what, more or less, all teenage girls are," that

"living together alone is hell between consenting adults," that "legitimate disgust . . . seizes any normal man at the sight of a baby," that
"a child is a sort of vicious dwarf, innately cruel, who combines the
worst features of the species, and from whom domestic pets keep
a wise distance," and so on.

And yet the best reason to read Houellebecq, the one I would
give if I were asked, anyway, is that his work produces the scandal-
ously rare impression of being relevant, of connecting to how life
is, rather than how it might be if there were more adventures. Pessimism is unfalsifiable, of course, which is what makes it so often
insipid. If someone is genuinely determined to look on the gloomy
side of life there is no turning them. The "honesty" of a depressive
realist is sapping and tedious in that way. All of Houellebecq's nar-
rators present themselves as hardheaded men willing to speak unpleasant facts (explicitly, in *The Possibility of an Island*, where Daniel
comments: "On the intellectual level I was in reality slightly above
average . . . I was just very honest, and therein lay my distinction;
I was, in relation to the current norms of mankind, almost unbeliev-
ably honest"), but their stories would be banal if their author weren't
deft enough to make them plausible—that is, realistic.

"Realism" is, to say the least, a bit of a tattered banner in fiction.
Part of the mythology of literature is that Serious Novels exist as a
weather vane to the age, informed by and informing the mood of
the times, simultaneously symptomatic and diagnostic, reflecting
the particular concerns of their spot in history and in turn informing the deeper concerns of human life. The "conceptual" difficulty,
so to speak, for the modern novel might as well be termed the difficulty of realism. Since at least 1919, when Virginia Woolf published
"Modern Fiction," there has been a loose but persistent consensus
among "serious" writers that the world has changed in ways that
make Jane Austen-type classic realism inappropriate, so that if you
really wanted to be realistic you would paradoxically find the best expression in science fiction or postmodernist aesthetics, or deny the
possibility of realism as an achievable or desirable aim (cf. the critic
Jerome Klinkowitz: "If the world is absurd, if what passes for reality
is distressingly unreal, why spend time representing it?"). The rea-

sons for this steady, though now almost itself retro, shift in feeling are much discussed but remain ghoulishly unaltered.

"The pain of consciousness, the pain of knowing, grows apace"— that is Jonathan Franzen's phrase, and it could hardly have been said better. If one were forced on pain of injury to try to say what is characteristic of the present moment, one serviceable answer would be: we know more. Our collective awareness is tremendous; it increases. The sum total of human knowledge has long outstripped the capacities of any individual, however brilliant they might be (it being said that the last person to know everything there was to know was Leibniz, which isn't true, but would be bad enough even if it were—he died in 1716). As a thought experiment, consider any subject (e.g. cooking) that you could claim some knowledge of. Consider how many people in the world could claim greater knowledge of that subject, how much expertise you lack. Now broaden your thought to cover all the fields of science and sport and art and language and mathematics and commerce and engineering and philosophy and history and geography and medicine. Imagine how much you don't know that is known. It is dizzying. The expanse of human activity and enterprise, and our consciousness of that expanse, are vital ingredients for the modern novelist's stew. The problem being that this enormous weight of collected data—or, more accurately, the fact that we are ever more aware that this gigantic weight of data is sitting out there, collected—has rather awkward consequences for writing novels.

The first, most obvious one is this: there is so much stuff! Far too much to fit into any book, too much for any single talent—how could any lone novelist capture what the world feels like when she has such flimsy snares at her disposal? But the days when there was any broad distinction between the local and the exotic seem gone, and so the pressure mounts on the novelist to pack her work full of data and exoticism, to take her books globetrotting, evoke the sensation that there is more going on in the world faster and everywhere: the interconnected, networked, speeding, modern kaleidoscope. But the actual breadth of the world—the diversity of character and locale that you could encounter just by, say, spending an evening channel-hopping or browsing the internet—humbles the imagination, and it seems impossible to do it justice. The present isn't so much a moving target as a multitude of twisting, slipping bodies that refuse to remain targets long enough to take aim.

A massive proportion of Western art in the late twentieth and early 21st centuries is, in one way or another, a reaction to the feeling of overload. But the issue isn't simply one of scale, as though in principle, and with enough imagination and effort, one could amass a large enough quantity of information plus character and put it all inside one long book—it is also a matter of fit. In some plain respects, novels just seem like the wrong way to depict life in the information age. A linear narrative without explicit audiovisual accompaniment doesn't rest easily in the job of conveying a time and place animated by flickering bangs and whizzes. It isn't merely the problem already sketched, that literature must compete with all sorts of other, extremely colorful, forms of entertainment for the attention of an audience with less to give or desire to give it. It is also that literature aiming to be "realistic" would have to depict all the up-to-the-minute parts of the 21st century that make it difficult for novels to be that. It is as though the timely 21st-century fiction would have to somehow internalize those elements that make novels seem irrelevant and out of step—that is, represent (in a novel) a form of life that novels do not appear to be representative of; like pushing square pegs against round holes. What would a long story be like where the hero worked all day and then spent all his spare time on the internet? Possibly very interesting, but also hard to imagine—as a rule of thumb, novels struggle to capture information-age paraphernalia, and very often seem wooden when they try.* The problem

---

* For one minor example: hip-hop, a decidedly modern music. Hip-hop never seems right reproduced in a novel. Part of this, I think, is that a novel that reproduces a rap verse invariably writes the words out line by line, which is fine but palpably not how the music (which is, on the face of it, one of the most "articulate" or "wordy" types there is) makes itself felt—often the rhythm of a rap song pulls you along in spite of the fact that you usually can't really separate or understand many of the words if you aren't already familiar with the verse. This "pull" just isn't there on the page, although it is there on the radio, television, street corner,

of fit is more serious by far than the problem of scale—it's the difference between having a long and arduous job on your hands and having a job you are wrong for. A novelist who feels her medium to be out of tune with the world around her is obvious prey for the specter of irrelevance. It's a big deal: "For a writer of fiction to feel that he does not really live in the country in which he lives—as represented by *Life* or by what he experiences when he steps out his front door—must certainly seem a serious occupational impediment," said Philip Roth, surveying an American cultural landscape that had become unprecedentedly ill-disposed to the means and methods of written fiction. That was in 1961—and like Sontag's remark about redundancy, it is ominously ageless (once you replace *Life* with Google and delete the need to leave the home).

The terrors of redundancy are part and parcel of the enterprise of fiction writing—what modern life does is amplify them. It has never been easier to feel anonymous. Houellebecq's books, which don't take a massive amount of interest in the world buzzing around them, manage to convey this atmosphere extremely well—the gap between real life and life as advertised, and how the sense of disappointment this generates has perversely become a bit of a cultural norm. "There are some authors who employ their talent in the delicate description of varying states of soul, character traits, etc.," expounds the narrator of *Whatever*:

> All that accumulation of realistic detail, with clearly differentiated characters hogging the limelight, has always seemed pure bullshit to me. . . . The world is becoming more uniform before our eyes; telecommunications are improving; apartment interiors are enriched with new gadgets. Human relationships become progressively impossible, which greatly reduces the quantity of

---

coming out of car windows, i.e. all the everyday circumstances where one has the opportunity to hear rap music and compare it favorably to how it comes across inside a novel. Further minor example: I find email exchanges "written out" in a novel almost unfailingly clunky and awkward, e.g. pp. 497–502 of *The Corrections*. Is it that email, too, simply feels wrong and not at home on the printed page?

anecdote that goes to make up a life. And little by little death's countenance appears in all its glory.

•

In *The Elementary Particles*—the story of Bruno and Michel, two socially isolated half-brothers—tremendous glee is taken skewering neo-hippies and New Age mystics. A thwarted hedonist, the forty-year-old Bruno spends a dismal fortnight holidaying in the Lieu du Changement, a semi-commune founded in 1975 with the aim of "providing a place where like-minded people could spend the summer months living according to the principles they espoused. It was intended that this haven of humanist and democratic feeling would create synergies, facilitate the meeting of minds and, in particular, as one of the founding members put it, provide an opportunity to 'get your rocks off.'" By the time Bruno visits in the late nineties the Lieu du Changement has become miserable, a microcosm for one of Houellebecq's central themes—the cruelty and exclusion of the sixties' sexual revolution. For the clientele of the Lieu, "as their flesh began to age, the cult of the body, which they had done so much to promote, simply filled them with an intensifying disgust for their own bodies—a disgust they could see mirrored in the gaze of others. . . . Dedicated exclusively to sexual liberation and the expression of desire, the Lieu du Changement naturally became a place of depression and bitterness." By the mid-eighties the commune has become a corporate business, supplementing its promise of sexual liberty with quasi-religious workshops and esoteric disciplines—"Tantric Zen, which combined profound vanity, diffuse mysticism and sexual frottage, flourished."

Bad luck in sex, the marginalization of anyone who fails to be erotically desirable, is the backbone of Houellebecq's oeuvre. *Whatever*, the most overtly philosophical novel, is narrated by an unnamed computer technician—a job that Houellebecq held before he made his living as a writer—on a business trip training provincial civil servants how to use their new equipment. His companion is another young technician, Raphaël Tisserand. "The problem with

Raphaël Tisserand—the foundation of his personality, indeed—is that he is extremely ugly. So ugly that his appearance repels women, and he never gets to sleep with them." The two men travel from town to town, retiring to bars and nightclubs after work, where Raphaël—affluent, but a total flop as a sexual commodity—meets progressively terrible frustrations. The issue, as the narrator diagnoses, is one of simple sexual economics: his colleague cannot offer anything on the marketplace. "Just like unrestrained economic liberalism, and for similar reasons, sexual liberalism produces phenomena of *absolute pauperization*. Some men make love every day; others five or six times in their life, or never. Some make love with dozens of women, others with none. It's what's known as 'the law of the market' . . . In a totally liberal sexual system certain people have a varied and exciting erotic life; others are reduced to masturbation and solitude." Lacking charm and resembling a toad wrapped in cellophane in his looks, Raphaël has nothing he can trade. Characters that suffer because of their biological makeup, the life sentence imposed by being undesirable, or the delayed punishment of aging, recur—sex, we are told, is life's only real motive. If you are disqualified, or "past it," then you will suffer unto death: "All energy is of a sexual nature, not mainly, but exclusively, and when the animal is no longer good for reproducing, it is absolutely no longer good for anything."*

Raphaël is killed in a car accident, driving home in the mists on Christmas Eve. At his funeral: "A few words were pronounced on the sadness of such a death and on the difficulty of driving in fog, people went back to work, and that was that." But for the narrator, who until then had taken a cold, if not gruesomely manipulative attitude toward his partner, the news of Tisserand's death sparks a mental breakdown. After checking himself into a psychiatric hos-

---

* Fair to say, Houellebecq's books don't shy away from what Wallace called "the bizarre adolescent idea that getting to have sex with whomever one wants whenever one wants is a cure for ontological despair." Interestingly, that judgment was part of Wallace's famous review of John Updike's *Toward the End of Time*; the same John Updike who disapprovingly quotes Houellebecq's bit about all energy being sexual energy in the rather sniffy review of *The Possibility of an Island* he gave for the *New Yorker*.

pital, the hero is confronted by a female counselor who chastises him for speaking in overly abstract, sociological terms. His effort at self-analysis emerges: "But I don't understand, basically, how people manage to go on living. I get the impression everybody must be unhappy; we live in such a simple world, you understand. There's a system based on domination, money and fear . . . there's a . . . system based on seduction and sex. And that's it. Is it really possible to live and to believe that there's nothing else?" Afterwards, he asks the counselor if she would sleep with him. She refuses.

Although Houellebecq shoots plenty of venom at the sexual revolution, it is not that he is a reactionary writer, exactly. He never suggests that religious faith is the solution to his character's dilemmas, for example; the books are all resolutely atheist. The only places in which traditional religion makes a significant appearance are in a subplot of *Whatever*—a Catholic priest, an old acquaintance of the narrator's, loses his faith over a failed affair with a young nurse— and at the climax of *Platform* in the form of Islamic terrorists.* In any case, Houellebecq's heroes are generally no less deviant than the sad revelers of the Lieu du Changement. What the sexual revolution stands for, rather, is the triumph of philosophical materialism: the worldview that erases the supernatural, making it impossible to believe in God and—at its logical conclusion—eradicating the possibility of communion altogether. The starkest material truth, after all, seems to be that we are all ultimately alone inside our skin: "elementary particles." In Houellebecq's fiction, the real brutality of post-sixties sexual economics is that it is based on fact; it is, in its way, progressive. One way of putting it is that in our enlightenment we are able to see ourselves as merely creatures, rather than God's creatures, and nature as purposeless matter, rather than divine plan.

---

* In 2001, French courts agreed to hear a formal case brought against Houellebecq by four French Muslim organizations on the charge of racism, after he was quoted (inaccurately, he claims) in an interview promoting *Platform* saying that Islam was "the most stupid of all religions." The case was eventually dismissed, but in between the publication of *Platform* and his appearance in court two planes smashed into the World Trade Center—which made Houellebecq's eye for subject matter seem like an uncannily sharp one, whatever else.

Humans are just animals, and, unsurprisingly, that knowledge gives precedence to biological impulse; to strength, health and beauty over weakness, infirmity and repulsiveness; and it makes self-interest paramount. Houellebecq's men find themselves incapable of considering anything but themselves, but they also apprehend, with some horror, the essential unsustainability of individualism. Living with nothing other than your own desires and urges makes your frustrations, increasingly awful and unavoidable as you age, torturous—and the prospect of death unmanageable. "Contemporary consciousness is no longer equipped to deal with our mortality. More than at any time or in any other civilization, human beings are obsessed with aging. Each individual has a simple view of the future: a time will come when the sum of pleasures that life has left to offer is outweighed by the sum of pain (one can actually feel the meter ticking, and it ticks inevitably toward the end). This weighing up of pleasure and pain, which sooner or later everyone is forced to make, leads logically, at a certain age, to suicide." It is, to paraphrase Houellebecq on a different topic, an insoluble condition, but not really a complicated one.

"Old age; there was not a new blossoming at the end of the road, but a bundle of frustrations and sufferings, at first insignificant, then very quickly unbearable . . ." *The Possibility of an Island* is probably the worst of the novels, a long and caustic monologue against a cardboard backdrop, but even it achieves a kind of demonic power thanks to the intensity of its will to communicate the slide of bodily decay, "the sadness of physical decrepitude, of the gradual *loss* of all that gave life meaning and joy":

> Not only did the old not have the right to fuck . . . rebellion was forbidden to them, rebellion too—like sexuality, like pleasure, like love—seemed reserved for the young and to have no point for other people, any cause incapable of mobilizing the interest of young people was disqualified in advance, basically, old people were in all matters treated simply as waste, to be granted only a survival that was miserable, conditional, and more and more narrowly limited.

Esther, the aging narrator's 22-year-old mistress, never strikes the reader as much like an actual person, but the hero's desperation as their romance comes to an end—an end that he does not think he will survive—is palpable to the point of suffocation; you want to put the book down for air. Love is very real in Houellebecq's fiction, "immense and admirable," the nearest thing there is to true communion, but it too is part of a game one cannot help but lose. Houellebecq is hardly above mining sentiment on this score. Indeed, the two best novels, *Platform* and *The Elementary Particles*, succeed because they approach classical romantic tragedy. Bruno's vacation in the Lieu is saved when he meets Christiane, a forty-year-old whose eyes "were blue and a little sad," who travels to the Lieu for the sex rather than the mysticism. "The whole spiritual thing makes the pickup lines seem less brutal," she admits, but is unreservedly cynical about its value otherwise:

> I know what the veterans of 'sixty-eight are like when they hit forty, I'm practically one myself. They have cobwebs in their cunts and they grow old alone. Talk to them for five minutes and you'll see they don't believe in any of this bullshit about chakras and crystal healing and light vibrations. They force themselves to believe it, and sometimes they do for an hour or two . . . but then the workshop's over and they're still ugly, still ageing, still alone. So they cry for a bit—have you noticed? They do a lot of crying here.

In spite of his maladjustment and her damage, Bruno and Christiane find tenderness with one another. As their relationship progresses, Bruno's bleak worldview ("second-rate Nietzscheanism," he calls it) begins to thaw. The two fall in love. During a happy week together in Paris: "They took a taxi to Les Halles and ate in an all-night brasserie. Bruno had rollmop herrings as a starter. 'Now,' he thought, 'anything is possible.' He had hardly done so when he realized that he was wrong." What he thinks of is not a rival lover or external interference, but rather the course of nature—the implacable reality of separation and decline. The end that Bruno and Chistiane's affair eventually comes to, wrenching as it is, is only an accelerated version of the fate of all affairs: sooner or later the body fails. "Though the possibilities were endless in [Bruno's] imagination . . . in reality his body was in a slow process of decay; Christiane's body was too. Despite the nights they spent together, each remained trapped in individual consciousness and separate flesh. Rollmops were clearly not the solution, but then again, had he chosen sea bass with fennel it would have been no different." The burden of materialism, and by extension atheism, is that it is less—not more—able to manage suffering and evil than religiousness. Nature is indifferent to human interest, cold and amoral without a God to make it good. What we are left with once the divine or supernatural is eliminated is not a life devoid of meaning but a life whose meaning is essentially dependent on bodily function: health, pleasure and physical ability. By nature, those things expire, and the hardships of being a vulnerable, fearful, mortal human thing are left bare. It's no accident that once the Lieu du Changement's business began to sag (as its customers' bodies sagged), the Zen workshops arrived.

The lone exception to Houellebecq's standard template for protagonists is Michel Djerzinski, Bruno's half-brother. A scientist of genius, Michel has little in the way of normal human appetites. His work shows, "on the basis of irrefutable thermodynamic arguments, that the chromosomal separation at the moment of meosis can create haploid gametes, in themselves a source of structural instability. In other words, all species dependent on sexual reproduction are by definition mortal." The solution to this essential fallibility is to remake human material—the epilogue of *The Elementary Particles* tracks an epoch-shifting transformation as Djerzinski's genetic research lights the way to the creation of a race of sexless, benevolent, neo-human immortals. The book ends with a tribute to humanity: a species that finally learned enough to be able and willing to engineer its own extinction.

•

Something that David Foster Wallace made much of in his career was the idea that literature served as a comfort to loneliness, and that this was maybe its most basic virtue. If you accept that loneliness is the great existential terror that we all, in our different ways, try to escape, it isn't hard to apprehend the fraught relationship that necessarily gives us to our own bodies, because it's our bodies that keep us so basically and dreadfully apart. It's interesting to note how often words used to express the value of literature (or art more generally) conjure up kinds of immaterialism: "seeing the world through different eyes," "being transported," forging a "psychic connection" with the author, "losing yourself" in a book—all of these are expressions that run against what seems to be the brute material truth: that we are prisoners inside our skulls. Nor is it a great challenge to draw connections between this and the spiritual immaterialism inherent in religion (think about the phrase "giving yourself to God"). Partly, these ways of speaking may be extensions of a vague but deep-rooted sense that what is distinctive and important about being human are things that find their best expression in non-biological, non-material terms—like when someone says that intimacy is the genuinely valuable part of sex. The villainy of materialism is that it undermines such talk—for instance, when it tells us that love is only a disguise for the urge to reproduce. Along this road we lose the use of a very fundamental and comforting terminology, or at least are obliged to admit that it gives a false or misleading account of human behavior. It emerges that there is basically no getting over yourself, no escaping your skull—and the more you are led to feel this way the more you are inclined to see life as isolated and vanishing.

Houellebecq's men don't think about God: all they think about—all there is—are the dictates of their biology, and their diminishing capacities to meet them. It is as if to say: the facts are what they are. So long as the facts are in your favor you can be happy, but there's nothing else to it. Not only is this position terribly lonely, it ridicules concepts of common good. Immanuel Kant, in arguing that God must be judged by the same morality as men, was saying, partly, that what is good would have to be as eternal and universal as God himself, because if what is good is only open to some—if it is dependent in any way on luck, for example—then it cannot really *be* good, since its contingency would be an evil. A value system like that of a hedonist, one that depends entirely on the working of the body, is akin to the kind of contingent good that Kant thought couldn't possibly be the real thing, i.e. it is good only for whomever it is good for. So sexual liberation is a boon *if* you are able to enjoy it, but that "if" carries with it the reality of all those people—the Raphaël Tisserands—who are left out. Moreover, materialism entails that Tisserand's condition is accentuated, but not unique. The picture Houellebecq paints across the nightclubs, resorts and restaurants of the West is of a society that understands the facts but won't spell them out—where concern for the body (health, beauty, sensation, etc.) has been raised to a cultural zenith, only without any corresponding apparatus to give meaning to decline and death. This, he opines, is the bleak consequence of the ongoing march of consumer capitalism—"which, turning youth into the supremely desirable commodity, had little by little destroyed respect for tradition and the cult of the ancestors—inasmuch as it promised the indefinite preservation of this same youth, and the pleasures associated with it."

Modern materialism has this strange kind of double effect on self-perception. On the one hand, it isolates the individual by (seemingly) dispelling various illusions of communion (the decline of religion being the paradigm example). On the other, progress in social sciences, psychology and neurology, which has seeped into the wider cultural air, encourages us to think about ourselves in various "external" fashions—as the product of genetic resources, social and economic starting position, etc. These modes of thought are uncomfortable, in that they imply that our view of things "from the inside" is illusory or distorted, and that what we experience as central and singular in our personal day-to-day are actually nothing more than instances of general truths about human behavior. To a certain extent, it is healthy to be objective about yourself (you aren't at the center of the world, despite appearances) but at its limits it becomes dehumanizing. "Flattening" is, for me, exactly the word for describing how the materialist double effect feels when you reach these limits—subjective consciousness is squished between the material barrier separating our inner life from those of others, and the inferential awareness that this inner life is itself the product of a hardwiring that we are subjectively blind to. The deeper way in which Sontag was right when she said that redundancy was the affliction of modern life is that the ascendancy of materialism not only attacks the meaning of this very precious "immaterial" vocabulary we use to talk about what it's like being human; it breeds biological fatalism, lending weight to the idea that our actions reduce to, and are determined by, dumb physical process—an ultimately pointless set of natural drives. Helplessness is the current running beneath all of Houellebecq's narratives, the soul-crushing inability to either find what you want or change what you want; to avoid death or believe that death is anything except bad.

"Is it really possible to live and believe that there's nothing else?" Thinking about a question like that is like trying to swim deeper and deeper underwater; oxygen becomes scarce and the pressure pushes you back to the surface. It is a shrill, self-pitying and impractical question, sure; and of course it would be nice to dismiss it, as it would be nice to dismiss the outlook in Houellebecq's books as so much moaning—except it's hard to evade the conclusion that the main reason for their success is that enough people identify with them; that they put into words things that people think and want to hear, but are either unable to articulate or unwilling to admit to. This, if it's true, is obviously kind of grim, because what Houellebecq has given voice to is such a downer—but then the curiosity of it is how the writing manages to be so powerfully invigorating. There is more life in *The Elementary Particles*, at least, than any number of contemporary novels—take the brilliantly banal awfulness of the scene recounting Bruno and Christiane's visits to Parisian sex clubs, where he "could not help but feel that many of the women they met in clubs were somewhat disappointed when they saw his penis. No one ever commented; their courtesy was exemplary, and the atmosphere was always friendly and polite; but their looks couldn't lie and slowly he realized that from a sexual viewpoint he just didn't make the grade." The combination of wit, pity and brutality is not common. But whether there's actually an imperative in Houellebecq for would-be novelists to digest is a difficult question. One's first instinct is to say something about the value of honesty, how maybe truthfulness is always fundamentally preferable in some way to its opposite. Certainly that is part of the appeal, and there is probably a good lesson to take in about trusting your instincts; if it feels true, it will be better writing than something that only feels like it ought to be true—literature isn't essentially normative. The downside is that actually taking what Houellebecq expresses seriously seems self-subverting. What good are books if you are sick, alone and un-loved? They are no good. At best they are make-believe to help us dis-guise the facts of life—unbearable facts. When Michel Djerzinski's lover, Annabelle, terminally ill and very frail, commits suicide, we are told that:

> She was far from accepting; life seemed to her like a bad joke, an unacceptable joke, but acceptable or not, that was what it was. In a few short weeks her illness had brought her to the feeling so common in the elderly: she did not want to be a burden to oth-ers. Towards the end of her adolescence, her life had speeded up, then there had been a long dull stretch; now, at the end, every-thing was speeding up again.

"Acceptable or not, that was what it was." Life carries on regardless until the day it doesn't—any question about what you make of it is secondary. How are you supposed to reconcile the human need to impose meaning on life, through art or other means, with the apprehension that life is arbitrary and beyond one's control? And how does it help to be honest about it if it is so? The dark joke at the bottom of the pessimist's project is that it ends up attacking its own grounds; ridiculing the futility of human action ultimately makes the art itself seem pointless—demonstrates the emptiness of its honesty. In *Platform*, the hero arrives in a Thai brothel, chancing across two other men from his package tour. One of these men, Rob-ert, is a weary cynic. The narrator's final judgment could be Houelle-becq's own:

> I nodded to Robert to take my leave. His dour face, fixed in a bit-ter rictus, scanned the room—and beyond, the human race—without a hint of affability. He had made his point, at least he

had had the opportunity; I sensed I was going to forget him pretty quickly. . . . I had the impression that he didn't even want to make love to these girls anymore. Life can be seen as a process of gradually coming to a standstill . . . In Robert, the process was already well advanced: he possibly still got erections, but even that wasn't certain. It's easy to play the smart aleck, to give the impression that you've understood something about life; the fact remains that life comes to an end. My fate was similar to his, we had shared the same defeat; but still I felt no active sense of solidarity. In the absence of love, nothing can be sanctified. On the inside of the eyelids patches of light merge; there are visions, there are dreams. None of this now concerns man, who waits for night; night comes. I paid the waiter two thousand baht and he escorted me to the double doors leading upstairs. [The girl] held my hand; she would, for an hour or two, try to make me happy.

It may be depressing that we live in a time where such a barren philosophy resonates; there is a tiny sliver of hope—possibly, maybe just—if at least it shows that resonance is still possible. Something is head-breakingly paradoxical about the concept of necessary illusions—but if we have them then, by definition, we cannot get on without them. Michel Houellebecq offers nothing that feels much like comfort, yet the force and the counterintuitive vitality in his work might allow that there is some irreducible solace just in feeling *as if* you are really connecting with someone, even if you can't—and even if it hurts.

No Such Thing?

MARGARET THATCHER
AND THE END OF SOCIETY

by Jonny Thakkar

ISSUE 7 | FALL 2013

When Margaret Thatcher died on April 8th of this year, my Facebook friends reacted with glee. Several posted a Glenn Greenwald article saying we should feel free to speak ill of the dead. Others rejoiced in a campaign to take "Ding Dong the Witch Is Dead" to number one in the U.K. charts (it made #2). Being both an expatriate and an academic, I often look upon British news with a certain degree of befuddled bemusement; questions such as whether Cornish pasties count as hot foods for tax purposes seem to lose their urgency when one spends one's life across the Atlantic reading Plato. But Thatcher's death was hard to ignore, and my friends' posts pricked something in me. Greenwald was right that it can be dangerous to allow political figures to become sanctified—as he observed, the bizarre fascination of American neoconservatives with Winston Churchill seems to have shaped their post-9/11 hysteria—and that insight would certainly have been worth sharing in the pages of the *Telegraph* or the *Mail*. But were *Guardian* readers, or any of my friends for that matter, seriously in any danger of idealizing Thatcher? It didn't seem likely. In left-wing circles Thatcher enjoys a level of prestige somewhere above Hitler but below Mussolini. What people like us needed to hear, it seemed to me, was precisely the opposite of what Greenwald said: that we should *refrain* from dancing on Thatcher's grave. From the perspective of a Plato or a Socrates, the first law of living well is to examine your own beliefs and way of life at every opportunity. By allowing a full human being to finally come into view, the passing of a once-hated political figure can occasion just such an examination. Interpreting an opponent's actions charitably can be hard, painful even. But it permits political life to disclose itself as the essentially tragic space that it really is, a space in which pursuing one value most often entails suppressing another. And in that light self-aggrandizement and demonization come to look like two sides of the same coin, both symptoms of our anxiety in the face of this troubling complexity. To sympathize with the other is, in the end, to sympathize with ourselves.

•

Why did we hate Thatcher so much, my friends and I? She was eminently detestable, there's no denying that. She gutted local democracy while claiming to be against big government; she fought inflation by deliberately running up unemployment; she labeled miners resisting the destruction of their livelihood "the enemy within"; she even managed to call Nelson Mandela a terrorist. And then there was her general bearing, which bespoke the strained snobbery of a lower-middle-class girl who had acquired a place at the top table and an accent to go with it and who now looked down her nose at those who hadn't. For Brits ashamed of their class structures, as all should be, Thatcher's whole manner was traumatic. She seemed to relish class warfare and to embody it. Even if she tried her damnedest to replace a system based on birth and schooling with one based on individual achievement, her apparent contempt for life's losers was if anything more galling than the old prejudices, and not only because the two systems seemed to map onto one another rather too neatly. The following story is most likely apocryphal but it's no surprise it stuck: at a private fundraiser in the eighties, Thatcher is said to have declared that "a man who, beyond the age of 26, finds himself on a bus can count himself a failure." Mitt Romney had nothing on that.

We had reason to hate her, right enough. But whence the intensity of our feelings for Thatcher? Whence the ongoing passion, more than 23 years after she was forced from office?

Some of it is personal, it has to be said. The most compelling reflection I found on Thatcher's death came from Russell Brand, surprisingly, writing in the *Huffington Post*. Brand certainly came to bury Thatcher, not to praise her—"Her death must be sad for the handful of people she was nice to and the rich people who got richer under her stewardship. It isn't sad for anyone else"—but what really drove the piece were his ruminations on growing up during her reign. His description of Thatcher's voice, "a bellicose yawn, somehow both boring and boring—I could ignore the content but the intent drilled its way in," captured the feeling of listening to her better than anything else I read, and the memoir was sprinkled with comic gold:

> As I scan the statements of my memory bank for early deposits (it'd be a kid's memory bank at a neurological Nat West where you're encouraged to become a greedy little capitalist with an escalating family of porcelain pigs), I see her in her hairy helmet, condescending on Nationwide, eviscerating eunuch MPs and baffled BBC fuddy duddies with her General Zodd stare and coldly condemning the IRA.

But there's a serious point in there too. In raging against Thatcher, our generation is, among other things, raging against the forces that shaped us—but rage as we might, they did still shape us, and they continue to do so. Brand himself is a case in point, as he well knows: he can lament the neoliberal erosion of the "unseen bond" of community all he wants, but at the end of the day he's not exactly Mother Teresa. He admits to feeling nostalgia for the Thatcher years, bound up as they are with his childhood, yet "what is more troubling," he owns, "is my inability to ascertain where my own selfishness ends and [Thatcher's] neo-liberal inculcation begins."

Might something similar be true for all of us who grew up in the neoliberal era? If so, might not our loathing of Thatcher—or its positive correlate, our longing for the primordial community she supposedly shattered—be rooted in anxieties about our own moral stature? It certainly rings true of me; I am, undeniably, one of Thatcher's *inheritors*. The bequest began in an oddly symbolic way: when I was seven or so, the other kids used to call me Thatcher on account of the similarity in our surnames (better that, admittedly, than a sub-sequent sobriquet that began with "f" and rhymed with "sucker"). Later on, in the complacent, pre-post-imperial environment of an elite boarding school, I came to rebel against the whole of Torydom; by blood I'm half-Indian and a quarter Irish and as a thirteen-year-old I was sure that gave me the nobility of the oppressed. But it's hard to maintain your victim status when you're on your way "up" to Oxford, and although many do seem to pull it off I wasn't equal to the challenge. As I gradually realized that I was and probably always would be on the winning side of Thatcher's great divide, I came to feel complicit in the cruelty of her supposed meritocracy. Privilege may not have been a gift that I ever asked for, but it was a gift I would receive nonetheless. Just as my younger self used to bristle at the accusation that I was spoiled, unanswerable as it was, so my eyes still water at Billy Bragg's reproach to Thatcher and her plummy progeny: "Just because you're better than me / Doesn't mean I'm lazy / Just because you're going forwards / Doesn't mean I'm going backwards."

•

The condition of being unable to respond, of being lost for words, or arguments, is perhaps especially traumatic in politics, where self-identification and self-justification are almost the same thing. So traumatic, in fact, that we tend to hide it from ourselves—but in others we can see it clearly.

I recently engaged in a deal with a right-wing American friend whereby each of us had to subscribe to a magazine from "the other side"; for me he chose *First Things*, a journal of Catholic thought devoted to something like "keeping religion in the public square." The magazine is basically pretty good, if somewhat predictable, and it's been well worth reading for an atheist like myself—but if there's one thing in God's creation the writers simply refuse to contemplate, it's how their opponents understand themselves. They consistently portray liberals as wanting to drive religion out of the public realm in order to undermine practice and belief and make way for some kind of hedonistic utopia. This may be true of some liberals. But in America the best and most influential arguments for religiously neutral public discourse have come from so-called "political liberals," like John Rawls, who actually take themselves to be *defending* religion. Only by remaining as neutral as possible with respect to religion, so the argument goes, can the state accord individual conscience, and hence religious belief, the respect it deserves. *First Things* writers never really take that argument on; they simply ignore it and bash the hedonists instead.

Let's assume, though, for the sake of argument, that political liberalism does in fact end up contributing to the secularization of public life; maybe citizens are more likely to maintain their faith if a religious worldview is taken for granted on public radio and so on. To someone like Rawls that will no doubt seem like an unfortunate side effect of his theory; to *First Things*, it will seem to have been the goal all along. Of course, the fact that you never intended something doesn't always excuse you for doing it—it just changes the nature of the culpability. Every point of view has its blind spots, and their location is always revealing; even if a general can never exactly foresee collateral damage, the rate of civilian casualties always says something about his priorities. But this is where it gets complicated. For what if you hate the side effects but have no alternative to the way of thinking that produces them?

It would be easier if your opponents were in power, especially if they didn't seem to care all that much about the collateral damage. That way you could blame them without having to account for your own position. If your own side were on top it would be much tougher, psychologically speaking. You would then be the ones producing the side effects you despise, and in principle you would have to be ashamed of yourselves. In practice, however, there is always one get-out: you can simply deny that you *are* in power.

The *First Things* crew have this technique down to a tee. If they're honest, they probably agree with the vast majority of what political liberalism has to say about toleration, devoted as they are to the image of America as a haven from religious oppression—had the 2012 election resulted in Mormonism being preached from the presidential pulpit, they would have been as horrified as the rest of us. What allows them to have their cake and eat it too is their ability to attribute the side effects of the liberal system of thought—their own system of thought—to godless elites who surreptitiously commandeered the country sometime during the sixties, the Depression or the Civil War. This is quite a feat of self-delusion, and it must take its toll on the psyche: to sustain such a fantasy, after all, you have to both demonize and aggrandize your opponents, and do so continually, in the face of reality, without end.

What does any of this have to do with Thatcher? Well, one of the greatest mysteries of the last three decades has been why leftist parties, so quick to criticize neoliberal policies in opposition, have consistently pursued them once in power. Since 1979, when Thatcher was first elected, almost all Western governments, left and right, have, to greater or lesser degrees, privatized public services and utilities while lowering taxes on corporate and individual incomes; inequality has risen inexorably; and the common perception is that citizens have become more consumerist and individualistic. In coming to terms with the failure of their elected representatives to arrest these trends, leftists have tended to cry corruption or cowardice; but the phenomena in question are too universal to be explained by personal vice alone. Either politics in general is just a cynical masquerade conducted by the rich and for the rich—a tempting explanation, to be sure—or there is something about the contemporary situation that makes it virtually impossible to resist neoliberalism. There must be various factors at work, but one of them is surely the absence of a compelling counter-ideal to neoliberalism in recent leftist thought. In the last three decades intellectuals and activists have mostly directed their attention toward foreign policy, climate change or identity politics rather than economic questions; when they have engaged directly with neoliberalism, it has typically been to offer what should technically be called *conservative* complaints, seeking to slow or reverse change rather than to suggest any new direction or ideal. And this, it seems to me, is because with respect to what we take to be our signature issue, economic equality, we have found ourselves in a similar position to *First Things*.

Economists of all stripes agree that the underlying cause of growing inequality in Western societies is the integration of the global economy, which has simultaneously increased the earning power of the highly educated while decreasing that of the rest. At the top end, HSBC can proclaim itself the world's local bank; at the bottom end, unskilled labor cannot compete abroad. Even if neoliberal tax cuts and privatizations have exacerbated the problem, they are by no means its source. This leaves leftist politicians, most of whom understand these facts perfectly well, in the depressing position of having to hold neoliberals to account for crimes against equality while having no idea how to avoid such crimes themselves. In such circumstances the only way to keep your hands clean is to stay out of politics altogether; that allows you to blame the whole thing on the political and financial elites who are *really in charge*, as per Occupy Wall Street. But the position of disdainful superiority is itself unstable. If millionaires on Wall Street are immoral for not wanting to give more of their wealth to the unemployed of Detroit, how can any of us justify not giving more of our own riches—for such they surely are—to the starving of Africa? And although globalization may produce rising inequality within Western societies as a side effect, wouldn't protectionism harm the poor in the developing world? Insofar as economic inequality is the left's principal field of battle in contemporary political life, the fact is that it has no real response to neoliberalism. Idealists without an ideal, moralists without morals, to be on the left today is frequently to be both helpless and hypocritical. Faced with such a predicament, hating Thatcher is the easy part.

Plato was very attuned to this kind of situation. One of the recurring themes of his dialogues is how angry people get when they realize their inconsistencies, or rather in the moments just before the fact of their inconsistency rises to the surface of their consciousness, as their self-image, their sense of what is due to them, begins to be squeezed by the pressures of reality. But Plato thought such humiliation was the precondition for arriving at wisdom, and I think he was right.

●

"There is no such thing as society," Thatcher infamously remarked. Coming across this statement for the first time it feels like you've discovered the secret memo that explains everything, as if Thatcher were a Bond villain who just couldn't resist explaining her entire evil scheme before enacting it. A common way of summing up Thatcher's legacy, exemplified in Pankaj Mishra's pronouncement that the London rioters of 2011 were "Thatcher's grandchildren," is that her policies and attitudes rendered Britons more individualistic and self-seeking. Russell Brand, who considers himself one of Thatcher's *children*, remembers being implicitly taught "that it is good to be selfish, that other people's pain is not your problem, that pain is in fact a weakness and suffering is deserved and shameful." And the evidence that both Mishra and Brand adduce for the idea that Thatcher wanted to impart such a lesson, the shorthand for it, is that she said "there is no such thing as society." The phrase is weirdly enigmatic, in and of itself; it rings of Yoda. Brand glosses it as "we are alone on our journey through life, solitary atoms of consciousness," as if Thatcher believed friendship or community impossible, and something of that interpretation is manifest in the way the phrase gets used as a trump card against neoliberalism from pubs to parliament. When David Cameron decided to name his political philosophy "Big Society" conservatism, for instance, no one doubted that he wanted to signal a move away from Thatcherism. "There is no such thing as society" has become a political Chernobyl.

Yet the phrase contains an important insight, I believe—one that might actually guide today's left. When you go back and look at the 1987 interview in which the phrase was uttered, it's obvious that Thatcher had no intention of glorifying selfishness.

> I think we've been through a period where too many people have been given to understand that if they have a problem, it's the Government's job to cope with it. "I have a problem, I'll get a grant." "I'm homeless, the Government must house me." They're casting their problems on society. And you know there is no such thing as society. There are individual men and women, and there are families. And no government can do anything except through people, and people must look to themselves first. It's our duty to look after ourselves and then, also, to look after our neighbors. . . .

There is no such thing as society. There is a living tapestry of men and women and people and the beauty of that tapestry and the quality of our lives will depend upon how much each of us is prepared to take responsibility for ourselves and how much each of us is prepared to turn round and help by our own efforts those who are unfortunate.

Once we've stripped away the ugly layer of contempt in which Thatcher encloses her remarks—"I'm homeless, the Government must house me"—something rather surprising emerges. For the central idea here, it seems to me, is not that there can never be any community between humans, nor that nothing can ever merit the name "society," but that community and society don't simply exist out there regardless of what we do; each of us, rich and poor, has to take responsibility for producing them. "There is no such thing as society" is a peculiar way of saying that, for sure, but then great rhetoric is often counterintuitive.

Plato is not a name one associates with Thatcher, to put it mildly, but he would have agreed with her on that point: there is no such thing as society—at least not at present. He thought of true society as an ideal, a goal, an aspiration; something that can be achieved but never assumed. Among the many topics addressed in the *Republic*, his masterpiece, is the question of what a true society would be like. To answer that question, he suggests that we need to think about why societies come into existence.

A society comes to exist . . . because none of us is individually self-sufficient, but each has many needs he cannot satisfy. . . . Because we have many needs, and because one of us calls on another out of need, and on a third out of a different need, we gather many into a single settlement as partners and helpers. And we call such a shared settlement a society.

The origin of society, then, its "real creator," is our need. Society comes into existence because we cannot satisfy our needs on our own; to do so, we have to contribute our laboring energies to the collective enterprise that is society. What society *is*, at the most fundamental level, is a cooperative scheme born of individual weakness. And the form of that scheme will determine not only the type of society we have but also the degree to which it counts as a genuine society at all.

But what are our needs, exactly? Thatcher seems to picture individuals as relatively self-sufficient. To succeed, in her view, is "to look after ourselves and then, also, to look after our neighbors," which presupposes that we can separate looking after ourselves from looking after our neighbors. Plato, by contrast, views us as *fundamentally* social creatures, relying on each other for even our most basic needs. He is clearly right that we need to share to survive. The more complex society becomes, the less likely we are to see this. But when you think about a simple society, like the one Plato has us imagine, it becomes obvious: if we each had to make our own shoes, clothes and houses we would have little time to do the farming. We depend absolutely on the division of labor.

Where Plato becomes radical, though, is in his view that we depend on the division of labor not only for our continued existence but also for our ultimate happiness. Nowadays we tend to think of our life prospects as relatively independent of one another, and that's what Thatcher assumes as well. But Plato thinks we sink or swim together. No one can be happy if his desires are not sound, his capacities developed and his opportunities felicitous; and our desires, capacities and opportunities are shaped by the people and institutions around us. In a bad society we can always hide ourselves away, but this will never shield us completely. In Book VI of the *Republic*, Socrates advises us to avoid political life in an unjust society, "like someone who takes refuge under a little wall from a storm of dust or hail driven by the wind." In Book VIII, however, he returns to this quietist, depicting him as a tragically impotent father, incapable of teaching his son to live well in the face of outside influences. We are all, in some sense, each other's parents. The ultimate goal of our social cooperation is therefore to create an environment in which virtue, and hence the possibility of happiness, can be reliably fostered. That would be a true society.

On Plato's view, then, society is a collective project aimed at securing the good life. It is as if we find ourselves thrust together with no option but to work as a team, at least if we are to survive and to prosper. But if the team is to function properly, each of us needs to *play for the team.* This is less a matter of fuzzy altruism—Socrates emphasizes that "if [citizens] share things with one another . . . they do so because each believes that this is better for himself"—than of having the discipline to carry out a particular role. Think of soccer. Defenders need to stick to their positions, and not wander around in search of excitement. If each player simply follows the ball (as often happens in pick-up games) there really *is* no team. Likewise with society: if everyone does his own job, and the jobs combine appropriately so that each contributes to the collective good, there will be a functioning society. If not, there will be no such thing.

•

Continental Europeans tend to drop the "neo" in "neoliberalism"—to them it is simply "liberalism." And from a Platonic perspective that's just about right. Where economic life is concerned, the contemporary political scene is split between *left-liberals* and *right-liberals.* What they have in common is an unwillingness to say anything about the goals of work. Provided they commit no crimes, how citizens choose to spend their laboring energies is seen as a private matter. What then comes up for debate is what to do with the proceeds: whether to force citizens to contribute to public goods such as infrastructure and education, for instance, or to improve the welfare of the poorest. In the Platonic view, however, all such debates are secondary to the question economic liberals invariably suppress: What do we actually do with our work?

If not all "societies" are real societies on Plato's account, then not all "jobs" are real jobs either. A hermit has work to do, but no job. Jobs exist only where there is a division of labor: you peel the carrots, I'll peel the potatoes. A division of labor in turn presupposes a collective enterprise, like an evening meal, towards which the various jobs aim, and in terms of which we understand what counts as a genuine job. For Plato, as we have seen, the goal of a society's labor is first to maintain that society in existence, and then to enable each citizen to lead the best life he can. And these goals determine what counts as a real job. Just as checking your email plays no part in preparing dinner, so blackmail doesn't contribute to a good society. Real jobs, by contrast, are *crafts*, skilled activities directed towards producing particular social goods; medicine, for example, is the craft that restores sick bodies to health. In a genuine society, Plato thinks, everyone—shoemakers and shepherds, soldiers and statesmen—will be a craftsman in this sense. But the statesman's craft is peculiar, since he is the one who regulates the other crafts to make sure they are really directed towards the social good. To return to the team analogy, the statesman is like a soccer manager, deciding which functions need to be carried out in a given situation: sometimes even the goalkeeper has to join the attack. The job of the statesman, then, is to decide what counts as a real job. He is a "philosopher-king."

Talk of "philosopher-kings" sounds far-fetched and utopian to the contemporary ear—yet Plato's vision of society as a team of craftsmen regulated by a master craftsman passed, partly through the influence of his pupil Aristotle, into the basic legal structures of medieval Europe. The idea of labor as teamwork aiming at the common good, rather than at one's own immediate gain, complemented the thought of the Christian Fathers: Christ had despised the rich; for Paul avarice was "the root of all evil"; and Augustine had seen lust for possessions as one of the three principal sins of fallen man. The medieval Church therefore held up an ideal—often flouted in practice, but an ideal nonetheless—of economic activity as subordinate to moral purposes. William of Auxerre, a thirteenth-century monk, was typical, for example, in arguing that private property was to be suspended in times of need, or that a contract resulting from unequal bargaining power was necessarily invalid. The central doctrine was perhaps that of the "just price," propounded in the second half of the thirteenth century by Albert the Great and Thomas Aquinas. Albert and Thomas argued that one ought always to sell an article for its true worth (understood primarily in terms of the labor required to produce it) rather than for the highest price the market will bear. If one village were struck by a crop failure, for example, the next village should not seek to profit by raising the price of their wheat. As Aquinas put it,

> If someone would be greatly helped by something belonging to someone else, and the seller not similarly harmed by losing it, the seller must not raise the price, because the benefit that goes to the buyer comes not from the seller, but from the buyer's needy condition: no one ought to sell something that doesn't belong to him.

Given human fallenness, however, this doctrine had to be inculcated by law and habit rather than mere preaching. It was therefore up to public officials to determine prices, wrote Henry of Langenstein in the mid-fourteenth century, since "to leave the prices of goods at the discretion of the sellers is to give rein to the cupidity which goads almost all of them to seek excessive gain."

When put into practice, then, Plato's economic thought quickly led to what we would now call *socialism*. The label seems perverse at first, since we tend to think of socialism as aiming at equality, whereas the largesse of the medieval Church was legendary and monks proved only too happy to sustain the feudal hierarchies at whose summit they naturally imagined themselves seated. But what else to call the price controls, limits on private property and so on that were instituted in the Middle Ages? Better to think of socialism as having a core sense beyond its more recent egalitarian incarnation—Plato's vision of society as an ideal, not a given, something that has to be continually created by citizens working towards the common good. With Plato, in other words, we can put the social back into socialism.

•

Today's economists would probably dismiss medieval strictures on price and property as primitive misunderstandings, much as they

now view twentieth-century command economies with more contempt than alarm—the first chapter of the most widely used text-
book, Hal Varian's *Intermediate Microeconomics*, consists of a simple
demonstration of why an economy with price controls will necessarily allocate goods and services inefficiently. But the sophistica-
tion of contemporary economics, unquestionable though it is, risks
blinding us to the fact that its medieval ancestor was barely concerned with efficiency at all. It was a branch of ethics. Citizens had a
duty to work for the common good, and it was taken for granted that
the purpose of economic regulation was to ensure this duty was performed. If the ethics-first approach to economics has come to seem
absurd to us today—if right- and left-liberalism seem like the only
live possibilities—then that represents an intellectual revolution.
And much of the credit must go to one man: Adam Smith.

Most institutions try to socialize us out of egoism; even competitive sports attempt to engender—or at least enforce—values and
habits that place the survival of institutions above individual success. Smith argued that the economy should be an exception to this
rule, a self-standing sphere with rules and norms that contradict
those of society at large. Bernard Mandeville, a Dutch doctor living
in London in the early eighteenth century, had argued in his *Fable of
the Bees* that a sufficiently artful politician could transform private
vices, like the desire for luxury, into public benefits. Smith took up
this line of thinking but freed it from its moralistic premise and its
reliance on individual dexterity. Replacing "vice" with "interest," he
argued that given appropriate institutional frameworks the general
welfare would be best served if everyone pursued his own private
interest in economic matters.

> By directing that [domestic] industry in such a manner as its pro-
> duce may be of the greatest value, [a businessman] intends only
> his own gain; and he is in this, as in many other cases, led by an
> invisible hand to promote an end which was no part of his in-
> tention. Nor is it always the worse for the society that it was no
> part of it. By pursuing his own interest, he frequently promotes
> that of the society more effectually than when he really intends

to promote it. I have never known much good done by those who affected to trade for the public good.

To pursue one's own interest in economic affairs is not only acceptable, on Smith's view, but noble. Whereas those who try to work for the public good end up being ineffectual, in a competitive marketplace those who serve themselves will inevitably end up serving others. If people want a given good, there will be an incentive to produce it; if they don't, there won't. "It is not from the benevolence of the butcher, the brewer, or the baker, that we expect our dinner, but from their regard to their own interest," Smith writes. "We address ourselves, not to their humanity but to their self-love, and never talk to them of our own necessities but of their own advantages." Self-love or self-interest, greed or avarice—call it what you will, the invisible hand promises to wash it clean.

Smith does not think we should always act selfishly, of course, or even that we do. If there is to be any kind of stable social order we must forbear from harming others; this is what Smith calls justice. More than that, we all have a natural interest in the plight of the badly off; this is what he calls charity. But what shapes today's economic thinking is not these nuances but Smith's central proposition, which is that in a competitive marketplace egoistic economic agents will raise productivity and thereby create a "universal opulence which extends itself to the lowest ranks of the people." Whatever our highest ends are, from alleviating misery to building opera houses in the jungle, wealth can only serve them. And if the opulence should turn out to be less than universal, well, we can always redistribute—whether through private philanthropy, as right-liberals recommend, or the state, as do left-liberals.

This way of thinking forms the unspoken background of Thatcher's "there is no such thing as society" interview. It's a vision of small shopkeepers like Thatcher's father, living in small market towns like Grantham, where she was raised, pulling themselves up by their bootstraps and encouraging others to do the same. "It is our duty to look after ourselves and then, also, to look after our neighbors." There's no room for large-scale capitalists or global corporations in this idealized marketplace of butchers and brewers and bakers, as liberals would happily point out. But there's also no place for the idea of work in Plato's sense—and that is an objection that tends to pass liberals by completely.

•

Imagine a debate between Smith and Plato today; ignore the anachronism, if you can. Plato would argue that the tradesmen Smith mentions in his famous example are not butchers, brewers or bakers at all, but what he calls "moneymakers"—they are guided by profit, not product. As such, he would claim, they will never create a genuine society.

In Book I of the *Republic*, Socrates insists that strictly speaking a doctor (and by extension any craftsman) must be distinguished from a moneymaker. Doctors do make money, of course, but Plato's point is that anything that counts as one activity will be governed by a single organizing principle, something that gives unity to all the sub-activities, and that for a true doctor this will be healing the sick. The true doctor still earns money, but since this is not the goal in reference to which he makes his professional decisions he should not be called a moneymaker; it is incidental to his activity that he earns money, whereas it is essential to it that he treats the sick. Imagine, on the other hand, a "doctor" who treats the sick with one thing in mind: earning money. Plato would say that this man *masquerades* as a doctor.

Smith would see no problem with that. After all, both doctors and "doctors" heal the sick. In a system where the incentives are correctly aligned, such as a competitive marketplace with perfect information, it should make no difference to a patient whether or not he is treated by a true doctor. But Plato might ask what happens if the incentives come apart. Imagine, for example, a country—let's call it America—where psychiatrists find they can make more money prescribing drugs than offering talking cures.* Some psychi-

---

* See, e.g. "Talk Doesn't Pay, so Psychiatry Turns Instead to Drug Therapy," the *New York Times*, March 5, 2011.

atrists believe that drugs are more effective than talk; imagine one who doesn't. This doctor really believes the best treatment he can give involves personal contact for sessions of 45 minutes or more, but knows he can earn almost twice as much by scheduling three fifteen-minute sessions for dispensing medication. All other things being equal, a true doctor will make a decision based on his patient's needs; a moneymaker will simply prescribe drugs. And since similar decisions are made every day in countless hospitals and clinics, it will matter a great deal whether a society has doctors or "doctors."

Since society is itself created and sustained only by the work its members perform on its behalf, like a team in which everyone has a role to play, Plato would also, as we have seen, distinguish between a society and a "society." If every citizen carries out his social work to the best of his ability, there will be a real society. But if each worker is a moneymaker who performs his role only incidentally, when the incentives happen to be correctly aligned, then society will be nothing but an incidental by-product of moneymaking. It will be a "society" rather than a true society. So what?—Smith might once again ask—we each get to do what we want, productivity is raised to unprecedented levels, and as a "collateral benefit" we produce something that to all intents and purposes looks like a society! Would you really rather live in the Middle Ages, toothache and all?

Wealth without virtue may indeed be pointless, as Socrates says in the *Apology*, but this rejoinder is unlikely to carry much weight in contemporary debate, however justified it might be in the abstract. As Deirdre McCloskey observes in *Bourgeois Dignity*, living standards have shot up since moneymaking began to be perceived as a respectable activity: in 1800 the global average income was just three dollars a day (in today's money); now it is thirty dollars, and in Norway it is as high as 137 dollars. Smith was right about productivity, essentially, and it's hard to see many of us choosing to swap its benefits for the rigors of virtue. As Thatcher used to enjoy repeating when pushed to defend neoliberalism, "There Is No Alternative."

Checkmate? Not necessarily. For even if Plato were forced to accept that labor should be allocated via the market and its price signals rather than conscious reflection on society's needs, he might still ask how we as individuals are to understand our roles in this system. Consider this reformulation of Smith's argument by Thatcher's intellectual hero, Friedrich Hayek:

> Profit is the signal which tells us what we must do in order to serve people whom we do not know. By pursuing profit, we are as altruistic as we can possibly be, because we extend our concern to people who are beyond our range of personal conception.

This is polemical of course—neither Smith nor his followers need say anything so extreme. But what it brings to the fore is the first-personal dimension of our debate. Should we respond to price signals *in order to serve others*? Or should we simply seek profit full stop? Do we consider ourselves as craftsmen or as moneymakers? Sometimes it is obvious that pursuing profit won't benefit others. The social function of financiers, we are sometimes told, is to ensure the efficient allocation of capital across society so as to spur economic growth. But suppose that for some reason or other the financial system actually rewards speculation that does *not* fulfill this function, speculation that actually *lowers* economic growth in the long run, and imagine—if you can—that our men of finance just happen to be moneymakers at heart . . .

•

Plato thought he could rely on a class of philosopher-kings whose craft would be to ensure that each part of society carried out a genuine job. But in *The Road to Serfdom*—a book that shaped Thatcher's ideology from her days as an undergraduate at Oxford—Hayek pointed out that a decentralized market economy will allocate social resources far more effectively than a team of experts ever could, since the price system instantaneously collates information about local conditions and needs. Besides, Hayek and other liberals argued, citizens tend to disagree about what is good for society or the individual, and hardly anyone still believes, as Plato did, that there is expert knowledge to be had about such matters. The basic tenet of social liberalism, that the state should not impose a vision of the good on individuals, is justified both in theory and in practice. Being able to shape your own course in life is a prerequisite for that life to be worth living; and experience shows that a society that does not respect individual freedoms will end in oppression. There is no way around liberalism.

The temptation is for socialists to repress the fact of liberalism, to blame elites for refusing to give economic life more ethical direction, and to cocoon themselves in hermetic discussions that pretend a top-down approach were still possible—to become, in short, the mirror image of the Catholics at *First Things*. Such escapism might well have its pleasures, but it also has its pains, not least psychically. And in any case there is no need: for economic Platonism is in fact compatible with social liberalism.

Socialists cannot force citizens to be craftsmen, true. Nor can they dictate a vision of the good life. But the state can legitimately encourage citizens to work according to their *own* conceptions of the good life. Just as it is a citizenly duty to look after the physical environment, throwing away litter, placing items in the right receptacles and so on, a duty that is promulgated but not enforced by the state, so it should be considered a citizenly duty to look after the social environment: to play one's part in producing the kind of institutions and goods that enable us all to flourish—not least our children, whom no parent, no matter how privileged he be as an individual, can isolate from society's influence. Granted, we may have different understandings of what would constitute a good environment and what would count as a contribution towards it. But within the framework of a liberal state, where no one forces anyone else to pursue a given way of life, we can live with that. This is socialism from the ground up.

The state must provide more than moral support, however, if such socialism is to become a reality. Imagine a stereotypical movie scene with an idealized worker—a fireman, say—nobly ignoring his own well-being for the sake of the common good and steadfastly refusing all congratulations: "I'm just doing my job," he says. Now imagine a real-life patient protesting to his psychiatrist that no, something really important has come up in the last few days and he just has to talk it over; the psychiatrist responds that he only has fifteen minutes to review the prescription; the patient gets angry and starts shouting; the psychiatrist tries to calm him down by saying, "Look, I'm just doing my job, all right?" What the phrase typically means in real life, in other words, is: "Leave me alone—it's not up to me." The psychiatrist might actually want to be a true doctor, yet be constrained to be a "doctor" by the insurers who pay his wage and the bankers who hold his student debt. To turn "doctors" into doctors will therefore require more than a change in their personal priorities; it will require changing the priorities of their institutions.

And this brings us back to the question that socialism has always raised, from the Middle Ages to the twentieth century, namely ownership. Businesses tend to serve the interests of those who own them, whether shareholders, workers or communities. To make institutions serve people rather than profit, we will therefore have to think about alternative forms of ownership: scholars like Erik Olin Wright and John Roemer have shown that social ownership can come in many forms, and these should be studied with an open mind.* What is vital, however, as we renew our assault on the neoliberal dogma of private ownership, is to remember that the ultimate goal is not to strengthen the central state or even simply to benefit the poor, but rather to free workers to use their own initiative to serve the common good as they see it.

•

When I think of Thatcher and the rage she induces in me and my friends, I can't help feeling that at the end of the day it's all quite simple: she won. In the face of her onslaught our arguments about equality feel abstract and phony. We know that we don't want too much inequality, but how much is too much? And what are we going to do about it? G. A. Cohen pointed out that if you really believe in redistribution, you don't have to wait for the right government

* See Erik Olin Wright's contribution to *The Point*'s issue 5 symposium on the left, "Toward A Social Socialism."

to get elected—you can start giving your money away this minute. His book was entitled *If You're An Egalitarian, How Come You're So Rich?* but the principle applies to most of us, especially when you start thinking on an international scale. However just the idea of worldwide redistribution may be in theory, few of us are principled enough to really countenance it. And we know that. Our accusations and our insults therefore sound shrill and frail. Lacking an ideal towards which to work, we are impotent and reactive—we can reject but we cannot affirm.

Nowhere is this more evident than in the matter of career decisions. We—my circle, at any rate—tend to despise those who take the "easy option" of corporate labor. As opposed to what, though? It seems to me that to earn a free pass from today's moralizers all you need to do is not sell out. It's considered absolutely fine, for instance, to while away your twenties in grad school playing video games, watching reality TV and occasionally turning your thoughts to the writings of some obscure author. A life like that actually gives you some kind of moral purchase vis-à-vis a banker or a lawyer—at least you're not increasing inequality. Even if we ignore the fact that a disdain for materialism has often been a marker of class distinction, it's clear that there's something fundamentally warped about this ethic. It tells us what is bad, but as to the good it is silent.

If leftists are to look neoliberals in the face with confidence rather than bitterness, we need an ideal that can orient us. Is Platonic socialism too distant to serve? I don't see why it should be. It gives us an overarching logic for resisting the march towards privatization, for one thing, above and beyond outrage at the corruption and incompetence that inevitably accompany such schemes; and it gives new focus to campaigns against personal debt. More than that, though, it gives us something to live by as individuals. For one way to bring about an ideal is to act as if it already existed. And in a service economy you can very easily ask yourself what service your work actually performs. Does it count as a *job* in the Platonic sense, a contribution to the collective enterprise of society as you see it? To be a craftsman you don't have to be a saint, running a soup kitchen or helping little old ladies with their shopping. But it might be hard, for example, to combine tutoring rich kids for their SATs with holding others in contempt for selling out, as so many twentysomethings try to. For Platonic socialism demands that you provide some account of how your work might help constitute a healthy social environment. You can always refuse that demand, of course, but you thereby accept Thatcher's bequest, however implicitly, and take your place in the neoliberal family alongside the bankers and the rest.

If, on the other hand, you do try to direct your labors towards producing a slice, no matter how small, of the common good, to make your product the best it can be while charging only as much as you consider fair—if you do all this you may end up contributing to the creation of a genuine society. Yet your work need not be in vain even if that larger goal remains unmet. "The highest reward for a man's toil is not what he gets for it but what he becomes by it," John Ruskin is supposed to have said, and Plato would certainly have agreed. In any case, however, society, like a team, is not an all or nothing proposition: every little helps. We may never produce a true society, sure. But what we can certainly produce is some such thing—and from where we stand right now, that will do just fine.

Forward with Fukuyama

by Daniel Luban

ISSUE 10 | SUMMER 2015

Francis Fukuyama was 36 years old in 1989 when "The End of History?" made him a star. At the time, there was little in his biography to mark him as anything more than another ambitious young Cold War technocrat. He had been hired by the RAND Corporation directly out of graduate school at Harvard (where he wrote a dissertation on Soviet foreign policy under the famous political scientist Samuel Huntington) and, aside from two stints at the State Department, had remained at RAND ever since, producing geopolitical analyses whose readership did not extend beyond the national-security bureaucracy.

But Fukuyama had always been philosophically curious—a bent nurtured by his undergraduate teacher, the Straussian guru Allan Bloom, and maintained throughout his time in the policy world— and the argument he made reflected that. Delivering the original lecture before a University of Chicago audience that included Bloom, he argued that the scientific revolution had unleashed unprecedented productive energies for satisfying human desire, energies that only capitalism could properly harness. On its own, this scientific-economic logic could lead "equally well to a bureaucratic-authoritarian future as to a liberal one," as he put it in his book-length elaboration, *The End of History and the Last Man* (1992). But humans are more than just desiring creatures seeking material satisfaction; they are also valuing creatures seeking recognition as equals, and only liberal democracy could satisfy this drive for recognition. The demise of fascism and communism left no coherent ideological challenges to liberal capitalist democracy, which stood revealed as history's endpoint.

The basic argument, as Fukuyama stressed, was not original to him; he had adopted it from Hegel, and specifically from Hegel's twentieth-century interpreter Alexandre Kojève. Timing alone, however, helped Fukuyama reach an audience unlikely to slog through Kojève's 1930s lectures on the *Phenomenology of Spirit*. His essay arrived in the months before the fall of the Berlin Wall, the book in the months following the collapse of the Soviet Union. Yet this timeliness was a curse as well as a blessing; if it guaranteed Fukuyama a mention in every intellectual history of the post-Cold War zeitgeist, it also meant that he tended to be more cited than read.

For a supposed embodiment of American triumphalism, the book's tone was strangely wistful, and in its latter parts Nietzsche replaced Hegel as the guiding philosophical influence. Liberalism offers satiation of our desires and universal recognition as equals, Fukuyama suggested—but what about our need for heroism as opposed to harmony, our urge to struggle for superiority rather than settle for equality? Weren't these more powerful drives, and in some ways more admirable ones? Won't some of us continue to "struggle for the sake of struggle," with a consequent "potential to restart history" at any moment?

These questions were too high-flown to interest most of Fukuyama's critics. After the initial celebration, he quickly lost favor, his argument often treated as little more than a rhetorical punching bag. Commentators of varying leanings could all agree that the end of history thesis was willfully naive, a relic of post-1989 triumphalism that had been rapidly overtaken by harsher political realities. Fukuyama, for his part, turned to somewhat more modest topics in the years after *End of History*, writing books on trust, biotechnology and U.S. foreign policy.

But now Fukuyama has returned to the scene of the crime—to History in its full sweep. In a two-volume work, *The Origins of Political Order* (2011) and *Political Order and Political Decay* (2014), he offers an extraordinarily ambitious account of human political life from prehistoric times to the present day. *Political Order* (as I'll call the volumes collectively) is undoubtedly his most significant work since *End of History*. Yet the reader could be forgiven some skepticism: Why slog through a thousand pages by a man most famous for being spectacularly wrong?

One answer is because he wasn't wrong at all, at least not in the ways that are commonly assumed by his critics on either the right or the left. Fukuyama's argument has its limitations, and *Political Order* helps bring them into clearer focus. But understanding those weaknesses requires us first to reckon with its genuine strength.

•

The backlash against the end of history thesis began almost immediately. Beginning with the 1991 Gulf War, critics noted triumphantly that events (important events, even!) were continuing to occur, an observation that was recapitulated after every major geopolitical occurrence of the past quarter century. But this represented a simple misunderstanding. For one thing, Fukuyama did not think that history had ended everywhere; much of the world remained "stuck in history," if only temporarily. More importantly, he was concerned not with history in the sense of the everyday flow of events, but with history as the story of the broader ideological frameworks by which we live. The only kind of event his theory ruled out was the rise of a world-historical challenge to liberal capitalist democracy.

The more serious critiques, found in both right-wing and left-wing flavors, came from those who charged that such a challenge *was* emerging. The right-wing critique, more prominent in everyday political debate, found its most famous expression in the 1993 essay "The Clash of Civilizations?" by Fukuyama's old mentor Samuel Huntington. (Huntington's piece, seemingly destined to be mentioned alongside Fukuyama's "End of History?" in perpetuity, likewise lost its question mark on the way to becoming a book, *The Clash of Civilizations and the Remaking of World Order*.) Huntington posited a number of distinct civilizations alongside the "Western" one that Fukuyama took to be potentially universal, but the most salient was

Islam. Fukuyama's ostensible failure to account for the rise of radical Islam became a commonplace on the right; as one hawkish critic jeered, "the 'end of history' ended on September 11, 2001." The consensus that radical Islam had taken the place of fascism and communism as the existential threat to Western liberalism reflected a genuine fear of terrorism, of course, but its appeal also reflected something deeper: the desire for an enemy that would allow today's Westerners to relive the Manichean conflicts of generations past. It reflected, in other words, something like the need to "struggle for the sake of struggle" that had worried Fukuyama all along.

The notion that 9/11 changed everything involved a fair amount of selective memory; the threat of radical Islam had been a major topic of public debate since at least the Iranian Revolution of 1979, and many of Fukuyama's critics had cited it against him from the beginning. His response throughout was measured and consistent: the most attention-grabbing forms of radical Islam were a fringe position even among Muslims, and showed no capacity to win adherents among the non-Muslims who make up the vast majority of the world. Terrorism was a product of modernity, bred primarily by Western societies' failures to integrate immigrant populations, rather than a deep-rooted feature of Islam itself. Above all, the West should remember that its own transition to liberal democracy had been long, uneven and violent.

In truth, Fukuyama's thesis had always been ambiguous with respect to international politics, for it could be interpreted in either an idealist or a realist direction. The idealist version (whether liberal or neoconservative) suggested that liberal democracy's triumph would be accompanied by peace, as commerce replaced warfare; perhaps national boundaries would even fade as the world approached Kojève's "universal and homogeneous state." This had been Fukuyama's own interpretation (although he never went in for fantasies of a world state), and in *End of History* he buttressed it with invocations of democratic peace theory, which maintains that democracies do not go to war with one another. (The theory is controversial for multiple reasons: empirically, because its truth depends heavily on the definitions of key terms like "democracy" and "peace";

politically, because it can, rather perversely, justify starting wars to impose democracy abroad.) But the end of history thesis could also be interpreted more minimally. It would not, on this view, deny the persistence of international conflict but only the persistence of conflict motivated by rival ideological systems, the grand "isms" of the twentieth century. Liberal states might continue to struggle among themselves, but these struggles would concern immediate interests rather than the value of liberal capitalist democracy itself—just as European states of previous centuries fought numerous wars that did not call into question the legitimacy of divine-right monarchy.

Fukuyama never fully defected from the idealist to the realist camp. Even in his most recent writings, he insists that states are not homogeneous pursuers of self-interest, for their internal structures and core values shape their foreign policies. But his political orientation changed over the years in subtler ways. Once a self-proclaimed neoconservative and man of the right, he broke with his former allies over the 2003 invasion of Iraq. His grander claims about the pacifying effects of liberal democracy faded away, and in his 2006 book *America at the Crossroads*, he made his break with neoconservatism official, arguing instead for a "realistic Wilsonianism" (even if he left unclear precisely what such a stance would imply). The book concluded by proposing as a model for American foreign policy not the neoconservative idol Winston Churchill but the realist icon Otto von Bismarck.

In a surprising way, the attacks from the right helped illustrate some of the less obvious virtues of Fukuyama's original thesis. He may have been complacent, but he was no crusader. The very triumphalism that his critics decried, his belief in liberalism's unshakable ascendance—and, perhaps, his bittersweet consciousness of living in a post-heroic age—helped inoculate him against the impulse to seek out new monsters to slay.

•

If the right attacked Fukuyama for being insufficiently fearful about political threats to Western liberalism, the left attacked him for being insufficiently hopeful about economic alternatives to it. Fukuyama's argument came on the heels of a set of developments that seemed to fit a pattern: the collapse of the USSR; Deng Xiaoping's decision to move China toward something that looked a great deal like capitalism; Margaret Thatcher's and Ronald Reagan's attacks on the postwar welfare state. The closing-off of systematic alternatives to capitalism coincided with capitalism's own transition from "Fordism" to "neoliberalism" (to use the now-conventional terminology), and Fukuyama seemed to exemplify both of these pernicious trends. To detractors on the left, his thesis was at best a failure of political imagination and at worst a highfalutin version of Thatcher's taunt that "there is no alternative" to the free market.

However unappealing Fukuyama's view may have been to the left, the lean years of Third Way liberalism and compassionate conservatism did little to disconfirm it. But more recent events have offered critics of the left, like those of the right, the chance to claim vindication by history. If the right liked to maintain that history had returned on September 11th, the left came to argue for September 15th: the day in 2008 when the fall of Lehman Brothers signaled that the Great Recession had arrived in earnest. The years that followed brought political disappointment, particularly for those who had grandiose expectations for the Obama presidency, but this very disappointment seemed to open the door for a resurgent radical left that would reject liberalism altogether. Marx is back, it was proclaimed—often by the remaining faithful, who had never allowed that Marx had ever been away, but sometimes also by new converts. Those looking for portents could find them all over the world. In Europe, the fight against austerity brought the largest left-wing economic mobilizations in a generation, exemplified by the recent electoral victory of the leftist party Syriza in Greece. In America, economically focused movements like Occupy had difficulty gaining much traction, but a resurgent left was visible elsewhere, above all in the recent protests against police brutality stretching from Ferguson to Baltimore. Everywhere, self-proclaimed radical voices became more prominent, driven by a new and adversarial activist culture centered on the internet.

But regardless of how significant this trend proves—and the fact that its participants tend to be young, educated and internet-savvy likely leads us to overestimate their numbers—its implications for Fukuyama's thesis are not entirely clear. The end of history does not require total ideological consensus or political stasis, for the overarching framework of liberal capitalist democracy is perfectly capable of including warring left-wing and right-wing variants. The relevant question is not the size or strength of today's left but whether it stands outside this framework.

One obstacle to answering this question stems from the persistent conflation of Fukuyama's thesis with Thatcher's "no alternative," suggesting that Fukuyama's position is specifically neoliberal. Of course, the meaning of "neoliberalism" is itself often obscure; increasingly, it is used as shorthand for The System as a whole, in which case it must include Fukuyama along with virtually everyone else. But in the narrower and more concrete sense of the term—the specific form of capitalism characterized by privatization, deregulation, austerity and so on—Fukuyama is no dogmatic neoliberal. In *End of History*, he argued that all societies will eventually accept the "basic terms" of capitalism, but denied that this must dictate "the extent to which they regulate and plan capitalist economies." The kind of capitalism found at the end of history rules out Soviet-style central planning but encompasses everything from extreme laissez-faire to robust social democracy.

It therefore encompasses virtually all of the left's economic battles in recent years. These battles have mostly been rearguard actions in defense of what remains of the old welfare state—against austerity, against privatization, against the continued upward redistribution of income. However necessary they may be, they do not take us beyond the end of history. The point was driven home with great clarity in a recent speech by Greek finance minister Yanis Varoufakis, the darling of the left since Syriza's electoral victory. The experience of recent decades, he argued, demonstrates the futility of hoping that crisis would inevitably lead to something better. "The left must admit that we are just not ready to plug the chasm that a collapse of European capitalism would open up with a functioning socialist system." As a result, Varoufakis suggested, Syriza finds itself in the unlikely position of trying "to save European capitalism from itself," however ambivalently it might approach this task. It is too early to tell how Syriza's story will end, but the recent experience of leftists in power (especially in Latin America) suggests that they will likely disappoint those hoping for a systematic rejection of capitalism.

A similar point holds for the leftist groundswell more broadly. Rejectionist pockets exist, but the dominant ideals are largely liberal ones. The most important left-leaning writers to emerge in recent years, like Glenn Greenwald and Ta-Nehisi Coates, tend to be masters of immanent critique, challenging actually existing liberal democracies from inside rather than outside their own premises. (Whether this is a matter of genuine belief or rhetorical strategy is not particularly important; what matters is that these are the arguments that resonate.) Issues like privacy, once disparaged as the quintessential bourgeois freedom, have become central concerns of the left.

To be sure, the generation that came of age after Obama has grown more willing to embrace the "radical" label, leading some centrists to warn darkly of an emboldened far left that (in the words of the journalist Jonathan Chait) "has borrowed the Marxist critique of liberalism and substituted race and gender identities for economic ones." But the radicalism of what we might loosely call the "internet left" has been primarily on the level of tone and tactics; there is little in the underlying vision that would shock John Stuart Mill. If its partisans are radicals, they are predominantly radical liberals. This is not, as some old-fashioned Marxists are prone to complain, because of a shift of focus from class toward race and gender; such categories can be analyzed from any number of political standpoints. The prevailing tenor (and perhaps the incoherence) of the movement stems rather from its specific ideological mixture: broadly pluralist and tolerationist ideals combined with maximalist tactics directed against those perceived to violate them.

None of this is to suggest that the left's current battles are not worth fighting. Nevertheless, the fact that these are the relevant battles tends to confirm rather than to refute Fukuyama's basic thesis. He may still be proven wrong—after all, for his argument to be correct, it has to be correct forever, and the future lasts a long time. But on the most basic level, we still inhabit the ideological landscape that Fukuyama described a quarter century ago. The end of history hasn't ended, yet.

•

Yet perhaps we are looking in the wrong place. Fukuyama and his critics, for all their disagreements, have shared a set of assumptions about history's overall shape. For both, history is directional and dialectical, continually generating new things and never precisely repeating itself. Whether we have reached the end of the road, or whether we have an unknown distance still to go, both can agree that we will never double back the way we came. Historical change comes about as one world-historical formation supplants another, dramatically and often violently. We remember such changes by the capital-r Revolutions that name them: American and French, Russian and Iranian, Agricultural and Industrial, Scientific and Digital. If Fukuyama is wrong, the logic goes, it is for failing to anticipate the next of these momentous changes—if the end of history ends, it will do so with a bang.

But what if it ends with a whimper instead? What if the alternative to the end of history is not a leap forward into the unknown but a slow slide back into what came before? Perhaps the last couple of centuries, with their warring -isms struggling to supplant one another, are the real anomaly. The task then would be to stop trying to discern the next -ism coming over the horizon, and instead focus on the multifarious problems of political life that take place on a less grandiose level. A return, not to the warring gods of the twentieth century, but to history as it has taken place for most of human existence.

These are the questions that are raised by *Political Order*, if only implicitly. Fukuyama rarely pauses to relate his new work to the ideas that made him famous, but it nevertheless sheds light on how his thinking has evolved over the last quarter century. The change is most obvious on the level of genre: while *End of History* was a work of political theory, with a distinctly Straussian undercurrent of hostility towards scientistic views of human life, *Political Order* is unabashedly social-scientific. It might be misleading to say that the new work is more concrete than the old—certainly it is no less sweeping and ambitious, aiming to give a history of human political life from prehistoric times to the present. The tone, though, is more practical, examining the concrete problems of building political institutions rather than the fate of the world. Just as significantly, the Hegelian and Nietzschean themes in the earlier work—the view of humans as value-creators, recognition-seekers, strivers after power—largely drop out. The people on display in *Political Order* are more prosaic creatures: rule-following, religious and community-oriented, somewhat venal but not otherwise vicious.

Fukuyama presents his new work as a revision of Huntington's *Political Order in Changing Societies* (1968). Huntington's book was notable for its rejection of the tidiness of classic modernization theory: far from political, economic and social development progressing in tandem and irreversibly, uneven development and political decay are perpetual possibilities and sources of unrest. Along these lines, Fukuyama tracks the various permutations by which societies have arrived at successful political institutions, or failed to arrive at them, or lost them. The ultimate task, he suggests, is "getting to Denmark." (The choice of social-democratic Scandinavia as the endpoint rather than market-mad America is probably not accidental.)

Political Order's thousand or so pages cover a vast amount of historical ground, far more than any review can survey. But one of the work's virtues is that for all its massive scope, Fukuyama is agreeably cautious as an analyst. He rejects monocausal explanations of historical change and warns against the delusion that we could ever predict future developments with any certainty, instead aiming to provide a "middle-range" theory that isolates a range of causal factors and generalizes about their relative importance. Rather than a grand theory of history, *Political Order* presents us with a careful and thoughtful observer picking his way through the grand theories of others.

As Fukuyama is well aware, however, there is no such thing as pure empiricism, and *Political Order* has an implicit conceptual framework. The directionality of *End of History*, with its closing image of humanity as a wagon train traveling into the future in procession, has become far more muted; so has the theme of technological change. Fukuyama sometimes notes the vast changes wrought by industrialization, the breakout from a zero-sum Malthusian world into one marked by new and untold production possibilities, but such changes do surprisingly little work in the overall argument; he views the problems of political development today as broadly similar to those of past millennia. History, once a directional process producing endless novelty, has become something like an oscillation between two poles—a story of nature and artifice, as humans alternately rise out of their primordial state and descend back into it. One pole, the goal to be attained, is rationally administered Denmark. The other, the primordial state perpetually threatening to return, is what he follows Max Weber in calling "patrimonialism."

•

Fukuyama begins his story before *Homo sapiens* even emerged, and the first hundred or so pages of *Political Order* race through the vast majority of human societies, first "bands" of hunter-gatherers and later "tribes" of farmers and herders. The distinguishing feature of these societies, he claims, is that they are organized around what he calls "natural human sociability." Contrary to the state-of-nature fantasies of early modern philosophy, humans have always lived in groups; contrary to the anachronistic assumptions of economists, their default mode is cooperation rather than the pursuit of individual self-interest. Drawing on voguish work in evolutionary psychology and game theory, Fukuyama argues that there are two basic and biologically rooted forms of such cooperation: kin selection, by which we favor others insofar as they share our genetic material, and reciprocal altruism, by which we help genetic strangers insofar as they help us in turn. This natural sociability is the basis of the general phenomenon of patrimonialism, the tendency to favor one's own family and friends. The bands and tribes that precede proper states are entirely organized around these decentralized patrimonial groups.

The tribal or patrimonial society, its structure dictated by biological imperatives, is thus the default mode of human existence for Fukuyama—the baseline against which we can measure our progress toward Denmark. The evolutionary flavor of the argument certainly suits contemporary intellectual sensibilities. But already difficulties appear which will trouble the project as a whole. It might be true, for one thing, that the biological imperative to pass on one's genes is responsible for the general ubiquity of kinship structures of some kind. But as many anthropologists have argued (the most recent being Marshall Sahlins), these kinship structures take a wide variety of forms that do not strictly correspond to the percentage of genes shared by members, meaning that there is no single natural or default form of kinship. Likewise, however interesting the game-theoretic models of the emergence of cooperative behavior may be, they bear a striking resemblance to the state-of-nature model that Fukuyama elsewhere rejects, and may not tell us a great deal about actually existing social relations. The structure of Fukuyama's narrative requires "patrimonialism" to be a unified phenomenon, one whose biological roots make it a constant possibility and hence the perpetual threat to effective political order. But its conceptual underpinning, natural sociability, seems to dissolve the closer one looks at it.

The other pole of the basic contrast that underlies *Political Order* is clearer: it is the modern state-level society. The contrast itself, as Fukuyama acknowledges, is essentially Max Weber's, and his narrative echoes Weber's story of the supplanting of "traditional" authority by a "bureaucratic" authority that is rational, efficient, autonomous and impersonal. Fukuyama rejects certain aspects of twentieth-century modernization theory, such as its Eurocentrism and its assumption of unilinear progress. But like modernization theory, his work remains structured around the categories set out by Weber and the other founding fathers of social theory: Maine's status and contract, Tönnies's *Gemeinschaft* and *Gesellschaft*, Durkheim's mechanical and organic solidarity. Fukuyama may vary the story, delinking the various processes of modernization and emphasizing that they are always contingent achievements, but the desired end state is ultimately not very different. History can be (even if it isn't always) a process of rationalization. And history still has an end, not in the sense of a stopping point but in the sense of a telos: getting to Denmark is history's purpose, even when the actual passage of time takes us further away from it.

Fukuyama isolates three institutions on the road to Denmark: the state, which involves consolidating power, and the rule of law and accountable government, which both involve tempering it. The rule of law requires that a higher body of preexisting law (whether constitutional, customary or divine) set limits to the ruler's power; accountability requires that rulers be responsive to the interests of society as a whole. Defining these institutions so broadly lets Fukuyama appreciate the ways that informal constraints have historically limited what rulers are able to do in practice, even in societies lacking the formal mechanisms of modern liberal democracies. It also lets him appreciate the critical role that religions have historically played in shaping political institutions. (Some of the most surprising chapters in *Political Order* describe how the self-interested policies of the Catholic Church helped create an atomized society in Western Europe at the dawn of the medieval period. It was this atomized social structure, he suggests—drawing on scholars like Marc Bloch and Jack Goody—that was the true source of Europe's distinctiveness, a thousand years before the rise of capitalism.) But at the same time, this ecumenical approach comes at a cost: it prevents Fukuyama from defining the rule of law and accountability with any precision, so that it is never entirely clear, for instance, whether they are a matter of rulers' subjective beliefs or of objectively enforceable limits on their power. Nor is it clear how much the two differ from each other, and he allows that they "have been closely associated with one another historically and promoted in common."

This imprecision may reflect Fukuyama's own preoccupations, for his primary focus is ultimately on the state—that is, on the creation of effective power rather than its limitation. The state-building chapters are the central ones in *Political Order*'s first volume, and the most willing to depart from the conventions of the "West and the rest" genre. While his broad-brush depiction of "tribal" society might suggest that his will be yet another story of modern European exceptionalism, he instead gives pride of place to classical China, arguing that the Qin and Han Dynasties (221 BCE to 220 CE) saw the birth of the "modern" Weberian state. More generally, he refuses to equate modernity with the growth of limited (Anglo-American) government or to identify what Europeans called "Oriental despotism" with backwardness and ignorance. On the contrary, he remarks wryly, "so-called Oriental despotism is nothing other than the precocious emergence of a politically modern state."

Impersonal administration is the goal and patrimonialism the threat, and Fukuyama is bracingly ready to follow this logic wherever it might lead—in the process rehabilitating some of the villains of traditional Whig history. Nowhere is this more striking than in his treatment of the form of military slavery that developed in the Islamic empires of the Mamluks and Ottomans, in which the military and administrative classes were composed of slaves separated from their parents and forbidden heirs of their own. The system may have shocked European observers; "no one is a tyrant there," Montesquieu marveled of the Ottomans, "without at the same time being a slave." But Fukuyama sees it as a rational solution to the problem of patrimonialism, ensuring a class of impartial soldiers and administrators without whom Islam would likely have perished as a world religion. It only failed when the slaves were allowed to make their positions hereditary, thereby allowing patrimonialism and corruption to reassert themselves.

•

The theme of rational administration besieged by biological sociability likewise dominates the second volume of *Political Order*, which covers the last two centuries or so. Noting that the world changed dramatically after 1800, as industrialization offered an escape from the Malthusian cycle, Fukuyama focuses on the political ramifications of this shift rather than on its economic, technological or environmental aspects. Increased prosperity brings social mobilization, as newly literate publics demand a role in political life and mass democracy replaces traditional mechanisms of accountability. But democracy is a mixed blessing, for it invites clientelism, the modern form of patrimonialism. Tammany Hall-style machine politics is, for Fukuyama, the natural outcome when a society (like nineteenth-century America) democratizes before it has a well-run state in place.

How then to achieve good governance? One answer is war: the pressures of military competition are a brutal yet effective mechanism for weeding out inefficient structures, and many of the most successful states (from classical China to nineteenth-century Prussia) were forged in its crucible. (Conversely, the relative lack of interstate war in Latin America, however desirable in itself, helps explain the persistence of the patrimonial structures inherited from the Spanish and Portuguese colonizers.) To an extent, then, Fukuyama endorses Charles Tilly's maxim that "war made the state, and the state made war." He does insist, however, that war is not necessary for effective state-building, since in some cases (notably nineteenth-century America and Britain) reform coalitions were able to emerge in the absence of a major military threat, which largely succeeded in purging patrimonialism and creating effective bureaucracies.

At least temporarily. Perhaps the most important lesson Fukuyama takes from Huntington is that political decay is always possible. The conservative and rule-bound nature of human beings means that institutions which arose as a rational response to one set of conditions persist well after these conditions have abated, and the biological imperative to favor one's own means that re-patrimonialization is always a threat. Here Fukuyama clearly has America in mind. The central theme of his second volume is how the United States, having briefly achieved something like an effective state in the early twentieth century, has subsequently let it slip away (a process symbolized by the rise and decline of the U.S. Forest Service). He tries to stay out of the polemics about size of government that define everyday American politics, instead emphasizing that the quality of government is more important than its size. But his book nonetheless represents a sustained argument against America's libertarian self-image, beginning with its opening epigraph: Alexander Hamilton's paean to "energy in the executive" from the *Federalist*. The problem with American government is that it "allocates what should properly be administrative powers to courts and political parties"—or, more simply, that it has "too much law and too much 'democracy' relative to American state capacity."

Should state-building therefore take precedence over democracy? That had been Huntington's answer; the most famous takeaway of his 1968 book was that developing countries might require an "authoritarian transition" to modernize before opening the democratic floodgates. Here, at least, Fukuyama is unwilling to follow his teacher. For one thing, it is easier to sing the praises of enlightened authoritarianism in theory than to find genuinely enlightened authoritarians. For another, although the demand for democratic participation is not historically universal, and only arises as a by-product of the modernization process, once it has arisen it can no longer be ignored. Democracy is a fait accompli.

This is the answer we would expect from Fukuyama; he became famous, after all, for insisting on democracy's inevitability. And here even his critics (at least his Western ones) are unlikely to disagree with him. The ascendancy of the concept of "democracy" is in fact one of the strongest pieces of evidence in favor of the end of history thesis. The old debates in political theory, from Aristotle onward—which took democracy to be one kind of regime among many, and argued for its superiority or (more often) inferiority compared to the others—are barely imaginable now. The premise that democracy is the only legitimate form of government has become so deeply ingrained that the only remaining question is who gets to claim the term for themselves. Contemporary debates in political theory pit "deliberative democrats" against "radical democrats"; social critics of self-proclaimed democratic regimes like the United States charge them with being "sham" rather than "real" democracies; even nakedly authoritarian states feel compelled to give themselves a democratic sheen. (Kim Jong Un rules over the Democratic People's Republic of Korea.) To that extent, we are all Fukuyamans now.

But is Fukuyama himself still a Fukuyaman? If he still insists on democracy as a sine qua non, the tone is a bit more hesitant, and the argument somewhat at odds with the tenor of *Political Order* as a whole. *End of History* had insisted that economic modernization alone cannot explain the inevitability of democracy, for the logic of capitalism is as compatible with a "bureaucratic-authoritarian" future as it is with a liberal one. Only by treating humans not merely as desiring creatures who seek material satisfaction but as valuing creatures who seek recognition can we understand why liberal democracy is necessary. Such Hegelian themes are far less evident in *Political Order*, and the bureaucratic-authoritarian future seems more of a live possibility. It is China, Fukuyama suggests, that poses "the most serious challenge" to the end of history thesis, although he insists that it is impossible to tell whether the Chinese model will be stable. Regardless, the dominant image evoked through the thousand pages of *Political Order* is of the modern Weberian state—rational, impersonal, bureaucratic—born in China and at home there for the past two thousand years.

•

For all that Fukuyama rose to fame by announcing the end of the Cold War, his categories remain deeply shaped by it. The authoritarian Weberian state rising to confront the liberal Weberian state, embodied in two global empires—the image is one that would be at home in the social theory of half a century ago. It may not be a coincidence that Fukuyama's fiercest critics tend to be those who want to refight the Cold War, regardless of which side is the object of their nostalgia. But perhaps this framework itself is no longer adequate.

As I write this piece on the South Side of Chicago, I have periodically stepped outside to feed the meter where my car is parked. It might seem like a classic example of the modern state's fiscal apparatus in action, down to the high-tech electronic meter itself. But my money is not going to the local government at all: in 2008, the city of Chicago sold off its parking meters to a consortium of private investors led by the financial giants Morgan Stanley and Allianz. In return for a one-time infusion of cash to the revenue-starved city government, the consortium received the right to run Chicago's parking for the next 75 years (a right, as it turned out, worth far more than what they paid for it). It is only an especially brazen example of a wider trend toward the privatization of core government functions.

Fukuyama has a ready way to explain such phenomena: they represent re-patrimonialization, the innate tendency to favor one's family and friends over the public good. The privatization of parking meters is not different in kind from the tribal leader using his power to reward kin and allies. And there is some merit in this explanation, at least in reminding us that many of the phenomena taken as novel features of the contemporary world have a long history. Indeed, in its broadest outlines the Chicago parking deal is simply a form of tax farming, the practice by which ineffective pre-modern states sold off the right to extract revenue from the populace to private actors; it would have been familiar to an inhabitant of the French *ancien régime*.

But Morgan Stanley is not a local chieftain, and the interest groups that dominate contemporary politics are hardly analogous to the kinship groups of non-industrial societies. If the Weberian state is losing its coherence, this may not represent a retreat to the particular, to the local, to some sort of vaguely defined biological sociability. It seems rather to represent a new kind of impersonality, still more impersonal than the territorially rooted governments that it is challenging. When I lose patience with the increasingly extractive Chicago parking authorities, I want more than anything to give a piece of my mind to those responsible—but who would this even be? Does it make sense to speak of "recognition" in such a context? Recognition by whom, of whom, as what? Does it make sense to describe this relationship as "liberal," or for that matter as "illiberal"? We still lack the vocabulary to describe what is happening around us, but perhaps this very lack is a sign that the end of history will not last forever.

II

AFTER FERGUSON

Who Will Pay Reparations on My Soul?

by Jesse McCarthy

ONLINE | SUMMER 2014

In the summer of 1960, James Baldwin wrote an essay he styled "Fifth Avenue, Uptown: A Letter from Harlem." Among the host of ills he observed in the neighborhood where he was born and raised, he gave a prominent place to the dynamics of racialized policing:

> The only way to police a ghetto is to be oppressive. . . . Rare, indeed, is the Harlem citizen, from the most circumspect church member to the most shiftless adolescent, who does not have a long tale to tell of police incompetence, injustice, or brutality. I myself have witnessed and endured it more than once.

Like so many of us watching events unfold on the live feed from Ferguson, Missouri, I thought about how depressingly familiar it all looked. How many times has this very script played out in our lives? What year wasn't there a prominent slaying of a black citizen under dubious circumstances, followed by an outbreak of rioting? Here is Baldwin in 1960, describing the archetype in his characteristically lucid way, with empathy but also a stern moral clarity:

> It is hard, on the other hand, to blame the policeman . . . He, too, believes in good intentions and is astounded and offended when they are not taken for the deed. . . . He moves through Harlem, therefore, like an occupying soldier in a bitterly hostile country; which is precisely what, and where, he is . . . He can retreat

from his unease in only one direction: into a callousness which very shortly becomes second nature. He becomes more callous, the population becomes more hostile, the situation grows more tense, and the police force is increased. One day, to everyone's astonishment, someone drops a match in the powder keg and everything blows up. Before the dust has settled or the blood congealed, editorials, speeches, and civil-rights commissions are loud in the land, demanding to know what happened. What happened is that Negroes want to be treated like men.

The vulnerability of racially marked bodies to power, particularly police power, and the lack of justice—the singular and persistent evidence of gross unfairness where race and the law intersect—reveals a bloody knot in the social fabric that is as vivid in Ferguson, Missouri today as it was in Baldwin's Harlem half a century ago. What can be done to end this awful cycle of violence? What still prevents so many blacks from being treated with full humanity—treated, in Baldwin's words, as men?

•

In German, the word *Schuld* means both *guilt* and *debt*. In the context of the American debate about race relations, "reparations" likewise reflects both sides of the coin. The principal difficulty with reparations, as with black history in America more generally, is that guilt is an unpleasant feeling, susceptible to clouding judgment. Guilt colors the whole conversation. Today nobody can deny that being charged with racism is one of the most incendiary charges one can levy in public life. People are genuinely mortified by the accusation; many fear to even approach racial topics, or tread through them like a minefield. This legacy of political correctness has proved double-edged. On the one hand, a certain kind of public discourse is far less poisonous and injurious than it was a few decades ago. On the other hand, we have made race a relentlessly personal issue, one that often shields and distracts us from the harder questions of structural inequality, racial hierarchy and social control.

Ta-Nehisi Coates, an editor for the *Atlantic*, has recently joined a long tradition of black American writers stretching back to David Walker by calling upon America to live up to its moral promise; to re-imagine itself, in Coates's words, through "the full acceptance of our collective biography and its consequences." His essay "The Case for Reparations" has renewed the enduring debate about the possibility of reparations as payment for racial injustice in the United States.

The popularity of the piece has led, predictably, to a consider-able backlash, notably among black conservatives, with much of the criticism grounded in the notion that the topic of reparations is harmful rather than helpful to a conversation about racial politics. But Coates is right to take us back: in "reparations," he has resus-citated a word with the rhetorical heft necessary to shift a conver-sation on race that has become too personalized, and too compla-cent. It is far more productive for us to argue about reparations than about, say, graphic suffering in *12 Years a Slave*, or how wonderful (or troubling?) it is that Lupita Nyong'o is now a fashion icon. Talking numbers, legal cases: all this may not be as jolting as the prostrate flesh at the whipping post. Yet it represents what we still don't seem to know: for whites, the extent to which blacks were defrauded and stolen from; for blacks, an oft-forgotten history of resistance, like Chicago's Contract Buyers League, laying the groundwork for re-newed action in the present.

At the same time, I want to seize on the opening Coates has pro-vided to suggest a different emphasis, one which ultimately comes down to thinking about reparations for racial injustice as a moral rather than a material debt, and one that must be repaid politically, not compensated for economically.

I should make a few things clear here. First, Ta-Nehisi Coates *does* think America owes a moral debt to African Americans; it's just that he believes one way of discharging that debt is through material compensation. I agree that compensation is owed, and, like Coates, I am not impressed by the usual objections, many of which Coates anticipates and counters in his own essay. Typically these involve throwing up one's arms over the practical conundrums of determin-ing who is owed what, how much, how to be accounted after so many years, etc. What about people of mixed race? What about recent immigrants? What about all the white Americans who fought with the Union and bled and died to defeat the Confederacy? (I won't respond to those here. For those interested Coates has good rebuttals to many of these objections, which he posted in a follow-up article.)

Ultimately, I think we ought to reject a program for material reparations in America for two reasons. The first is that no amount of monetary compensation can rectify a debt that consists in the broken promise of a social contract; this contract is a moral good, and therefore its abrogation a moral debt.

What do I mean by a moral debt? It is not fashionable these days to talk about the principle of a social contract. But the American founders were intimately attached to the idea, and placed it at the center of their reasoning and justification for creating a democratic republic. That this framework for freedom and flourishing was built over and against a massive system of black enslavement is at the heart of the American contradiction, our original sin. There is a strong belief today that the civil rights movement redeemed that sin for all time. But a real democracy doesn't live on its laurels—it has to be "worked out in terms of the needs, problems and conditions of . . . social life," as the philosopher John Dewey reminds us. Can anyone today seriously maintain that there isn't urgent work to be done to integrate poor black communities politically and socially, or that there is not a strong case for favoring such work over other potentially worthwhile objectives?

My second objection is pragmatic, although not in the sense described above. Despite the justifiability of the case for material reparations, it is vastly improbable that they will ever be mandated politically, whereas reasonable new initiatives in education, policing, prison reform, community empowerment and sentencing reform, even if difficult, should all be realizable within the horizon of contemporary politics.

Ta-Nehisi Coates knows that the chance of restitution resulting from a reparations bill passing in Congress is nil; the gambit is that even without enforcement the required return to forgotten history could provoke "a national reckoning that would lead to spiritual renewal." I agree that we need to have the kind of conversation that would lead to a national reckoning. I just think the issue of monetary loss and compensation is not the right angle from which to pursue it.

Let me be clear: Coates is not wrong to address the wealth gap. Far too few Americans understand the way black poverty has been systematically contoured and shaped by white power, by whites refusing black populations access to the levers of upward mobility that they then endlessly complain blacks fail to take advantage of. Yet Coates's overarching emphasis on material loss can make it seem as though our affective reaction should primarily be motivated by material inequality. Coates writes that "no statistic better illustrates the enduring legacy of our country's shameful history of treating black people as sub-citizens, sub-Americans, and sub-humans than the wealth gap." The wealth gap is obviously a significant metric for blacks today, but I would argue it is not nearly as significant as the black incarceration rate, as the death rate of blacks at the hands of police, as the number of failing schools in black school districts. The "Colored Only" sign says to a black person that they have been robbed of much more than what could or should be in their wallet.

Toward the end of his article, Coates draws a comparison to the case for German reparations after the Holocaust. The comparison is thought-provoking but inexact. One obvious problem is that, in the German case, the reparations were paid to the state of Israel. A state can collect and allocate large-scale resources in ways that can generate gainful investments benefitting the population it speaks for. In the case of reparations to American blacks, there is no state organ on the side of the collector. More importantly, the Israeli Jews on the receiving end of German reparations were citizens of a separate nation from the one that was paying them. The reparations we are concerned with here are not for foreigners, or a group of African Americans with their own state in, say, Liberia. The taking and giving in this instance would be from the same people; black American taxpayers would be handing money back to themselves. Within its own borders the way for a state to do justice to an oppressed minority is not by paying it off, but by creating the conditions for it to flourish equally.

Reparations as cash equivalent, even if justified, would be inherently superficial in this sense. But there is another way of thinking about reparations. Instead of arguing about wealth, we could talk about freedom from domination, community control and justice before the law. Reparations in the form of political and legal reform, a recognition that blacks still need and deserve greater control over their communities, and the resources to make that control efficacious. The disturbing images from Ferguson are clear: a police force with a local power structure that is overwhelmingly white coupled with jurisdiction over a community that is predominantly black is a recipe for disaster. None of this should be surprising given our history—but that does not make it intractable. We have addressed such problems with democratic principles and reform-minded politics before.

•

"They were seeking the protection of the law," Ta-Nehisi Coates explained, describing the reason Clyde Ross left Mississippi for Chicago. Ironically, Mr. Ross would find himself again the victim of unjust housing policy in the North. The protection of the law is not something that white Americans are used to thinking of as a luxury. But for black Americans the law has only rarely functioned as a protection, and then only after it has been struggled for mightily. I don't use the word *luxury* casually. It's astonishing how often people talk about civil rights without considering how deeply illogical it is that civil rights needed to be passed in the first place—how it took a hundred years after Emancipation for blacks to have protections to which they understood themselves entitled even in bondage.

The hypocrisy of white power in the United States has long flowed through illegal, extralegal or flagrantly immoral channels. It is black Americans who time and again have called for ensuring truer and broader justice in the land—for America to live up to the formidable ideals of its charter and not just pay lip service to them.* That deep

---

*The tradition goes back to the founding. David Walker, in his Appeal of 1829, invoked the broken social contract when countering Thomas Jefferson's racist pseudo-science in *Notes on the State of Virginia*. The theme is the thunder

sense of corrective justice suffuses King's "Letter from a Birmingham Jail" with its profound meditation on just and unjust law, and with its memorable and timely chiding of the "white moderate, who is more devoted to 'order' than to justice; who prefers a negative peace which is the absence of tension to a positive peace which is the presence of justice." From Ida B. Wells's anti-lynching campaign, to Freedom Summer, to the ongoing campaign against the unconstitutional "stop-and-frisk" policy in New York City, black Americans have relentlessly advocated for a nation of laws, for respect for constitutional rights and for freedom from domination, the cornerstone of republican participation and inclusion in the social body.

And yet the poisonous dynamic that Baldwin described hasn't shifted an inch. Blacks in the most vulnerable and poorest areas of America continue to experience the law as a raw power relation, the police as a hostile enforcer to be distrusted or openly resisted. People continue to be astonished at "no-snitching" attitudes, even as police continue to justify coercion and abuse by framing their captives in the same light as the Bush and Obama administrations have painted terrorists: folks beyond the reach of the law, folks that bad things (like torture) happen to, because—implicitly—they deserve it. This situation, one of negative tension rather than positive justice, has all but drowned out the voice of Mr. Ross. But his desire to simply be "protected by the law" has always burned behind black demands for *access* to the law, for an instrument that respects their moral agency and values their lives accordingly.

We would do well to recall images that we have allowed ourselves to forget. Like that famous photograph of old Mose Wright, stand-

---

in Frederick Douglass's blistering philippic, "What to the Slave is the Fourth of July?" And it is why Dr. King, in his last speech, directed mostly to an audience of illiterate sanitation workers, could get such a clamoring response when he said, "somewhere I read of the freedom of assembly. Somewhere I read of the freedom of speech. Somewhere I read of the freedom of press. Somewhere I read that the greatness of America is the right to protest for rights." None of the workers there had likely "read" the founding documents; but they could read King's irony perfectly. They were striking for a fair wage, but it wasn't just about money. Someone wearing a sign that says "I AM A MAN" is not merely asking for a pay raise. At stake in Memphis was a claim on a civil birthright.

ing and pointing in the courthouse in Tallahatchie, Mississippi to identify the men who abducted and murdered Emmett Till. He risked his life to do what was right, and in faith that the law would bring justice. It did not. The all-white, all-male jury acquitted the killers who left the courtroom smiling. People who watched and re-watched videotape of police beating Rodney King in 1992 were sure the LAPD would finally have to be held accountable for a practice blacks knew was routine in their neighborhoods. The police were acquitted. LA exploded. In 1999 Amadou Diallo, a black immigrant from Guinea, pulled out his wallet to produce identification and was shot 41 times by police who claimed they saw a gun. Officers were acquitted. In 2006 Sean Bell was leaving his bachelor party when he was gunned down by plainclothes officers, also acquitted. In 2009, Oscar Grant was shot in front of a packed rush-hour train while lying facedown with his hands over his head on the subway platform. Riots had to be suppressed in San Francisco. Blacks felt sure that in 2012 with a black president in the White House, his-tory could not repeat itself in the case of Trayvon Martin. But it did. Even the O. J. Simpson case of 1994, a "victory" that proved terribly pyrrhic, revealed how deeply American blacks wanted to believe that they could have the power of the law serve them.

Earlier this summer, the death of Eric Garner—a black man sell-ing illegal cigarettes—at the hands of police who were videotaped taking him down in an illegal chokehold revived racial tensions in New York City. A report from the New York District Attorney's office that adolescent inmates at Rikers Island have for years been system-atically physically abused and had their rights violated will perhaps shock some white New Yorkers, but it is only a small part of a pattern that is common knowledge to the city's blacks. The cases continue in their ugly procession. Today the nation knows the name of Mi-chael Brown, dead at the hands of a white policeman in Ferguson who shot the unarmed teenager six times in broad daylight.

These are only the most publicized cases, the tip of the iceberg. There are innumerable examples that don't grab headlines, like that of sixteen-year-old Corey Stingley—who in December 2012, about ten months after Trayvon Martin's death, stupidly shoplifted some wine bottles he was too young to buy from a corner store in suburban Milwaukee. He was restrained at the store by three older white men, and held in a chokehold that ended his life. In an excellent documentary Vice News produced on the case, Corey's father, Craig Stingley, says, "I'm not going to stop pursuing the justice that my son deserves, until I know that there is no justice . . . And that will be an indictment on the system in and of itself."

Would the local D.A. have taken the case to trial, instead of dismissing it, if Corey were a sixteen-year-old white boy and had been pinned down by three grown black men? What if the D.A. had been black instead of white? Forget the racial dynamics for a moment. Consider simply that Corey's father is moved with extraordinary calm to seek justice in the law; all he asks is that his son's death be allowed to go to trial. Even that has been denied. The father has spoken on what that lack of justice means. But the failure of justice spreads like a ripple, and for Corey's white girlfriend Maddie, and particularly the other black citizens of Milwaukee, a wave of ominous questions must now cloud their lives.

Injustice has an affective, emotional dimension that is deeply corrosive, but which can never be quantified. The rage and pain that blacks feel when white officers are acquitted has no useful coefficient—yet I would submit it is precisely this kind of injustice that most seriously frays black confidence in integration, by reinforcing already deeply ingrained attitudes towards institutions. The point is that injustice inflicts primarily a moral cost, and only incidentally a monetary one. Thomas Piketty may have recently revived a conversation about inequality of income, but many Americans fail to fully recognize that a well-segregated subset of their fellow citizens still do not see equality before the law.

Such a blow can be literally fatal. The deaths of unarmed black men at the hands of police cannot be attributed to the wealth gap: plenty of poor whites come into police custody all the time. But the deaths of black men at the hands of police can, by destroying and warping moral confidence in society, contribute in very real ways to the persistence of a wealth gap. If black men feel confirmed in their status as outlaws, as rejected and unwanted bodies, it's more likely to harden patterns of antisocial behavior that will isolate and impair them. How can you in good faith enter a society that treats you more like an enemy combatant than a citizen?

•

It is undeniable that the ghettos experienced a brutal shift in the eighties and nineties, as the government ramped up the so-called War on Drugs and the neoliberal state retreated from social care in favor of what sociologist Loïc Wacquant has called "punishing the poor." This climate of violence and fear damaged solidarities and communities in ways we still haven't come to terms with. You can hear the shift in black music, as hip-hop hardened between 1988 and 1994. Biggie's "Things Done Changed," Tupac's "Keep Ya Head Up" and a litany of similar tracks show a deep awareness of a change in conditions that isn't about poverty, but about violence, incarceration and drugs. When Nas says in the song "Halftime," from *Illmatic* (1994), that he raps "in front of more niggas than in the slave ships," the historical continuity is telling. It speaks volumes that his imagination can seamlessly recast the projects as nothing but the long, hardened shadow of the slaver's hull.

When I used to teach at a high school in Red Hook, Brooklyn, I would assign a beautiful book by the photographer Jamel Shabazz called *A Time Before Crack*. Shabazz grew up in Red Hook in the late seventies and eighties, documenting the nascent hip-hop generation that was coming up around him. My students loved seeing images of an optimistic youth that had "swag" but didn't appear to look or feel criminalized, "gangster." They saw images of a generation that was ready to live, not ready to die. They couldn't recognize themselves in it. The issue wasn't money—the kids in the pictures didn't seem any poorer or wealthier than them. Something else was missing.

•

The Princeton political theorist Philip Pettit has been a proponent of a return to republican (with a small "r") values in political philosophy. Republicanism, a tradition founded in classical Rome that flourished in the city-states of Renaissance Italy, conceives the relation of the individual to the state primarily as a subject bound by laws and duties. But its most essential feature, according to Pettit, is non-domination. In his 2012 book *On the People's Terms*, he reminds us that for republicans "the evil of subjection to the will of others, whether or not such subjection led to actual interference, was identified and indicted as the iconic ill from which political organization should liberate people." This evil was described as "being subject to a master, or *dominus*"—suffering domination—and was contrasted with the good of *libertas*, liberty. The state must guarantee citizens freedom from domination from each other, but, importantly, "it also needs to guard against itself practicing a form of public domination." For republicanism to work the people must "demand a rich array of popular controls over government."

It is no accident that blacks in the United States would be attracted to a republican conception of politics. Black Americans are the only population in U.S. history to have known complete lack of lawful protection in regular peacetime society, a condition described by Giorgio Agamben as the "bare life" of *homo sacer*: the human being whom the sovereign treats as existing beyond the reach of the law, capable of being terminated at any time and without any legal or moral cost. (Sociologist and cultural historian Orlando Patterson famously named this condition "social death.") The black man in America has often been imagined as an outlaw, but in truth blacks more than any other group have fought for the sanctuary of the law, seeing in it their best weapon for securing freedom from domination.

Arguably it is that intangible freedom that subtends the possibility all other goods; where it is eroded or negated, all else fails. It won't help Mr. Ross to pay off his mortgage with a reparations check if he has to continue living in a neighborhood that is patrolled like a war zone. No material reparation of any kind would have made a difference to Michael Brown's fate as he ran from an ugly encounter with a cop. His family cannot be consoled by a check in the place of a son going off to college. And the black citizens of Ferguson cannot trust they are safe, or believe they are equal, if they don't see justice.

Think about how the world looks from one of the black ghettos we hear about—say, on the South Side of Chicago. Think of the real pressures of domination that shape the perspective of so many young black men, who by reasonable inference from their immediate environment see themselves in an overtly antagonistic relationship to a Foucauldian state that expends considerable resources to discipline and punish them, and none to secure a basic foundation for their flourishing. They are born squeezed between what Hobbes would have recognized as a war of all against all, where life is "nasty, brutish and short," and what Michelle Alexander has called "The New Jim Crow," a society that has shamefully crowned America with the highest incarceration rate in the world, with the federal inmate population increasing by 800 percent between 1980 and 2013. Unfreedom is everywhere, nowhere is safe, justice is the law of the gun. Let's focus on changing these conditions. When we do, I'm confident blacks will reconstitute all the wealth they need.

•

Gil Scott-Heron has a beautiful song I wish Ta-Nehisi Coates and all of us would listen to again. It's called "Who'll Pay Reparations on My Soul?" The title is also the refrain, but the force of the rhetorical question lies in its pithy yoking of materialism and slave capitalism to a logic that transcends the material. This is also the crux of my dissent: What can reparations mean when the damage cannot be accounted for in the only system of accounting that a society recognizes? Part of the work here is thinking about the value of human life differently. This becomes obvious when commentators—including Coates—get caught up trying to tabulate the extraordinary value of slaves held in bondage (don't forget to convert to today's dollars!). It shouldn't be hard to see that doing so yields to a mentality that is itself at the root of slavery as an institution: human beings cannot and should not be quantified, monetized, valued in dollar amounts. There can be no refund check for slavery. But that doesn't mean the question of injury evaporates, so let us ask a harder question: Who will pay reparations on my soul?

Black American music has always insisted upon *soul*, the value of the human spirit, and its unquenchable yearnings. It's a value that explicitly refuses material boundaries or limitations. You hear it encoded emblematically in the old spirituals. Black voices steal away to freedom. They go to the river. They fly away. Something *is* owed.

But the very force of this debt lies in the fact that it cannot be repaid in the currency that produced it. There is a larger question at stake, a question of values and social contracts, and about dismantling the intimate relationship between white supremacy and capitalism, which threatens to make a mockery of the republican promise of freedom from domination.

Reparations should be about bending the social good once again towards freedom and the good life. The War on Drugs and its corollary, mass incarceration, represent a massively unjust and abusive use of state power with massive consequences. I firmly believe it will go down as a blight on American history. For the work of reparations, dismantling its legacy and restoring confidence in a demilitarized social life is urgent. Thankfully, there are some signs that—however belatedly and feebly—Eric Holder's Justice Department is inching in that direction.

In other areas, too, there are divinations of progress. The nation is slowly recognizing the absurdity of its sentencing guidelines, with New York's judge John Gleeson serving as a powerful voice to reform mandatory minimums with infamously disparate racial impacts. In Newark, newly elected mayor Ras Baraka is championing citizen involvement and empowerment at the neighborhood level, in part by organizing concerned citizens to monitor and patrol high crime areas in coordination with city police, making them stakeholders in neighborhood safety and not just collateral damage to police enforcement. Prison reform that would track juvenile nonviolent offenders into spaces isolated from a harder prison population should be explored. Accountability and reform that prevents the physical and sexual assault too often endured by American prisoners is needed. Examining the hiring and training of local and state police, and ensuring that communities have a say in how they are policed, and who is policing them, is an urgent business. And black Americans must strive to reinvigorate a communal, grassroots politics that brings pressure from below, a pragmatic social politics that black intellectuals like Eddie Glaude, Jr., Cornel West and Tavis Smiley have been advocating for years now. These practices and demands of civic inclusion are what a republic is supposed to embody: a freedom where people care for each other and hold each other accountable.

•

After Ta-Nehisi Coates's essay was published, the popular liberal pundit Ezra Klein interviewed him for Vox. There is a touching and awkward moment in that interview when Coates tells Klein that he is interested in the question of whether a state can have the kind of memory that a parent has for a child: a love unconditional, but that doesn't shy away from recognizing vices and flaws. Klein takes up the point, but not the metaphor. It struck me as a fascinating moment because in some ways this is a very "black" way of thinking about society, of the body politic, one that makes perfect sense for Coates to evoke, but which Klein would likely never articulate in quite that manner.

Black Americans have long maintained an understanding and practice of kinfolk acknowledgment, born from the condition of subordination in a racially hierarchical society, that extends kindred belonging to all those in need of it. Black men who don't know each other are "brothers"; a black woman I give directions to in the street will say, "Thank you, baby." And we've never had any other choice than to make white America a part of the family; our self-understanding as Americans depends in part on it. Chris Rock makes the joke that Uncle Sam is kind of like the uncle who molested you, then paid your way through college. Everyone knows that Jefferson and Washington are more likely than not to be black family names.

Blacks have often understood family, and the love of family, as a metaphor for society, an affective relationship based on mutual respect and realistic expectations. The American state, initially constructed by and for whites only, has never fully relinquished its conviction that blacks are subjects who need to be dominated. There is no way forward, no path to King's "table of brotherhood" where we sit together as family, without demolishing the remnants of that mindset. We won't see a republic of socially responsible, free and equal persons until the ugly damage of racial domination in America is repaired.

Linked Fate

by Melina Abdullah

ISSUE 11 | WINTER 2016

Black boys are being targeted, and those are ours . . .
those are ours . . . those are ours.

STACI MITCHELL

I don't know what it was. I don't know if it was gazing into the eyes of that sweet-faced boy whose picture kept visiting my television screen and believing that the world must also feel his tenderness and feeling the need to defend this child—even posthumously. I don't know if it was the clearly false sense of self and delusional state of the one who would steal Trayvon's life. I don't know if it was the hope that all of our protests—for Trayvon Martin, Oscar Grant, Amadou Diallo, Sean Bell, Margaret Mitchell, Devin Brown, in Sanford, Oakland, New York, Los Angeles and so many other cities—would mean something, would have an impact. I don't know if it was the faith that somehow our prayers as Black women would move the jury. We waited, daring to hope for justice, but the verdict came not as a slow, healing breath but as yet another punch to the stomach. Well into the night on July 13, 2013, George Zimmerman was acquitted in the killing of seventeen-year-old Trayvon Martin—the teenager that he stalked, harassed and shot dead in his gated community in Sanford, Florida.

For decades and generations our community has been abused, brutalized and murdered by a policing system that sees us as subhuman. Black people arrived to the Americas as chattel—the prop-

erty of White landowners who built their fortunes on stolen Indigenous land and stolen African labor. But we never submitted to our
oppression and dehumanization. We rebelled. The infamous words
of Harriet Tubman to "be free or die" challenged every fiber of our being. We resisted by maintaining Indigenous cultures—most apparently in places like the Sea Islands—by taking our own freedom as
runaways, by launching insurrections and by positioning ourselves
as what Robin D. G. Kelley calls "race rebels," or perpetual resisters.

To be clear, the enslavement of Africans in America was not
simply about labor exploitation. Chattel slavery actually transformed people into property by law and practice, but not simply as
"human proprietary objects." Rather, what distinguishes American
slavery is what Orlando Patterson terms the "social death" of the enslaved. No feature was more illustrative of this phenomenon than
natal alienation, the denial of blood and kinship ties that create ancestral linkages and familial bonds to descending generations. This
meant that mothers had no legal claims to their children, which permitted the severing of families at the will of slaveholders. As Angela
Davis noted, the nineteenth-century "idealization of motherhood"
did not extend to slaves: "In the eyes of slaveholders, slave women
were not mothers at all, they were simply instruments guaranteeing
the growth of the slave labor force. They were 'breeders'—animals,
whose monetary value could be precisely calculated in terms of their
ability to multiply their numbers."

The narrative of Black women as breeders did not end in 1865 with
the passage of the Thirteenth Amendment, or in 1964 with the passage of the Civil Rights Act. The construction of Black women with
children as something less than mothers is still deeply entrenched
in the larger social order. Most clearly outlined in Ange-Marie
Hancock's seminal work, *The Politics of Disgust: The Public Identity
of the Welfare Queen*, the relegation of Black women to dehumanized breeder status is embedded in the "welfare queen" moniker
assigned to those whose primary traits are assumed to be "hyper-
fertility and laziness." I would argue that such identities are not only
imposed on Black women who receive welfare benefits but are extended to Black mothers as a whole.

Black women have not submitted to these imposed identities, although we are burdened with the oppressive policies and treatment that come along with them. Somehow, despite the constant assault on our identities as mothers, the constant reiteration of our dehumanized status, the brutality of state systems meant to disrupt our families and criminalize our very existence—despite all of that, we stand as people, as mothers and as defenders of our children. And even more, our identities as such extend beyond biological boundaries, embracing the African practice of collective mothering, or what Patricia Hill Collins calls "other-mothering."

It was this realization that hit me the hardest, I think: the depth of the problems we face as Black mothers of Black children. When Zimmerman shot Trayvon, and the policing system and the court condoned his killing, it was not simply the most egregious of assaults on Trayvon and the Martin family, but an assault on our collective son. While the personal pain and anguish felt by those who knew and loved Trayvon is more than I can begin to fathom, what Michael Dawson calls "linked fate" binds us all together as African people who share in suffering. We still live in a state that denies the humanity of Black children, of Black mothers and of Black people. We still live under a system that sees us as socially dead, dehumanized beings with no rights—even to our own children.

•

Black mothers know what it is to pour our hopes, dreams, prayers, love and adoration into a life that has come through our very bodies, to summon every lesson handed down by generations of foremothers, to shield him with every knowing and protection and to be bound to his life as an extension of our own. To have our son's body stolen from us is a shattering of our Spirit, forming a wound that will never heal. It is that universal mothering that moved us to mourn, to wail from the deepest parts of our Souls. That ancestral cry was the cry of our African mothers, whose children had been stolen by white-faced men who invaded their homelands; it was the weeping of enslaved women who were denied the sacred ties of mother and child as babies were ripped from their breasts and sold away; it was the screams of mamas who were held back and beaten as they attempted to stop lynch mobs from abducting, terrorizing and killing their adolescent sons in the most savage ways; it was the sorrow of mothers left to search for their children's lifeless bodies in trees and rivers.

Like our foremothers, we recognize that we are in the midst of war. After the court acquitted Zimmerman, there was no time to allow ourselves to be paralyzed by trauma. Through our tears, we straightened our backs and planned our defense.

That night, as I made my way home from weekend errands, I methodically outlined what had to be done: feed my three small children—ages three, six and nine—then bathe them, put them to bed and find someone to sit with them. I arrived home and through the fog of despair I performed these perfunctory motherly duties. Now well beyond evening, I called three other mamas, who joined me at my home. We held each other for a moment, breathing in our shared pain, acknowledging the humanity that the world was trying to deny us. Then we went into defense mode. Into the streets. Into a sea of grieving mamas, a groundswell of rage and pain.

We filled and poured out of Leimert Park—our Congo Square— the cultural and political hub of Black Los Angeles. Plans and directions were whispered and then shouted, rippling through the assembly of people determined to make our despair felt beyond the psychic walls of South Los Angeles. For three days we marched— dodging police in riot gear, armed with batons, Tasers, pepper spray, beanbag guns, standard issue handguns and rifles. We jumped yellow tape, bypassing the lines of police cars parked to barricade us into our hoods. These new-millennium slave-catchers wielded their power most brutally at night. The day brought some cover; the media and non-Black allies offered a semblance of protection. A broader array of demonstrators found the risk minimal enough to be present for daytime marches, and many of us mamas brought our children.

Like our Ancestors freeing themselves from bondage, there was only one direction for us—north. Our people pressed so far north on the second night that they arrived at Hollywood and Highland, the great tourist mecca. There protesters stood audaciously, feet firmly planted on the names of the Hollywood stars whose memorials peppered the sidewalk, and yelled "No justice, no peace" and "*Tray-von*." White faces panicked and New-Balanced feet froze mid-stride, unsure of what they were witnessing.

On the third day, we were led to the 10 Freeway. First a few people entered, then in an instant the thousands of Black people who had been marching down Crenshaw Boulevard poured out onto the exit ramp—young folks walking with purpose and excitement, older folks who thought they had won the battles of the sixties and seventies only to discover that while "strange fruit" no longer commonly hang from trees, the extrajudicial killing of Black bodies was occurring with the same regularity. The most powerful among us were our young lions, the boys—twelve, fourteen, seventeen years old—with brown faces that glistened in the sun, white t-shirts, jeans that sagged and tapered at the ankle. They had names like Jamal, Michael, even Trayvon, with eyes that squinted like his and an energy dancing between joyful boy and proud warrior.

I paused, clutching the hands of my daughters, holding tightly to the shoulder of my son. He was three years old now, no longer a baby, old enough to breathe this in. Thandiwe, my nine-year-old, pulled me—"Let's go, Mama!" she pleaded. I shook my head, placed her hand on the wall of the overpass, told her to hold on, and retrieved my vibrating phone from my purse. It was a text message that whispered simple instructions: meet at 9 p.m. at St. Elmo Village, a local community art center. It felt like a message from the Underground Railroad, just a few words that pointed the way to freedom. I shared the clandestine plan with the dozen or so "Spirit-children" of mine who were among the thousands who filled the freeway.

Shifting my gaze back down to the dancing eyes of my oldest child, I explained that we were here for Trayvon, to uplift him, to be his hedge of protection, even in death. As we stood for Trayvon, I came to understand that we also stood for my children. As we demanded justice for Trayvon, we knew that it could only be attained through justice for Thandiwe, Amara and Amen, my young ones. Justice for Trayvon would come by making the world safe for other Black children—Black boys who sometimes wear gold teeth and hoodies, Black boys who eat Skittles, watch basketball and love their brothers and fathers. This means transforming the system that seems to enlarge each time a Black body is murdered, as well as awakening our children to their own power. As I locked eyes with my daughter and declared that we were there for Trayvon, I also communicated the sacred bond that she and I shared and that we shared as a people.

But there was something even more immediate: I was to be Thandiwe's protector, and her siblings' protector—and that meant, for now, that we would not be entering the freeway. I turned Thandiwe away from the now-barren street. We looked toward the interstate and saw our people—thousands of them—standing in front of cars, calling Trayvon's name, denying the movement of those who chose to close their eyes to our pain. I lifted my phone and snapped a photo in an attempt to capture the insurrection that was moving through our people, and my Soul filled.

•

That night we gathered, like our foremothers, like Harriet, inside the wooden, vibrantly painted structure that was the center of St. Elmo Village. I arrived later than 9 p.m.—I had once again to feed, bathe and put children to bed. As I entered the space, I was embraced by my young warriors—I'd adopted them, years and months before, taken them on as my Spirit-children and students. While the existing social structure emphasizes boundaries and individuality, I was raised in the Black mothering tradition, the African practice that positioned us all as *family*.

A strong-faced woman spoke—with sensuous lips, dimples that sunk deeply into her smooth brown skin, tattooed arms and a voice raspy, powerful and deep. I'd known Patrisse Cullors loosely for years. The Ancestors had always walked with her—it was a tangible thing. She spoke of liberation and building an ongoing movement, of assigning roles and developing groups: artists, healers, social justice workers. She talked about how we had to sustain this energy and build our power if we were to truly honor Trayvon and get free.

Then she led us out of the building into the warmth of the summer night. A million stars were out that night. The sky was especially dark. Dozens of us circled up, held hands and felt the magnetic energy of one another.

I was one of two mamas there. I locked eyes with the other, Shamell, and we each understood that this was for our own children and for all of us. This moment was the moment that we claimed freedom, that the Spirits of our most powerful Ancestors would inhabit us and use us in the unfinished war for our liberation. The wails that we shared on July 13th had been transformed into a roar as we repeated the final chorus of Assata Shakur's call for resistance:

It is our duty to fight for freedom.
It is our duty to win.
We must love and protect one another
We have nothing to lose but our chains.

After Ferguson

#BLACKLIVESMATTER AND THE LEGACY OF CIVIL RIGHTS

by Brandon M. Terry

ISSUE 10 | SUMMER 2015

Six in the morn,' fire in the street / Burn, baby, burn . . . that's all I wanna see / And sometimes I get off watchin' you die in vain / It's such a shame, they may call me crazy / They may say I suffer from schizophrenia or some-thin' / But homie, you made me . . .

KENDRICK LAMAR, "The Blacker the Berry"

As night fell over Missouri on November 24, 2014, the streets of Ferguson erupted in protest and then riot. The occasion was the announcement that Darren Wilson, a white officer in the Ferguson police department, would face no criminal charges for killing Michael Brown, an unarmed black teenager, the preceding August. Bob McCulloch, St. Louis County's prosecuting attorney, delivered the news in a performance notable both for its condescension and its violation of the canonical norms governing the relationship between prosecutors and grand juries. Shortly thereafter, the perpetually flammable contents of moral outrage and civic distrust, accumulated resentment and plain human grief ignited the violent conflagration that nearly all, it seemed, had come to expect in the saga of Michael Brown.

As Prime Beauty Supply and Hunan Chop Suey burned through the night, a small Midwestern town took its improbable place alongside Watts, Newark, Detroit and South Central Los Angeles in the annals of urban unrest that form an especially contentious chapter in the history of race and class division in America. Meanwhile, several hundred miles away, the first African American president stood wearily behind a podium adorned with the seal of his office. The cable networks, faced with the choice of broadcasting Barack Obama's remarks or the unfolding riot in Missouri, decided instead to display them simultaneously. No picture better captured the dialectic between expectation and frustration, hope and nihilism that characterizes black political life today.

The president, bearing a visage troubled by reluctance, exhaustion or both, began his remarks by counseling that, though we may be disappointed, we must remember "we are a nation built on the rule of law." No harm, therefore, must come to person or property in dissent. This responsibility suitably discharged, the president pleaded for peace and understanding, reminding us of the mutual goodwill he has made a career of insisting lies beneath the *Sturm und Drang* of racial recrimination. But as Obama spoke, uncomfortably posed alongside the burning remnants of police cruisers on television, it was difficult to surmise what work he thought those words might perform that evening.

This is not to deny that there remains, even now, totemic force in the combination of the presidential seal and a black body. This is particularly true for the descendants of American slaves, far too many of whom had been led, by an interminable diet of "not in my lifetime" prognostications, to settle on Bill Clinton as a provisional standard-bearer for the race. But the insurgence of *les damnés de la terre* into the familiar ritual of power that evening was unmistakably jarring and undeniably diminishing. The ordeal evinced a cruel irony: the prophet of racial reconciliation was invoking the sanctity of the rule of law to no effect on white impunity and with no authority against black impudence.

How could it be otherwise? Since August, this municipal regime had deployed the hand-me-down war matériel of the military-industrial complex to defend itself against its own citizenry. These efforts were met not with capitulation but with entrenched resolve. Ferguson witnessed daily youth-led demonstrations, often punctuated by rapper Boosie Badazz's "Fuck the Police"—the unofficial anthem of their dissent.

Although Brown's slaying—followed by the Sophoclean indignity of his corpse lying in the street for over four hours—was the immediate impetus to mass protest, relations between the city government and its residents had long taken on a near-colonial character. According to the U.S. Justice Department, each year Ferguson expects to produce a significant and growing portion of its budget (23 percent in the pre-uprising fiscal plan for 2015) from the aggressive pursuit of municipal fines and fees. The scale of the enterprise and its concentrated focus on African Americans led the Justice Department to declare that the city viewed its residents "less as constituents to be protected than as potential offenders and sources of revenue." While many in the news media focused on the report's documentation of racist "humor" in official emails, the notion that individual prejudice is solely responsible for the situation in Ferguson is a profound error.

"Ferguson," Cornel West declared in the wake of the November unrest, "signifies the end of the Age of Obama." This, at least from the vantage point of African American politics, appears appropriate. Though not many wanted to say it at the time, a notable chill fell over progressive and radical black politics from 2007 until roughly 2012, the year of Trayvon Martin's slaying. This deep freeze stemmed from strategic concerns about Obama's reelection prospects and political standing, genuine outrage at the intransigence and hostility he has faced from some Republicans, broadly shared affective investments in his and his family's symbolic import, and an optimism born of the improbable fact of his electoral success.

The Ferguson eruption and the movement that arose in its aftermath are only the most spectacular evidence that these factors appear to be less constraining on African American politics than at any time since Obama's ascendancy. For a rising number of African Americans and their racially egalitarian allies, the reactions to the deaths of Michael Brown and Eric Garner—and the non-indictments of those responsible—dramatized the need for another path. That the protesters in Ferguson were met with such an enthusiastic and imitative response across the country signals the thawing out of the black protest tradition and a rejection of more conciliatory and

consensus-oriented conceptions of black politics. Once again, extraordinary effort is being devoted to building militant, independent social movements with organized African American participation, capable of transcending the limits of conventional electoral
politics and effectively channeling black rage and resentment.

•

*We so elated, we celebrated like Obama waited / until his last day in office
to tell the nation / brothers is getting their reparations, hey—/ A man can
dream can't he? / No disrespect, in terms of change I haven't seen any /
Maybe he had good intentions but was stifled by the system / And was sad
to learn that he actually couldn't bring any . . .*

J. COLE, "Be Free (Live)"

Unlike the groundswell around the first Obama campaign, the activist energies of our moment have coalesced under a capacious sign—
"Black Lives Matter"—rather than a specific organization, program
or leader. Indeed, the disparate efforts might best be described as
sharing a determination to defect from the vision of racial justice
and reconciliation articulated by our 44th president. As prominent
figures within Black Lives Matter activism, like Alicia Garza, decry
black poverty, mass incarceration and police violence as forms of
"state violence" that leave African Americans "deprived of our basic
human rights and dignity," it is remarkable to remember that just
seven years ago the most vital forms of black political participation
were geared toward the election of a man who famously proclaimed:
"There's not a black America and white America and Latino America
and Asian America; there's the United States of America."

Beneath the president's stubbornly optimistic rhetoric on race
is a political theory that betrays cold realism. The American pol-
ity is starkly polarized, particularly on issues that appear to call
for the reconfiguration of public goods or practices in response to
African American claims of injustice. Social psychologists, for example, find that presenting white Americans with data that shows
racial disparity in incarceration or death penalty sentencing, even

in ways that suggest these disparities may be partly unfair, tends to increase support for more punitive policies. These findings give rise to a suspicion, which the Obama administration has fashioned into a principle of governance, that criticism of racialized inequality or injustice is only likely to embolden and intensify opposition, and thus, as practical politics, is self-defeating. Consequently, the president traditionally avoids emphasizing the amelioration of racial injustice or deep poverty, focusing instead on the "universal" impact of social policies and foregrounding technocratic problem-solving, pragmatic compromise, efficiency and cost-effectiveness. In addition, the administration pursues policies that elide public justification altogether, seeking to advance racial equality through the arcane labyrinths of the executive branch (e.g. the Justice Department, the Department of Agriculture, etc.) where they are less likely to generate scrutiny. Both approaches reflect a judgment that "results," defined as comparatively immediate improvements in the life chances of African Americans, are more important than an ethical commitment to transparency or the practice of public reason.

There are two major exceptions to this approach, both of which in their own way confirm the rule. The first are those efforts, like My Brother's Keeper and the White House Initiative on Historically Black Colleges and Universities, which can be framed palatably because they promote equality of opportunity by repairing social capital deficits among blacks through education, job preparation and cultural socialization. The second are those occasions where Obama feels obliged to comment on potentially explosive racial incidents. There, his default instinct seems to be to immediately personalize the issue. In discussing his own experiences with racial profiling, or in proclaiming, "If I had a son, he'd look like Trayvon," Obama has attempted to reassure black supporters while also using the symbolic power of the presidency to displace the stigmas that frustrate interracial sympathy.

This symbolic power is not easily dismissed, and its integrity has been a core concern of black politics in the Obama era. For many African Americans, 2008 enlarged the political imagination and emboldened expectations. The massive increase in black voter turnout and participation is a powerful reminder of the emotional, aesthetic and moral force of democracy. At its best, democratic life offers the chance—a rare one in the history of the human species—to see ourselves as co-authors of a society where we can feel at home. As was perhaps inevitable, however, these raised expectations soon crashed headlong into the enduring realities of American civilization. These include not only racial and economic inequality and the limits of executive authority, but also the power of capital to bend government to its ends, the tragic entanglements of the American military and national-security state at home and abroad, and a cultivated disregard for the equal value and significance of non-white lives that has helped to build, among other horrors, the largest carceral system in the history of the world.

If Ferguson is indeed where we will come to mark the eclipse of the Age of Obama, it is in large part because the crisis exhibited to a stunning degree both the deep interpenetration of these factors and the limited ability of this presidential administration, or perhaps any administration, to lead the confrontation against them. There remains hope there, perhaps, but not of the audacious sort.

•

It would not be accurate to say that the direct actionists speak for all Negroes under all circumstances. It is fair to say that their philosophy is ascendant, that their influence is becoming pervasive and that their voices are heard with increasing respect and diminishing dissent in Negro communities. Those voices are harsh and strident, and jarring to the liberal ear.

LOREN MILLER, "Farewell to Liberals" (1962)

Those who persist in search of that elusive quality of audacity, however, seem to have rediscovered it in the ecstatic experience of resistance in Ferguson. While the death of Trayvon Martin and subsequent acquittal of his killer, George Zimmerman, in 2013 gave rise to some of the most significant protest organizations of the moment (e.g. the Dream Defenders), as well as the original use of #BlackLives-Matter as a social-media hashtag, it was the crisis in St. Louis County that ignited political organizing, direct-action demonstrations and identification with the rhetorical cry of "Black Lives Matter" nation-wide. In the latter half of 2014, Ferguson became a hotbed of polit-ical exchange and collaboration, with professional activists travel-ing in from all over the nation for events like the August "Freedom Ride" and the dramatic Columbus Day weekend of protests known as "Ferguson October." These efforts were led, in many respects, not by familiar charismatic male religious figures, but by women, labor organizers, local community members and queer-identified activ-ists. In addition to the media coverage these actions generated, the vibrant digital public sphere known as "Black Twitter" amplified their impact far beyond Missouri—reflecting both an evolving ter-rain of organizing as well as the innovative and idiosyncratic efforts of new media citizen-journalists like DeRay Mckesson and Johnetta Elzie, publishers of the online newsletter *This Is the Movement*.

Intellectually, the disparate efforts unfolding across the country under the banner of Black Lives Matter share two unifying commit-ments, both of which entail ethical and political rejection of the accommodations counseled by the Obama administration and its civil rights allies. The first entails foregrounding *white supremacy* and *state violence* as categories of critique and analysis in opposi-tion to "racism" and "discrimination." The second is to *unapologetic blackness.*

"Racism," at least in everyday discourse, tends to refer either to discriminatory acts and intentions or to prejudicial beliefs. The vo-cabulary of white supremacy and state violence, however, seeks in-stead to emphasize forms of racial degradation, domination and disadvantage that are not reducible to individual intent or episodic acts. The focus is instead on the systematic and cumulative charac-ter of racial hierarchy, and on the barriers it erects to human flour-ishing. In a recent essay, for example, Garza describes black poverty, mass incarceration, welfare and education policy, immigration pol-icy and the "unique burden" of "black queer and trans folks . . . in a hetero-patriarchal society," among other social problems, all as forms of state violence.

Although these terms perform corrective work in drawing at-tention to the coercive quality of slow-moving social threats, like residential segregation and lead-paint exposure, such invocations of "state violence" risk obscuring forms of disadvantage that do not have origins *only* in the actions of government agents or institutions, or so inflating the concepts of "state" and "violence" as to obscure more precise and persuasive analyses of racial injustice. But perhaps this sacrifice of analytical clarity is in the service of a more important moral claim, which we would do well to confront forthrightly. The claim, quite radical in its implications, is that a government's failure to protect its members' civil liberties, the social bases of their dignity and their material security from the unjust distribution of social burdens simply *is* a form of injury morally equivalent to arbitrary violence—and must be resisted accordingly.

The second commitment, to what I call "unapologetic blackness," is an axiomatic rejection of political, sociological or moral "post-racialism." It insists that race is indispensable for explaining the origins and reproduction of social inequality and injustice in America. Further, it endorses the idea that black political solidarity—especially *within* broader coalitions—is empowering and expansive, rather than divisive, distracting or morally objectionable. This solidarity is defended as an indispensable element of an emancipatory politics capable not only of confronting the unique challenges facing African Americans, but also of illuminating the ways that "racial" injustice is inextricably intertwined with other forms of injustice. As Garza writes, "#BlackLivesMatter doesn't mean your life isn't important—it means that Black lives, which are seen as without value within White supremacy, are important to your liberation. . . . When Black people in this country get free, the benefits will be wide reaching and transformative for society as a whole."

These positions undoubtedly echo important strands of thinking from the Black Power era, which also emerged, (in)famously, in the wake of urban rioting. Prominent figures and organizations within the current movement, including Garza, the St. Louis rapper-activist Tef Poe, Ashley Yates of Millennial Activists United and Phillip Agnew of Dream Defenders, often gesture toward Malcolm X, Stokely Carmichael, Assata Shakur and other black radical icons of the mid-sixties. A joint list of demands from the groups Hands Up United and Black Lives Matter quotes almost verbatim from the 1966 Black

Panther Party Platform in calling for, among other things, "full employment of our people," "decent housing fit for shelter of human beings" and an "immediate end to police brutality and murder of black, brown and all oppressed people."

Such rhetorical echoes of sixties-era African American social movements, alongside activists' insistence, following Michelle Alexander, that present-day carceral and police practices amount to the "new Jim Crow," have prompted comparisons between #BlackLivesMatter and the civil rights movement. Many of these comparisons have been unfavorable. The economist Glenn Loury, for example, has argued that unlike the struggle against Jim Crow segregation, there is now no clear law to oppose, and no existing "legislative agenda activists can point to as a plausible remedy for the conditions we all lament." Worse yet, Loury criticizes activists for treating as "issues of race" what are really "structural problems—too few jobs, concentrated poverty, failing schools," and therefore not the proper target of a "black movement."

In making this comparison, critics like Loury project a streamlined coherence backward onto the aims of civil rights activists that was in fact, where achieved, the hard-earned work of theory and praxis or, more tragically, an unintended result of their more radical demands being ignored and written out of history. In "Organizing Manual No. 2," the pamphlet written largely by Bayard Rustin summarizing the goals and strategy of the 1963 March on Washington for Jobs and Freedom, the focus is precisely on those structural problems that Loury describes as outside the bounds of "traditional" civil rights or "black movement" concerns. Rustin writes of "the twin evils of racism and economic deprivation," which "rob all people . . . of dignity, self-respect, and freedom." They "impose a special burden on the Negro," however, who is "denied the right to vote, economically exploited, refused access to public accommodations, subjected to inferior education, and relegated to substandard ghetto housing." To combat these problems, march leaders demanded not just anti-discrimination laws, but also "a massive federal program to train and place all unemployed workers—Negro and white—on meaningful and dignified jobs at decent wages," as well as a national minimum-wage act. Today's activists, many of whom have backgrounds in organized labor, are similarly aware of "root causes," and are once again forging alliances with minimum-wage campaigns like the nationwide Fight for $15 demonstrations.

It is similarly anachronistic to imply, as Loury does, that it was always clear during the civil rights protests who bore the "responsibility for changing the law," or that "the moral conviction at stake" was never in doubt. In fact, in the fifties and early sixties, the question of responsibility was precisely the issue; civil rights protesters not only challenged the constitutionality of state-mandated segregation statutes but forced a constitutional crisis over the unsettled question of whether privately owned enterprises, including restaurants, theaters and private holding companies operating mass transit, were legally obligated to refrain from customs of racial discrimination and segregation if the state did not explicitly forbid them. To confront the latter principle, as activists compelled the nation to do, was hardly to follow an existing map of legal responsibilities and duties; it entailed bringing a tremendous array of the everyday operations of American consumer society into our fundamental understanding of the meaning of equal citizenship.

Of course, this is not the only terrain on which critics judge Black Lives Matter to be deficient in comparison with its civil rights predecessors. In notable contrast to the enduring image of the heroic activist and "respectable" citizen Rosa Parks peacefully submitting to unjust arrest in Montgomery, many of the victims of police violence ritually invoked by current protests have criminal records, attempted to flee or resist arrest and were alienated from politics. Given how Michael Brown died—as a suspect in a robbery, and likely in a mutually aggressive interaction with an officer—even sympathetic commentators have called into question, as Loury writes, "whether his case can be a viable focal point for change within the limits of ordinary politics [or] whether protests resulting from Brown's death can lead to real improvement in the quality of American democracy." John McWhorter likewise relayed his fear that "the facts on this specific incident are too knotted to coax a critical mass of America into seeing a civil rights icon in Brown and an institutionally racist devil in Wilson."

McWhorter may be right, of course, but what of it? The FPD, like departments in Baltimore, Chicago, New York and elsewhere, has a record of excessive force and other unconstitutional practices that fall disproportionately on African Americans. Meanwhile, familiar stories of black deviance and statistics demonstrating the level of community violence function as default explanations—not just for any specific dispensation of violence, but for why no explanation should be needed in the first place. At its sparest, Black Lives Matter is a reaction against this kind of partitioning in American democracy. It seeks to expose the contempt and resentment with which far too many public officials and fellow citizens treat the idea that the basic structure of society, and especially law enforcement, should be accountable to the assent of African Americans. "Hands Up, Don't Shoot" may indeed be a lie, but this deception does not make the Ferguson police truthful, nor does it make Michael Brown's death legitimate.

The movement aspires to nourish forms of sympathy and solidarity even with those members of society that may be, at present, our most violent, with the understanding that they often began life among the most vulnerable. Loury is right that no attempt to shoehorn these efforts into "ordinary politics" will produce the kind of "real improvement" in American democracy that would reach the next Michael Brown. Ordinary politics treats these deadly encounters between citizens and police as causal inevitabilities—high crime begets intensive policing, which brings unfortunate tragedies. But why stop there? What we need is an extraordinary politics informed by ordinary lives, one capable of provoking, and responsibly guiding, a process of civic reflection in a moment of moral crisis.

•

Clock ticking backwards on things we've already built / Sons and fathers die, soldiers, daughters killed / Question ain't "do we have the resources to rebuild?" / It's "do we have the will?" / Perilous dissidence evening up the score / Do we even know what we're fighting for?

D'ANGELO, "Till It's Done (Tutu)"

That some comparisons between the civil rights era and our current moment may be judged invidious does not mean that today's activists have nothing to learn from exemplary moments of black political struggle. Unfortunately, the prevailing narratives often obscure the philosophical complexity of the civil rights and Black Power movements, especially as it relates to their staging of protests, direct-action demonstrations and other public, performative gestures. In my own work in political theory, I argue that when serious attention is paid to the way African Americans have wrestled with questions of when, how and why to protest, the ethical, political, affective and aesthetic dimensions of these choices come to the fore. Above all, one sees how the demands and dramaturgy of the most powerful protests of the era managed to be at least three things at once: *provocative, pedagogical* and *political.*

Those who celebrate the demonstrations of the civil rights era often fail to ask why such images were so provocative to the public. Why did they disrupt everyday routine and arrest public attention? It is not simply that the orderly procession of stoically marching black bodies singing spirituals was inherently moving. The force of these demonstrations involved the powerful merging of black prophetic Christianity's spiritual fervor with left-liberal politics, as well as the powerful contrast between the evident dignity and discipline needed to mount such spectacles and widely held stereotypes of black incompetence and cowardice. Further, the omnipresent threat of violence was of undeniable importance to the movement's success in provocation.

This latter point is crucial. It is well known that Martin Luther King, Jr. and other activists deliberately provoked violent repression to expose the state-sanctioned terror upholding segregation. But their efforts often inadvertently contributed to black violence as well—most significantly in Birmingham, Alabama. In the wake of King's home being bombed, thousands of blacks rioted, leading to the death of a policeman and a frantic request for both National Guard troops and civil rights legislation by the White House. Months later, fear that the now-sacrosanct March on Washington would explode into violence led the city to close schools, ban alcohol sales and cancel the Washington Senators' baseball games. Residents and shop owners fled the city, while the federal government placed nearly twenty thousand troops on standby. The same fascination with violence that directs attention to Ferguson or Baltimore today was at work then. As the historian Timothy Tyson writes, "one of the enduring ironies of the civil rights movement [is] that the threat of violence was so critical to the success of nonviolence."

Not all provocations are created equal, however. The most effective were those that also employed what might be called a moral and civic *pedagogy*. In the Jim Crow South, for example, the array of legal techniques, bureaucratic justifications and forms of extralegal violence used to prevent blacks from casting ballots was purposely disparate and deceptive. Lyndon B. Johnson, in his 1965 "We Shall Overcome" speech, described the myriad obstacles to black voting as representing "every device of which human ingenuity is capable." In retrospect, what is remarkable about the voting rights struggle is that civil rights activists were able to communicate their claims in such a way that the phrase "voting rights" could be recognized to refer to a set of coherent and intelligible demands at all—a point brilliantly dramatized in Ava DuVernay's film *Selma* (2014). If illegibility is often characteristic of injustice, part of what protest must entail is the disclosure of things otherwise unseen. As regarded voting rights, this was achieved through theatrical demonstrations designed to render the systematic nature of these "ingenious" obstacles more visible, trenchant criticism of the illegitimacy of these practices, and persuasive portrayals of the radical democratic vision of near-universal suffrage.

Only once the particular nature of a problem is made legible, and visions of how to resolve it brought into view, can the political function of protest be fully realized. I do not mean by this that protest must press immediate, clearly defined legislative demands— although it can, and it is often quite useful to do so. The suggestion is rather that effective protest must find some way to integrate its demands into a broader political vision that either helps orient one's judgment about justification and strategy or paints a compelling portrait of an alternative social order. With King, for example, nonviolent direct action was not just a theological commitment or a pragmatic concession. King believed the strategy would be effective because it "does not seek to defeat or humiliate the opponent, but to win his friendship and understanding," leaving open the possibility for "redemption and reconciliation" within a political community. To do otherwise, even where it might win short-term victories, might undermine the higher aims of political struggle altogether.

The lunch-counter sit-ins of the early sixties can be seen as having achieved a remarkable synthesis of these three dimensions. Their provocation consisted in the spectacle of black students, clothed in the accoutrements of respectability, disrupting the settled habits of everyday life. The sit-in activists demanded acknowledgment, challenged the boundaries of the political and undermined expectations of both black acquiescence and black violence.

Their pedagogy was similarly effective. We tend to remember Jim Crow as a practice of total exclusion, and the most prominent images of the era, like "whites-only" water fountains and schools, reinforce the idea that "separation" was at the heart of discrimination. But Jim Crow capitalism was in fact sustained by a complex admixture of commitments, often in tension, to the imperatives of profit, the obligations of law and the mores of white supremacy. The metaphor of "exclusion" can obscure this complexity, and we might easily lose sight of how a great many businesses navigated this terrain, incorporating ritual humiliation and exploitation into everyday consumption. Thus, at this Woolworth's, Negroes may freely purchase school supplies at the store counter, but they may not purchase and consume food at the dining counter. At this restaurant, Negroes may order food, but they must be served in the back. At this department store, Negroes may purchase clothing, but they may not try items on before they purchase them. At this movie theater, Negroes may attend the screening, but they must sit upstairs in the balcony. The sit-ins revealed these practices of domination and acquiescence as connected problems, and they dramatized their moral stakes. By creating a crisis of order, they dismantled the public/private distinction, revealing how the state—and, by extension, the broader nation—was complicit in *enforcing* these ritual humiliations insofar as it was compelled to punish those who dissented.

Lastly, the activists managed to fuse their provocative and peda-gogical dimensions with an inspiring political vision. By adopting an inclusive style of protest and appealing to the possibility of future reconciliation, in method as well as in rhetorical content, the sit-ins successfully conveyed a reformist (rather than a revolutionary or re-taliatory) attitude, and thus undermined the kinds of suppression that might otherwise have been brought to bear against them. The activists leading the movement identified the most significant barri-ers to racial equality as racist attitudes and habits among Southern whites, the legal architecture of Jim Crow and the degrading accom-modationism of black people themselves. If one accepts these views (it should be said that there are good reasons for rejecting them), then one can see the brilliance of a mode of direct action that suffers violence willingly without retaliation, accepts arrests and justifies itself in the language of constitutional law and Christian morality. It is a stunningly powerful way to transform the fear and disgust of interracial proximity into feelings of human sympathy in the face of cruelty, which the activists hoped would serve as the affective ba-sis for a reconstructed democracy.

•

The problem isn't racial division or a need for healing. It is racial inequal-ity and injustice. And the remedy isn't an elaborately choreographed pag-eantry of essentializing yackety-yak about group experience, cultural dif-ference, pain, and the inevitable platitudes about understanding. Rather, we need a clear commitment by the federal government to preserve, but-tress, and extend civil rights . . .

ADOLPH REED, JR., "Yackety-Yak About Race" (1997)

To draw attention to the exemplarity of these acts of protest from the civil rights era is not to suggest that they can be reprised in the same form today. At the same time, such reflection can help us evaluate current efforts. A very real fear is that Black Lives Matter will manifest the same limitations as the Occupy movement. This would mean that although it might succeed in influencing the po-litical agenda and discourse, it would ultimately exercise a limited influence on the political and institutional formations that emerge in response to its provocations. Occupy, of course, was enamored with an idea that the political theorist and legal scholar Bernard Harcourt calls "political disobedience." In Harcourt's description, this is a strategy characterized by a total refusal of "the very way in which we are governed . . . the structure of partisan politics, the demand for policy reforms, the call for party identification, and the very ideologies that dominated the post-War period."

Underlying this "total refusal" is the idea, prominent among today's left, that suggesting policy reforms, developing organizational infrastructure, promoting spokespersons or even articulating utopian political visions is likely to lead to unintended complicity in the oppression of marginalized groups. This suspicion is supported by the revisionist historiography of the civil rights movement and the New Left, which criticizes those movements for marginalizing minorities, women, LGBTQ communities and the poor. It is accompanied by a corresponding belief that anti-institutional politics is the best way to facilitate the "organic" and egalitarian development of political consciousness. In terms of the approach to protest, this seems to have inspired a remarkable faith in the power of transgressive performance as such to call into question the existing social order and facilitate conversation capable of dispelling indifference and mobilizing resistance.

In this intellectual atmosphere, protest politics and organizations become unmoored from the most serious questions of responsibility, judgment and vision. The abdication of responsibility for building organizations capable of mobilizing resources and resisting state suppression is seen as a progressive virtue. The justifiable criticism of patriarchal, racial and charismatic notions of leadership drifts into the suggestion that leaders are not needed at all, or the rhetorical mystification that "strong people don't need strong leaders." Protest itself takes on the character of contemporary performance art, investing the transgression of social norms with a power it is unlikely to have unless linked to the cultivation of particular affective responses and the development of countervailing political practices.

This alchemy produces bizarre consequences. Often protest gets evaluated essentially on its ironic or spectacular character, as opposed to on the political pedagogy it enacts, the emotional response it engenders or the strategic vision it advances. This makes it difficult to hold organizations accountable for their political judgment or for non-members to decide which organizations to join or support, much less to evaluate the practical success of their efforts. More perniciously, it becomes easy to obscure the subtle, surreptitious ways in which those organizers who most loudly proclaim that "everyone" is a leader become—by any functional, sociological account—de facto leaders, precisely because their quiet, unaccountable authority is purchased with gestures to egalitarianism.

One of the exciting elements of Black Lives Matter is how demonstrators have managed to develop forms of protest that are genuinely provocative and arresting, holding our attention and making many feel that something profoundly personal and political is at stake. The dramatic actions at athletic events, at the Brooklyn Bridge, on Oakland mass transit and at shopping malls on Black Friday have shaped public debate and empowered young African Americans and other allies to courageously confront injustice. Where these protest actions have most obviously gone awry—attempts to disrupt the "white privilege" of Sunday brunch, blocking I-93 in Boston or the chaotic "Primal Scream" protest at Harvard, where students tried to interrupt a nude run that occurs on campus the night before finals— there has been a failure to turn the affective responses of demonstrators and spectators (e.g. anger, resentment, confusion, discomfort) into productive political energy and understanding. None of these acts persuasively disclosed the key obstacles or aims of reform, nor did they channel their provocations into critical self-reflection.

The challenge for today's inheritors of the civil rights example, I want to be clear about suggesting, can be met not only by *exposing* the mechanisms of injustice through spectacular confrontation, but also by *disclosing* the limits of existing institutions—which entails the advancement of new models for the organization of society. For all its shortcomings, the Black Panther Party was remarkably adept at this latter task, providing armed patrols to watch police and prevent brutality, medical services like ambulances and clinics and schools that emphasized African American history. These drama- tized the failures or weaknesses of existing institutions at the same time as they modeled the possibility of a world in which these com- munities would receive crucial social services without humiliation or disdain. There exist some contemporary efforts in this vein— Hands Up United has started a Freedom School and breakfast pro- gram in Ferguson—but not yet enough of them to sufficiently en- large the imagination of their audience.

•

I want to say to you as I move to my conclusion, as we talk about "Where do we go from here?" that we must honestly face the fact that the movement must address itself to the question of restructuring the whole of American society.

MARTIN LUTHER KING, JR., "Where Do We Go from Here?"

These, it should be apparent, are friendly criticisms. They should be taken as midpoint contributions to the development of an im- pressive movement still in its inchoate phase, but with the potential to have enormous import. My arguments here, like most of what has emerged from the crucible of creativity and contestation that is Black Lives Matter, share its fundamental premise: namely that tak- ing the strivings and sufferings of black people seriously may lead us to reshape our political order and social life in ways more consonant with equality, justice, dignity, freedom and human flourishing. The hope is that from the wreckage of Ferguson and Baltimore we might build new theories of policing and punishment, refound criminal justice and rescue some semblance of community from the cruelty of the neoliberal state.

There are, as always, reasons for apprehension. The movement's efforts may run aground on rhetorical excess, poorly chosen alli- ances at home and abroad, personal enmity, disagreement or re- pression. The obstacles to radical change are enormous, and all the invocations of "white supremacy" and "state violence" in the world will not wave away the hard practical issues—the underground economy and real crime, bureaucracy and federalism, collective bargaining and labor politics—that are involved in any serious attempt to transform the police, let alone society at large. The country remains polarized in ways that protests, violent or nonviolent, may only exacerbate, and human beings, even those impassioned by justice, are easily exhausted. As the movement spreads and evolves, it will inevitably encounter, among new recruits and claimants to the mantle of black political leadership, old habits that can derail any progressive movement, including patriarchy, homophobia and elitism. And as demands inevitably become more specific, divisions between competing factions of the movement could become insurmountable.

There are, nonetheless, important reasons for hope. The habits of citizenship that long anchored our collectively muted and moderated response to what the poet Claudia Rankine calls the "wrongfully ordinary" phenomenon of police brutality have been unsettled by the technological innovations of social media and digital technology. So too has an impact been felt from shifts in public opinion regarding the fairness of the criminal justice system. These things alone are not, and could not be, decisive. In light of the last three decades, however, they amount to an unprecedented political and cultural opportunity.

Indeed, the waves of activism and unrest seem finally to be impacting the agendas of mainstream politicians. Following the funeral of Freddie Gray, a 25-year-old African American resident of my hometown of Baltimore, who died from spinal-cord injuries sustained in police custody, television cameras once again zeroed in on the spectacle of urban protest and rioting. On April 28th, President Obama commandeered a joint White House press conference with the prime minister of Japan to speak to the unrest that unfolded roughly forty miles away. While the president assailed rioters as "thugs" and "criminals," he nonetheless conveyed sympathy for peaceful demonstrators and uncharacteristically blunt outrage against police misconduct and the injustice of ghetto poverty. Obama exasperatedly declared that "we, as a country, have to do some soul searching" about the plight of inner-city youth, excoriating those who think that instead of providing economic opportunity, ameliorating poverty, treating drug abuse and reducing incarceration, "we're just going to send the police to do the dirty work of containing the problems that arise." The next day, Democratic presidential candidate Hillary Clinton announced her support for police body cameras and an "end to the era of mass incarceration." This entailed explicitly disavowing—alongside her husband, former President Bill Clinton—the "tough on crime" politics of their administration.

On the ground in Charm City, Marilyn Mosby, a rising Democratic Party star and the 35-year-old African American state's attorney in Baltimore, became a national sensation after an emotionally charged press conference where she announced that six police officers would face criminal prosecution for Gray's death. With the city teetering on the edge of more violence, and thousands of National Guard troops patrolling West Baltimore, Mosby spoke explicitly to "the youth of the city" and "the demonstrators across America." Implicitly identifying herself with these efforts, she exhorted the public to hold "peaceful and productive rallies that will develop structural and systemic changes for generations to come," declaring that "as young people, our time is now."

All of these remarks contain striking concessions to—and in Mosby's case, identifications with—a social movement that currently relies far more on moral authority, social panic and public provocation than organizational capacity and long-term political strategy. They represent small victories, to be sure, but not irrelevant ones. It is clear that the activities of Black Lives Matter, and their associated unrest, have, for now, the attention of the politicians and the public—but to what ultimate end? What strategic provocations, civic pedagogies and political visions can be developed to leverage these gestures of recognition into concrete victories and the enduring exercise of responsible political power? How might these struggles best develop, and be informed by, the most incisive ideas concerning the reformation and reconstruction of our fundamental institutions and modes of citizenship? These, it seems, are among the most urgent questions facing Black Lives Matter; and they are unlikely to have easy answers. Yet as James Baldwin wrote, "not everything that is faced can be changed, but nothing can be changed until it is faced."

III

FINAL FANTASY

Understanding Is Dangerous

by Kathryn Lofton

ONLINE | FALL 2016

I am at a dinner party and I am annoyed. Nothing about this is exceptional, but still I find myself annoyed that I am annoyed. Nearing middle age, I should be in charge of my life enough not to end up in places where I will sulk. And so I am bored at my annoyance, mad at everyone's outfits, disgusted at the cheesecake with the blueberry compote, hateful of the word *compote*.

It is a double-barreled dinner party—not only a party organized by a dinner, but also a dinner organized as a tribute to one of those at the table. We are supposed to be fawning and on message. We are supposed to admire the food and agree to more wine. We are not supposed to slip out early. And, given the epoch in which we find ourselves, we are supposed to be aghast about Donald Trump.

You have been in so many of these conversations that I don't need to tell you the content for you to hum along. The conversation never starts straight. It never begins with someone saying, "Well, what about this election and this remarkably unusual Republican nominee Donald Trump?" It begins sidelong. Nobody intends to go there but they are *so glad* the opening is made so the phrases they've been practicing in their cars and in front of debates can get public hearing. But they don't want to show eagerness, so everyone speaks in knowing punch line.

I don't want to speak about Trump. I am concerned that our focus *on* him adds to the thing he needs to stay alive, namely our attention. I do not want to feed his reality—a reality defined by punch line, by non sequitur, by compulsive distraction from the subject at hand. If I get past that and assume attention is necessary, I worry that the *way* we talk reiterates, in every phrase and posture, why those who follow him do. He has got our goat. And when our goat is got, we talk in ways that show how he came to be by showing why he is someone who others—those not sitting at this dinner table—want.

This time Trump came up because someone mentioned Brexit. Brexit! *Can you believe it?* someone says. Eyes are rolled. Why are people voting against their interests? How has ignorance taken over the Anglophone world? What *is happening?* In reply, I do a thing that nobody likes at a party: I give an account of the punch line that isn't a joke. I begin well enough, nodding at the outrage, and then referring to a story I heard on NPR about a British baker who claimed that after Brexit he could export more cheaply to Europe. If I'd just leave it at that, fine, but I keep going, as if I'd become a scholar of this NPR story and this Brexit-voting baker: he also said that the potential relaxation of employment laws would bring greater flexibility to adjust his labor force; he also said that the increase in customs procedures didn't bother him; he also said that the diminishment of skilled immigrant labor could be a problem in some sectors but not his; he also said that he knew the tech companies and other newer industries would be hurt the most but that in general expected that any of these losses were nothing before the gains to be had by the decline in the exchange rate between the pound and the euro.

In this minute, I am being the worst. The worst because I can't stop talking, and the worst because everyone at the table is clearly getting nervous that I am a little too committed to the Brexit baker. Whose side am I on, anyway? The guest of honor speaks up: *Well, he'll be shown wrong.* And the woman on my left, the one who'd spent three years in England, the one with the gumdrop pearls and moss-green cashmere layers, observes that racism drives it all. *All of it.* See how the baker doesn't care about immigrant labor? Racism. And everyone at the table nods, knowingly. We know what is wrong in the world, and it is Donald Trump and his offensive forms of speech, his offending acts of racism, his offensive certitude relative to our own.

Understanding is dangerous, here. You are worried maybe now that I don't agree. That I don't know that Donald Trump is a world-class bigot who has insulted Mexicans and Muslims, who doesn't do his homework or honor his debts, who thinks immigrants are leeches and women are walking pussies. You are nervous, I assume, for the same reason that room was nervous: because they comprise that portion of the electorate decidedly disgusted by Donald Trump, and to be a member of that collective you have to understand things that I seem unwilling to see. I don't get how Brexit is about race and I don't get, therefore, why we so easily segued at that terrible dinner party from my babbling monologue about the baker into a zippy exchange of pre-auditioned quips about Trump's racism.

So I fell silent. I didn't have it in me to keep going with the shallow talk of elite people avoiding comprehension in favor of the pulse of commiseration. At that table, the cohering principle of togetherness was a commitment to the senselessness, the irrationality, the uncomprehending ignorance of it all. Staying shocked at the Donald keeps us all in it, eroticized by our own disgust. What a drag it would be to cease being shocked by his ascendancy, and pursue instead an explanation of how we contributed to it, contributed to it by our very knowing: mine, theirs, ours.

•

To be a scholar of religion is to participate in a hermeneutics of the incomprehensible. That isn't exactly right: what scholars of religion do is account for why groups of people consistently agree to things that other people think are incomprehensible, irrational, even senseless. Images illegible relative to contemporary notions of geometry or perspective; abstractions so abstract they twist the brain; doctrines so specific they seem impracticable; myths so fantastic they seem extraterrestrial. Through documentary engagement, linguistic specificity, historical and sociological and economic analysis— scholars of religion make those things legible as human products of human need.

It is therefore unsurprising that I, a scholar of religion, am invested in an account of Trump that renders his absurdity less so. It is, perhaps, my sole specific obligation: to figure out the reason in his seeming madness. To ask, too: Why does he seem mad to some, and not at all to others? The history of religions has long suggested the one does not exist without the other, that to be inside something requires someone else being outside. And, too, that making the strange familiar inevitably ought to make the familiar strange. But here I get ahead of myself.

To begin, the work of explaining Trump has already been done. The sheer tonnage of analysis on Trump outpaces any other modern presidential candidate, not merely because of his own peculiarity but also because of the seizing algorithmic enormity of the internet, where the long-form essay on Trump has become a rite of passage for anyone with a byline. Nearly every account of Trump's success works economics into their explanation, arguing that those who favor him are those who have experienced the negative effects of globalization, and the corresponding economic anxiety and stagnant median wages of 21st-century life. Oh, yes: and those refugee flows from the Middle East, bringing with them the toxic two-step of potential terrorist cells and low-wage competition for jobs. (It is unclear which is worse: the immigrant as cheap labor or the immigrant as suicide bomber.)

The problem with this economic theory of Trumpism is that no evidence supports it. Hard numbers complicate the argument that income or education levels predict Trump support, or that working-class whites support him disproportionately. The results of 87,000 interviews conducted by Gallup showed that those who liked Trump were under no more economic distress or immigration-related anxiety than those who opposed him. Moreover, Trump supporters don't have lower incomes or higher unemployment levels than other Americans.

The religionists are nodding. Not because we necessarily knew those statistics, but because we've been through this before. There is no religious movement in human history that has not been explained by outsiders to it through recourse to economics. People are always assuming that if you believe in Marian apparitions, throw yourself on a funeral pyre, pray five times a day or speak in tongues, you do so because you're poor and hungry for epic consequence, or because you're poor and want to pay obeisance to omnipotent powers who could make you otherwise. Such observers think religious activities are done by the desperate to compensate through immaterial means for material lack. Many of them, using Marx weakly, often dragoon him to their case.

It just isn't so. Earlier this year, primary exit polls revealed that Trump voters were, in fact, *more* affluent than most Americans, with a median household income of $72,000—higher than that of Hillary Clinton or Bernie Sanders supporters. Forty-four percent of them had college degrees, well above the national average of 33 percent among whites or 29 percent overall. These facts haven't stopped pundits and journalists from pushing story after story about the white working class's giddy embrace of Trump. We like that story, because it comforts us into believing that a liberal education begets liberal political thinking, and that a living wage could soothe the vulnerable. It's harder to understand why the world-class physicist is also an evangelical, or why the college-educated Army officer is voting for Trump.

What the research does show is that those who support Trump do so for reasons that are not well-captured by income brackets. It presses us to think differently about what organizes mass groups of people to adhere to ideas that seem senseless to outsiders. "The charismatic leader," wrote sociologist Max Weber, in 1919, "gains and maintains authority solely by proving his strength in life." Late-nineteenth- and early-twentieth-century American evangelists marketed their strength through the evidence of the adversity they survived. Whereas other Christian leaders advocated theological exploration or creedal recommitment, these ministers endorsed "Lessons from the School of Experience" or the "university of rail-splitting." "Great preachers cannot be made by technical pedagogy," explained the famous evangelist Sam Jones's biographer, George Stuart:

> They are developed amid adverse and favorable circumstances, currents and eddies, storms and stresses of life. Scholars, debaters, exegetes, and homilists may be produced in universities and

theological seminaries, but preachers who reach and save men come from the school of experience which acquaints them with the varied heart throbs generated in the toil, hardships, sacrifices and sufferings of themselves and their fellows.

I invoke the history of evangelicalism here to point out the way in which Trump is familiar to a nation forged through evangelical idiom. Pundits wring their hands over whether evangelicals will or won't vote for him, musing snidely that if they do, they should be ashamed of themselves—after all, who could possibly claim Christ's message and also claim Trump? But every time Trump does something mortifying, he only shows how true is his truth. Evangelicals don't understand sin as an incapacity for leadership. Obsessing over facts, revealing anxiety, worrying about correct speech and footnotes: these, in the evangelical paradigm, are the signs of faltering faith. Certitude in the face of bedevilment is the surest mark of the saved.

In January, political scientist Matthew MacWilliams reported findings that a penchant for authoritarianism—not income, education, gender, age or race—predicted Trump support. The questions that MacWilliams used to discern voters' preferences focused on child-rearing, asking whether it is more important for the voter to have a child who is respectful or independent, obedient or self-reliant, well-behaved or considerate and well-mannered or curious. Respondents who pick the first option in each of these questions are strongly authoritarian. It may seem contradictory at first to understand why respondents who would prefer a child to be respectful, obedient, well-behaved and well-mannered would be likely Trump voters. None of those would be among the words one would use to describe the candidate. Yet recall that the purpose of the survey was to see what makes a voter *pick Trump*. And the results suggest that the voter wants someone whose authority makes others around him submit to his will. We don't care if he's offensive if he gets the job done. Even more to the point, his level of offensiveness is exactly what it needs to be to jostle the world out of its false niceties. His crassness is the other side of our polite pluralism.

Later on in the evening of the dinner party, I wonder what I ought to have done differently. I think of an essay by my colleague, Noreen Khawaja, "Religious Truth and Secular Scandal: Kierkegaard's Pathology of Offense." Khawaja uses the Danish Muhammad cartoon crisis to launch an exploration of the value of offense described in the writings of Søren Kierkegaard. After a Danish newspaper, *Jyllands-Posten*, published a dozen cartoons under the headline "The Face of Muhammad," hundreds of thousands of people protested the cartoons, leaving nearly 250 dead and eight hundred wounded. The prohibition against illustrating the Prophet Muhammad began as an attempt to ward off idol worship, which was widespread in Islam's Arabian birthplace. A central tenet of Islam is that Muhammad was a man, not God, and that portraying him could lead to revering him in lieu of Allah. The editor of the Danish paper would eventually apologize, saying that the cartoons had "indisputably offended many Muslims," but that they "were not intended to be offensive."

Khawaja asks that we pause over this editor's phrasing—a phrasing so familiar it might pass us by. She asks us to think about what it can mean not to *intend* offense. Using the writings of a Kierkegaard, Khawaja demonstrates that the editor is showing a failure of understanding in this moment. As Khawaja says, cartoons of the Prophet Muhammad cannot be absolved of creating the possibility of offending. They offend precepts central to Islam. Certain practices of apparently secular freedom or reason are, by the very definition of their secularity, offensive. Kierkegaard asks us to understand offense not as a sign that something wrong has happened, but as an indication the truth is beginning to be identified. In our effort to avoid the hurt that offense produces, we may also avoid the foundational claims exposed in its production. "The point is simple but astonishing," Khawaja writes. "Being a Christian means not to reject the world but to employ the world—indeed, actually to need the world—as that toward which one's conduct may be understood as offensive." Kierkegaard says that being Christian is itself a posture of offense toward the world. Although the word "Christian" is especially important to Kierkegaard in that sentence, Khawaja's demonstrates the extent to which secularism represents another idiom of the same form.

In her recent excellent account of Trump supporters in West Virginia, Larissa MacFarquhar goes further, saying that when Trump's enemies criticize him for his gaffes, this pushes his followers to him. As one of her informants says, "When [voters] see that the media elite is driven out of their mind at the success of Donald Trump it makes them want to root for him. It's like giving the middle finger to the rest of the country." The offense of the media elite at Trump shows that their secularism has specific rules of engagement, and Trump is in violation of them. Yet they also need his offensive behavior in order to demonstrate their reason: to show again what they know relative to what he doesn't.

As MacFarquhar shows, this is a dangerous dynamic. Every time some secular authority tries to top Trump's authority with their forms of corrective reason, they offend again those who perceive this practice of secularism as a form of condescension. And Kierkegaard would say: our only mistake is not recognizing the offense of secular neutrality. Observing that Trump voters might be less educated than Clinton voters may seem to many to be a simple sociological observation. But for Trump voters, this is akin to telling a Biblical literalist that the text called the Bible is an amalgamation of a vast number of texts assembled by human editors and written by human authors. Facticity is its own offense in the realm of magical thinking. (It is, also, a kind of magical thinking all its own.) Khawaja, through Kierkegaard, tries to press us to see offense as productive. That it should be the beginning of reckoning and recognition, not a reason for further distance and recircling of the tribal wagons.

Scholars of religion often try to combat prejudice by showing how universal are the principles shared among the religions of the world. But this act of flattening comparison does nothing to assess or address the fact that belonging to a religion—belonging to a collectivity—is a radical act of distinction. Religions sanction conspiracy. If we are to use religion not only as a subject for diagnosis, but also as a tool of relation, we need to imagine a concept of encounter that is less phobic of offense. Less certain of the safety of difference. More interested in the tough work, the impossible wrestling with alien concepts until we make them legibly human, again.

Hurtling down the highway, muttering about the dinner party, I realize that the worst crime of the night wasn't the verbalized self-satisfaction of my companions; it wasn't the unchecked assumptions about Trump voters or Trump or Brexit. It was my offended distance, my self-soothing internal monologue, telling me that I was beyond their nonsense and unreason. It was my smug certitude that I was on the side of the angels simply because I had the better facts. I wish I could go back and do it again. To listen and reply. To try, in whatever stumbling way, to understand why their understanding seemed to me so far-flung from my craven own.

Midwestworld

by Meghan O'Gieblyn

ISSUE 13 | WINTER 2017

It was the kind of day in Detroit, late in the course of a temperate summer, when the heat rebounds and the humidity returns with a vengeance. We drove in on the freeway, past marshland and inoperative steel mills and townships whose names—Romulus, Troy—recalled the imperial ambitions of a more hopeful era. We were headed not to the city but to the simulation: the reconstructed historic town known as Greenfield Village. At nine, when we arrived—my mother, my sisters, the children and I—the parking lot was already packed. School had started a couple weeks earlier, and it appeared as though districts across the metro area had chosen the day for their inaugural field trip. Children poured out of Detroit Public Schools buses and shuttles stamped with the logos of Jewish day schools. There were Syrian and Yemeni kids from the Dearborn schools and kindergarteners dressed in the Hogwartian uniforms of parochial academies—all of them boundless and boisterous and shepherded by adults who bore the unexpressive fatalism of people who work professionally with children.

Saddled with diaper bags and water bottles, three small children in tow, we joined the throng at the gates and were promptly ushered into another world. Women in bonnets strolled down the thoroughfare. We passed tinsmith shops, farmhouses, horse-drawn buggies and a man who had been paid, in the name of historical authenticity, to stand in a shadowless field in three layers of tweed, pretending to pick beans. We had come here, supposedly, for the children, who belonged to my two sisters, though we were really here for my mother, who was in the delirious throes of early grand-motherhood and insisted that this was a family tradition. She led the way with the kids, while my sisters and I lagged behind, each of us pushing an empty stroller and redundantly lamenting the heat. We had, in fact, loved this place when we were young, but as adults we became uncharacteristically cynical each time we returned, eager to call attention to the park's lapses in verisimilitude: the milliner surreptitiously texting beneath her apron; the two men dressed as farmhands, believing themselves out of earshot, discussing cyber-terrorism as they forked hay into a wagon.

Greenfield Village describes itself as a "living history" museum. Unlike most museums, where artifacts are displayed in vitrines, the park is emphatically "hands on." Not only can you visit a nineteenth-century print shop where a man dressed in overalls operates a proof press with real ink, you can also attend one of the interactive work-shops and make antique broadsides with your own two hands. On that summer morning, the Village was alive with the bustle of people mak-ing things. There were men tinkering in workshops, bent over boot-jacks. There were women in calico dresses peddling flax wheels and kneading actual bread dough to be baked in functional coal ovens.

The park, completed in 1929, was the vanity project of Henry Ford, a man who years earlier had declared that "history is more or less bunk." Later, he would clarify: *written* history was bunk, because it focused on politicians and military heroes rather than the common men who built America. Greenfield Village was his correction to the historical narrative. It was a place designed to celebrate the inven-tor, the farmer and the agrarian landscape that had given rise to self-made men like him. Ford had a number of historically significant buildings relocated to the park, including the Wright brothers' cycle shop and Thomas Edison's laboratory, both of which still stand on its grounds. But the park was never really about history—not, at least, in any objective sense. It was a sentimental recreation of the landscape of Ford's boyhood. To this day, patrons can visit his family homestead, the one-room schoolhouse he attended and the work-shop where he built his first car, buildings he not only relocated to the park but also faithfully outfitted with the decorative props he recalled from his youth.

Ford was evidently not alone in his longing for this bygone era. The park's opening coincided with the Great Depression, a time when many people felt disillusioned with modernity and its narratives about progress. The Village, which evoked a way of life recent enough to have persisted in the memories of older visitors, attracted scores of Americans who felt alienated from the land because of urbanization and factory work, and who longed to return, if only momentarily, to the slower, more satisfying pace of pre-industrial life. In the forties, park guides began their tours by encouraging patrons to "forget the hustle and bustle of the atomic age and return briefly to the simple, rugged life" their forefathers knew. The irony, of course, was that the way of life the park romanticized was precisely that which Ford had helped usher into obsolescence with the invention of the automobile and the modern factory. The Village was modernity's elegy for an America that no longer existed, built by its most illustrious titan of industry.

Now here we were, some eighty years later, at the coda of another economic downturn. Throughout the worst years of the Recession, a crisis that hit Michigan particularly hard, Greenfield Village and its sister site, the Henry Ford Museum, had become more popular than ever. At a time when tourist attractions across Michigan were struggling just to keep their doors open, the Village actually saw a surge in attendance. This was the first time I'd been back since the financial crisis, and I'd never seen the park so crowded. We spent most of the morning standing in lines, uselessly fanning ourselves with park brochures. At the machine shop, we waited almost an hour so that my niece could use a turret lathe to make a brass candlestick. It was a tedious process that involved several complicated steps, each of which was accompanied by the docent's plodding commentary. In the end, though, there was something undeniably satisfying in seeing raw material transformed into a concrete object. I remarked to my sister, as we watched her daughter operate the lathe, that it must be some comfort knowing that if the whole global infrastructure collapsed, at least one person in the family would be able to make decorative metalwork.

"It's character building," she replied.

There was, certainly, a moral aspect to these demonstrations. As the costumed docents explained each archaic skill, they stressed the time and care that went into each of these primitive crafts. The park seemed designed to be not only educational but also edifying; children were brought here so they could become acquainted with all manner of "traditional" virtues—hard work, diligence, collaboration, perseverance—whose relevance to our current economy was not, it occurred to me, entirely apparent. But maybe that was the point. If the park still persisted as a site of nostalgia, it was because it satisfied a more contemporary desire: to see a market that depended on the exchange of tangible goods, a world in which one's labor resulted in predictable outcomes and the health of the economy relied on a vast collaborative workshop powered by the sweat of common people. There are, of course, different kinds of nostalgia, some more flexible than others. On that day, there was a restive energy throughout the park, as though the collective longing that had brought us here was undergirded by something more desperate.

•

It is difficult, in a place like Detroit, to avoid thinking about the past. The city is still associated with an industry that peaked in the middle of the last century, and has since succumbed to all the familiar culprits of urban decline—globalization, automation, disinvestment and a host of racist public policies. Perhaps it was destined from the start to collapse beneath the weight of the metaphorical import placed on its shoulders. During the Depression and throughout the years leading up to the Second World War, the city stood as a symbol of national strength, a thrumming life force pumping blood into the economy—associations that persist in the city's epithets (the "arsenal of democracy") and its industries' ad campaigns (the "heartbeat of America"). For decades, the auto industry boasted the highest-paid blue-collar jobs in America, making Detroit a magnet for working people from all over the country.

Among the first waves of migrants was my great-grandfather, who in the twenties abandoned his family's tobacco farm in southern

Kentucky to build Model Ts for the wage of five dollars a day. His son, my grandfather, grew up on Warren Avenue during the Depression, shoveling coal for nickels to help with his family's expenses. These men, father and son, remained lucid and hale well into my adolescence. Between the two of them, plus a coterie of uncles who had given their best years to Chrysler, my childhood was steeped in nostalgia for the city's glory years. Hardly a family holiday went by when my siblings and I were not made to remain at the table after the food had been cleared to listen to their recollections of the city. "They used to call us the Paris of the Midwest," my grandfather would say. These were men who spoke of Henry Ford as a demigod, and for whom work, with all its attendant Protestant virtues, was a kind of religion. Their stories expressed a longing for a time when the country still relied on the brawn of men like themselves who had, despite coming from humble origins and not going to college, managed to lift their families into the middle class. But they were also meant for us children, the beneficiaries of all that hard work, whom they perhaps feared were growing up a little too comfortably in suburban exile.

From time to time, my grandfather would load us kids—my brothers and sisters and me—into the back of his Town Car and drive us downtown to see his old neighborhood. By the late nineties, the area was a characteristic stretch of bricked-over storefronts and condemned buildings, but it had once been a thriving residential area built for the city's auto workers, a neighborhood of single-family homes where Southern transplants like his family lived alongside immigrants from Mexico, Poland and Greece. "People came here from all over the world," he told us. "Everyone lived together and got along." It was a remark he repeated every time he took us downtown, and one that seemed to me, even as a child, suspiciously rosy. In fact, the racial zoning laws that segregated the city were already in force during the decades he lived there. It's possible that he was being sentimental, infusing his recollections with the same sort of romanticism that had colored Ford's vision of his pastoral boyhood. But I think he was also deliberately refashioning these memories, the way one does when imparting lessons to children. He was not speaking to a historical reality so much as evoking an ideal, one that has long been associated with Detroit: it was a place where anyone—regardless of education, race or how recently they had come to this country—could, through hard work, enter the middle class.

Nostalgia was on my mind that day as we walked along the dusty roads of Greenfield Village. The country was entering the home stretch of a historically tumultuous election season, one in which Detroit had been revived, once again, as symbol. This time, in the imagination of Donald Trump, the city—along with places like Cleveland, Pittsburgh and the Pennsylvania coal country—became an emblem of bungled trade deals and inept Washington bureaucrats, representing an America that had been left behind in an era of breakneck change. Pundits dubbed this the "politics of nostalgia," but it was a yearning that felt different from my grandfather's wistfulness for the city of his youth. To be sure, many of Trump's platform points echoed grievances that had been loitering for decades in the op-ed pages of the *Detroit Free Press* and at dinner tables across Wayne County. But on the campaign trail these arguments were fed by something new, the raw energy of conspiracy and xenophobic scapegoating—a melancholia that longed to resurrect not only the economic landscape of mid-century America but also its racial and gender hierarchies.

Throughout the summer, I had watched many of my family members—men who, like my grandfather, had once extolled the city as a diverse and booming metropolis of yore—fall captive to these nativist reveries. If my sisters and I felt particularly uneasy about being at the Village that day, and more eager than usual to expose its artifice, it was because the park could, in some sense, be read as a lurid expression of that constituency's vision of a nation made Great Again: a world before globalization and the advent of civil rights; a time when black Americans were relegated to tenant farms and women were hidden within the narrow confines of galley kitchens.

But the park had taken pains to revamp its sites in an effort to preempt this more thorny form of nostalgia. Throughout the eighties and nineties, the Village amended its mission to offer a more progressive view of history. In place of Ford's celebration of self-made manhood, the sites now emphasized "community life." The bucolic romanticism of Ford's day had likewise been replaced with a focus on the shifting technological landscape of nineteenth-century America and the innovations that led to the first wave of the industrial revolution. The Village had become, in the words of its former president, "the great American museum of change." An African-American Cultures program was added to address the history of racial injustice inherent in the park's representations of the past, and the guide scripts had been expanded to highlight the contributions of immigrants, minorities and women.

Some of these revisions were a bit of a stretch. At the general store, a female docent showed my sisters and me an early wholesale catalog and insisted that women's demand for consumer goods significantly shaped the economic landscape of the nineteenth century. I turned to my sisters to impart some ironic remark and was surprised to find them listening with attentiveness. By this point, we had caught up with my mom and the kids, and my sisters had become mothers again. They were watching the faces of their daughters; it is difficult to be cynical in the presence of children. We were, on that day, among hundreds of them—kids who had come from all parts of the city to learn about their nation's history—and the park docents were doing their best to impart a version of that story that included everyone. If nothing else, we owed them this attempt.

•

In her 2001 book *The Future of Nostalgia*, the critic Svetlana Boym, who grew up in the Soviet Union, traces the different forms of nostalgia that emerged in post-communist Europe. Boym argues that the word's two Greek roots—*nostos*, or the return home, and *algia*, or longing—embody two types of nostalgia that tend to arise in modern cultures: "reflective nostalgia" and "restorative nostalgia." Reflective nostalgia thrives on the feeling of longing. As much as it might idealize or romanticize the past, it is a flexible form of nostalgia that interacts, in creative ways, with the present and the future.

Much like the revised narratives of Greenfield Village, or my grandfather's memories of Detroit, this brand of wistfulness is aware on some level that its visions of the past are illusory.

Restorative nostalgia, on the other hand, dwells in the feeling of *nostos*—returning home. It seeks not only to remember the lost homeland, but also to rebuild it. This more rigid orientation toward the past lies at the root of nationalist movements, and unlike reflective nostalgia, which can be ironic or playful, it tends to be severe, if not authoritarian. Those who are drawn to this kind of nostalgia, Boym notes, "do not think of themselves as nostalgic; they believe their project is about truth." Rather than meditating on the sense of loss, restorative movements exploit this longing by blaming certain groups of people who have supposedly caused the loss of the homeland. The Nazi pogroms, Stalin's Terror and McCarthy's Red Scare, Boym argues, all appealed to restorative accounts of history. Such narratives are often fueled by conspiracy theories and a mythology of persecution.

Nostalgia almost always stems from an anxiety about modernity: the fear that progress is happening too fast, and that the past will be irrevocably lost. But restorative tendencies are more likely to emerge during especially dramatic periods of upheaval. Restorative movements often take root in the aftermath of revolutions, though they are also common during times of social and economic turbulence, particularly those that unsettle existing narratives about national identity. It is in such times, when the distance between reality and myth becomes unbridgeable, that nostalgia can coarsen into resentment and people begin hunting for someone to blame.

Here in Michigan, it's hard not to sense that something fundamental shifted, or perhaps snapped, during the Recession—not necessarily at its nadir, but during the years that followed, when the news touted the "recovery" of the market while people throughout the state continued to lose their homes and their jobs. Any lingering belief that Detroit stood as symbol of the nation—that its prosperity and the rest of the country's were intertwined—was shattered in 2013 when the city declared bankruptcy the same week the Dow and the S&P closed at record highs. The city had been through hard times before; but if the crisis had a particularly demoralizing effect this time around it is because it undermined, in a way that even the Great Depression had not, the populist myths that have long animated the region. There is an uneasiness here, a needling suspicion that the fruits of the economy do not correspond to the exertions of the nation's labor force; that prosperity, once envisioned by Diego Rivera as an endless collaborative assembly line stretching into the future, is now a closed loop that ordinary people are locked out of. From such desperation, the natural tendency to reflect can evolve into a misguided effort to restore.

By the time we left the general store, the heat had become oppressive. The children were growing fractious, and the docents, with their Victorian cheeriness, were beginning to seem sinister. We made our way to the center of the Village, where there was a restored carousel, and each of us chose a painted animal; the children shared an antique bench carved to look like a swan. As the carousel began moving, the pipe organ churned out a kaleidoscopic rendition of "After the Ball," and soon the Village, and its visions of the past, became a blur of green. On a gilded unicorn, a man in a United Auto Workers cap snapped a selfie with his unsmiling granddaughter. A mother idly straightened her daughter's hijab. Everyone looked extremely tired.

The music stopped and the carousel slowed. People began collecting their bags and sliding their children off the wooden animals, but then the platform jolted and the carousel kicked back into gear. "Not over yet!" someone exclaimed. The man with the UAW cap joked about getting a two-for-one, and it became apparent that he was right: the ride seemed to have started over again. The organ played "After the Ball" from the beginning, though the tempo seemed slower this time and the melody began to warble, as though it were slipping into a minor key. As we wheeled around toward the operator box, I tried to determine whether anyone was manning the controls, but it was impossible to see inside. The other passengers seemed blithely resigned to our fate. It was hot, and the spinning created a welcome breeze. My mother was riding sidesaddle on a painted camel, texting. The children were narcotized, hair pasted against their temples, their eyelids weighted and fighting sleep. It was only when the music ended and we continued circling in silence that people began to look up with a dawning sense of alarm and seek out each other's gaze, as though everyone had collectively begun to wonder how we were going to get off.

Letter on Our President

by The Editors

ISSUE 13 | WINTER 2017

It became a commonplace last summer for political commentators to exclaim that they did not know some portion of the American electorate, hence that they did not know some portion of their own country, America. Some lamented (or pretended to lament) this irrefutable development, as if it were simply a hazard of being educated or knowledgeable in a country so big and benighted. Others ventured out into what they called "Trump country" and "RightLand" and "the heart of the Tea Party." They described their time on this alien planet as a "through-the-looking-glass experience" (Roger Cohen, the *New York Times*), or bemoaned their discovery that "we are now two separate ideological countries" (George Saunders, the *New Yorker*). In the introduction to the lengthiest production of the season, Arlie Russell Hochschild's *Strangers in Their Own Land*, the Berkeley-based sociologist conjured an "empathy wall" that stood between her and the Southern voters she met and interviewed. Thankfully, Hochschild had moved around a lot as the daughter of a Foreign Service officer: such experience, she related, had come in handy when she attempted to make inroads into the "foreign country" of rural Louisiana.

What these writers found on the other side of their empathy walls depended on the brand of binoculars they brought from home. Some concluded that the inhabitants of RightLand were reactionaries fearful of change; others that they were casualties of the global economy confused about their true interests; and others still that they were renegades in revolt against liberal condescension.

The accuracy of the conclusions didn't much matter—after all, Hillary was ahead in the polls. What mattered, insofar as a given entry wished to take its place among the genre's exemplars, was that the author refrain from ever questioning the premise that America had now to be considered as (at least) two distinct populations: populations that spoke different languages, listened to different radio stations and harbored irreconcilable assumptions about what made their country great. With this granted, or assumed, the suspense consisted in seeing how this particular journalist, academic or *New York Times* columnist, deploying her finely trained capacity for empathy and deductive reasoning, would manage to twist some new drop of insight out of what had become, by the end of the summer, a deadeningly dry tale.

Once Trump was elected, the tone of the think pieces changed but their central conceit remained. What had been a subject of benign, if fervid, intellectual curiosity was suddenly, as the editor of the East Coast's preeminent lifestyle magazine put it just after 1 a.m. on November 9th, cause for "revulsion and profound anxiety." The world, it was proclaimed, had been made unsafe by democracy, but we could at least take comfort from the knowledge that the New Yorker who would ascend to the White House was "not our president." He belonged rather to that other tribe, the one that roamed outside the train window, behind the strip malls, over the smoke stacks, in the midst of the megachurches. Now it is "those of us on the liberal left," Hochschild said, deftly repurposing her title for the altered post-election zeitgeist, "who are strangers in our own land."

•

Internal to the setup of the election-year travelogues was the familiar idea that certain groups of Americans have more in common with Parisians than they do with Pennsylvanians. Simple facts—facts right in front of us and therefore apparently impossible to see— have always challenged this tempting hypothesis, and when the exit polls came in they offered more trouble for it still. Plenty has already been said about the countless Rust Belt voters who, after helping to reelect Barack Obama in 2012, presumably declared dual citizenship by breaking for Trump four years later. Less has been mentioned about another cross-cultural phenomenon just as obvious: the tremendous fascination that the new president holds for supposedly uncomprehending liberals.

After the election many criticized the news networks for having given so much "free media" to the Republican nominee, but this could not help doubling as a form of self-criticism. When CBS CEO Les Moonves said Trump was "damn good" for business, he was merely stating the obvious: Americans—and not just conservative or "non-college educated" ones—could not get enough of Trump. Overall, ad revenue for the three political news networks climbed 26 percent compared to the last election year in 2012. Raising its viewership by 36 percent from 2015, Fox leapfrogged ESPN to become, for the first time, the most-watched cable network in 2016. CNN (77 percent) and the left-leaning MSNBC (87 percent!) experienced even larger percentage increases. This is not because either devoted themselves to the careful examination of the candidates' policy papers. A *BuzzFeed* report in July 2015 found that MSNBC had covered Trump even more disproportionately than the other networks, with its anchors uttering his name over four hundred times in a single week (CNN came in second at 340).

Viewership does not imply endorsement, and doubtless many had complicated reasons for tuning in to the daily soap opera. But the breadth of the fascination over two long years suggests it does not take some special exertion for those of us who live in cities or on the coasts to comprehend Trump's appeal. Of course we already knew this from our social-media feeds, crammed as they were with running chronicles of Trump's daily crimes and misdemeanors, video clips from his latest campaign stop and close readings of his most recent outburst on Twitter. (Did we require such information in order to make up our minds about the candidate?)

A similar story could be told about so much of the culturally charged "evidence" in what has become a *de rigueur* ritual of election-year taxonomy. In 2004 George W. Bush's chances were said to hinge on the "Nascar voter," a hick with a taste for carnage who was pitted against those who knew to draw the line at the rolling concussion protocol known internationally as "American football." Last year the mindlessness and vulgarity of the Trump voter was daily condemned by those who spend their weekends playing Candy Crush and marveling at "high-concept" rape and pillage vehicles like *Game of Thrones* and *Westworld*. The point is not that we should all be equally ashamed: as those shows themselves set out to demonstrate, a taste for violent pleasures is hardly unique to any particular demographic or time period. The advantage of living in the country that invented demolition derby and the Hollywood Western is that you can safely drop the pretense of having evolved beyond them.

Of course the truly definitive differences between our two Americas are supposed to inhere in something deeper than taste. The liberal left might even admit its occasional attraction to cathartic domestic pastimes—who doesn't love a gambling weekend in Vegas!—so long as they can be safely separated from the retrograde prejudices of those for whom such activities (so we hear) are habitual. Hence the high psychological stakes for those ensconced in the comfortable neighborhoods of Chicago or Los Angeles, cities persisting in a condition of de facto apartheid, in denouncing the irredeemable racism of Southern whites. Likewise the urban parents paying $30,000 per year to keep their children out of unruly public schools, who lecture suburbanites on the necessary tradeoffs between diversity and security. From college campuses duly cleansed of challenges to enlightened liberalism, the children of those parents will one day inveigh against the intolerance of the evangelicals.

A popular interpretation of the 2016 election holds that it disproved our outgoing president's vision, first articulated in his famous speech at the 2004 Democratic National Convention and reiterated in his farewell address this January, of an America that was, in fact and not just in aspiration, one country. And there is little question that the special ugliness of the contest between Trump and Clinton was due in part to the fact that both candidates— aided by the latest filtering algorithms and poll-based targeting techniques—opposed their preferred version of America to the one they disparaged as inauthentic or deplorable. But a more plausible, if less comfortable, way of interpreting what happened in 2016 is to say that it exposed those features of the American character that Obama had been too hopeful, or too prudent, to identify.

Indeed, the comparisons drawn, in recent months, between America's new president and right-wing populists in Europe, such as France's Marine Le Pen and Germany's Frauke Petry, only sharpen the outlines of Trump's distinctive brand of Americana. Le Pen and Petry are ideologues with views many consider extreme and dangerous, but they look and act like politicians of a fairly conventional kind. Trump has no ideas whatsoever, ignores every convention of political self-presentation and is a proud member of World Wrestling Entertainment's Hall of Fame. Having announced his candidacy from the lobby of his gold-plated Manhattan tower—a fitting symbol of the "vast, vulgar, and meretricious beauty" to which he had, Gatsby-like, devoted his existence—he embraced a persona that was part Benjamin Franklin, part P. T. Barnum and part Oprah. On stage, he combines elements from our hallowed national traditions: vaudeville, battle rap, the coach's hokey halftime exhortation. To the supplicants waiting in the cold outside his campaign rallies in Des Moines, IA, Manheim, PA and Roanoke, VA, he seemed to resemble one of those itinerant preachers whom Tocqueville encountered "in all the states of the Union" during the Great Awakening, "peddl[ing] the divine word from place to place."*

It is hard to imagine Trump's performance charming Europeans, yet in America it made him mesmerizing—and then it made him president.

•

We did not need the 2016 election to know we lived in a divided country. Since its inception, America has been on the brink of being torn apart by its differences—and national elections have often served as referendums on the divergent attitudes toward race, religion and government power that once precipitated a civil war. Trump's pres-

* "Religious follies are very common there," the Frenchman concluded.

idency poses a unique threat because he treats these divisions as opportunities to be exploited rather than obstacles to be overcome: his promise to return the government to "the people" is explicitly a promise to return it to *his* people. But that strategy can succeed only if the rest of us choose to be complicit in it. One way we become complicit is by indulging, above and beyond our experience of the things that differentiate us, in a flattering fantasy of them.

Acknowledging the familiarity of Trump's appeal does not mean ceasing to struggle against his agenda (such as one can be discerned), or being naive about the sinister potential of his presidency. Nor does it require of any of us that we renounce our commitments to pluralism, social justice or HBO. It might encourage us to trade a hollow moralism, aimed always at that "other" America that has not yet learned the right manners, for a recognition that our new president is a product of forces and feelings with deep roots in both our history and ourselves.

At times in that history there have been populations compelled, by law or by force, to suffer under the authority of a president they could credibly claim was not theirs. But to declare today that we bear no responsibility for the elected leaders of our democracy would be merely laughable were it not, in this case, so potentially self-destructive. This land has always been strange, but we are not strangers to it: Donald Trump could be the president of no people besides ours.

Pleasure Won

A CONVERSATION WITH
LAUREN BERLANT

Interview by Bea Malsky

ISSUE 13 | WINTER 2017

Lauren Berlant is a literary scholar and cultural theorist who works primarily on questions of belonging, citizenship, intimacy and affect. Her writing on fantasies of the good life—how people formulate and pursue desires under precarious political, economic and social conditions—has become a touchstone in contemporary critical theory and cultural studies. Berlant has been teaching at the University of Chicago since 1984 and is the author of several books, including *Cruel Optimism* (2011) and *The Female Complaint* (2008). In 2016 she was awarded a Guggenheim Fellowship for a project on "flattened" forms of affect called *Matter of Flatness*.

Berlant speaks the way she writes: in full paragraphs, punctuated by phrasal asides that nod toward rabbit holes of references before returning to their sentence's original point. Her thoughts are often structured around some kind of punch line. I first met Berlant at a gallery show where she was quoted in the artist's statement on the wall; later on in college I took her Theories of Gender and Sexuality class, in which I reserved a section of my notebook for phrases I thought were funny or beautiful but didn't yet understand. In December, at the Chicago Center for Contemporary Theory, I asked Berlant about the recent election, political emotions, and what America is for.   *Bea Malsky*

•

BEA MALSKY: *When I first asked you about being in this issue of* The Point, *you responded that you didn't know what America was for, but that the question reminded you of a joke: "What's a meta for?" Can you explain the joke?*

LAUREN BERLANT: It reminded me of a joke for the same reason that "What do women want?" is a joke to me. I understand that when Freud asked this it was a serious question, but when I hear it it's a funny question, because it's a ridiculous question. What's beneath "What is America for?" is: Why do we need the nation form? What does it mean to use an object? How do we think about fantasy in the production of sociality? You know, a question like that means so many things it's not actually asking.

One of the things that excites me about comedy is the comic disturbance of the shared object. Like, you think you know what it is but you don't, and you get to delight in that. It allows in the room a multiplicity of kinds of possible effects and affects, and that flooding itself is funny. So a question like "What is America for?" opens up so many possible ways of responding to it, including . . . nothing. Or, a shrug. I just started laughing at it and it became a joke to me.

So that's why I'm interested in comedy. I'm also interested in thinking about politics as comedic, by which I don't mean delightful or funny in the easy Schadenfreude sense. I'm interested in the comedic dictum, which is that disturbance doesn't kill you, it forces you to live on. The thing about trauma, as I always say to my [Literature of] Trauma students, is that it doesn't kill you and you have to live with it. And that's the thing about comedy, too. The comedy is that you get up again after you fall off the cliff, and have to keep moving. You have to live with the brokenness, and you have to live with surprise, and you have to live with contingency. And you have to live with the pleasure of not knowing, if you can bear it. But how you have to live with it is another story.

Comedy is a lot about the question of whether you can bear it, in a way that tragedy isn't. Because in tragedy the world can't bear you.

BM: *Right, in tragedy you die.*

LB: Exactly, there's that. America tries to be a comedic force, in the sense that it tries to organize a kind of optimism about living politically. About a greatness, about a transcendence, about the practical or concrete utopia. About the history of the nation form as a space of justice.

And saturating the space of justice is so important in America's modernity that it's like a failed pun or something: it doesn't work. I always have had respect for people's desire for there to be a form that will solve the problem of living. America is one of those forms—the nation is one of those forms. And form can't solve the problem of living. The constant disappointment at that fact is a lot like the constant repetition in a comic sequence of a slapstick event. Except the violence of the disappointment is not funny! And it has really bad, painful effects on people's lives.

BM: *You've been writing a lot about humor lately, including a piece in a recent issue of* Critical Inquiry *on humorlessness. Why is humorlessness important to your thinking about comedy?*

LB: Whenever I tell someone I'm writing a book on humorlessness, they always laugh. Because humorlessness is so unbearable. I think that's interesting! A liberal model of humor and humorlessness would suggest that you should always try to cure humorlessness with humor, because humor is what keeps things warm between people and it makes it possible to move together in the social. But of course, our political commitments are also humorless. They're the things that we would like to be intractable about.

One of the ways that I define humorlessness is as the sudden withdrawal of a cushion in a social relation, the sudden experience of the intractable where you thought things were tractable. I don't think of it as a moral thing. I think we're all humorless, and we've made friends with our humorlessness in certain places. So when making charges of humorlessness, what people think they're saying is, "I have humor, I'm flexible, I could change. But you, on the other hand, are immovable." But in fact we're all unmovable in places, and a lot of politics is a negotiation of different forms of immobility and commitment.

This is why there's a lot of humor in anti-politically correct discourse. The PC debates have been incredibly interesting since PC was invented as a way of self-policing—PC was an aspiration when we first started using it as a phrase! Because you were trying to un-learn your default sensorium of misogyny and racism and xenopho-bia and class privilege. Being PC was a reminder that your visceral responses were not justice. Of course, all of us are trained as modern subjects to think our visceral responses are justice. But they're not.

It mattered to me that Al Franken, when he was on Air America Radio before he was a senator, used to always call Rush Limbaugh "the comedian Rush Limbaugh." I learned a lot from listening to that and thinking about that. Because what he meant was that Rush Limbaugh has a comedian's commitment to the joke—if he says something outrageous, he's going to follow it through to its logical end, even if the logical end is completely untethered from the real. Because affectively, it demonstrates something for him, whereas ref-erentially, it has no traction. And I think the alt-right is all about that. It's all about affective truth that has a distorted tethering to how people live.

I can give you an anecdote that ties this up somewhat: about six months before the election I started having panic attacks from polit-ical triggers. It's not usual for me, and I didn't really know why. But after some reflection one day, I realized it was because I knew that whoever won, the atmosphere of the Trump campaign had let out of the bag an amplifying pleasure in white supremacy and American exceptionalism and misogyny and xenophobia that, no matter who won, was not going to get stuffed back in.

We are now in, on the one hand, an unchanged world—because white supremacy's not new, and structural violence is not new, none of that is new just because Trump got elected—but the pleasure in it *is* intensified. They took enormous pleasure. Pleasure won this election, you know. Pleasure and violence are all bound up in each other for this election.

BM: *How have you been talking about the election with your students?*

LB: This quarter in my undergrad gender and sexual theories class I tried an experiment. We had a unit on citizenship, three weeks of reading about citizenship and sexuality and gender, and then their midterm project was based on citizenship.

And I said to the class, for how many of you is citizenship an active topic of thought? One person. And I thought that was incredibly interesting, because I've been working on citizenship since I started doing my graduate work, but I myself had been dialing back from it and thinking more about social membership and belonging and all these more diffuse bindings. And then many different social and political crises since 2008—from the economic crisis to Twitter citizenship that enabled the Black Lives Matter movement and other organized refusals to allow the ordinary destruction of life to just be the thing you knew as realism—started to make citizenship an active category for me again.

BM: *How had you first approached that concept of citizenship?*

LB: It was partly that I was eleven in 1968, and a precocious—wild— eleven. So I went to anti-war rallies, and my political consciousness came up during a period of radical experimentality about what it was possible to do as a member of a social world, politically. And so I went to a commune when I was fifteen, I went to rallies, I hated Nixon appropriately, and I had socialist proletarian grandparents on one side of the family.

I understood that there were alternative ways of living. And they were, in a material sense, alternative—it wasn't like someone had a theory about alternativity. It was that people had lived alternatively, and that people were living alternatively. And so it became really important to me to ask the question of what I would now call normativity, but I didn't have that language at the time.

Then, in the seventies, the British feminists were all socialist feminists. I went to England when I was a junior in college at Oberlin— you just paid your regular tuition, which I barely paid any of since I was really poor and on my own. They gave me $45 a week and paid my tuition and I got to go to England and take courses. I took these night classes with secretaries, and radical socialist feminists were teaching them at the University of London. And my eyes were completely opened to the collaboration of nationalism and capitalism, and to imperialism, which I had known as a state of exception for the Vietnam War, and later realized to be not exceptional at all.

I got to graduate school and I started reading a lot of historical novels and Marxism. The rise of the historical novel and the rise of Marxism were at very similar time periods, but also Marxist literary criticism was very involved in thinking about the historical novel as a way of understanding the subjective history of class, capitalism and the nation. And there's the sexuality component, which is that any time you read any criticism of a historical novel it would say, "And then there was this stupid love plot." So I was curious: Why did there need to be sexuality in the historical novel? And so I started thinking a lot about the mediation of politics through the body, and that's how I became me.

BM: *A couple years ago I was in the Theories of Gender and Sexuality class that you co-taught with [sociologist] Kristen Schilt. One of my favorite sessions was when we discussed the video of Obama announcing that his presidential library was going to be on the South Side of Chicago— the things it was saying about the family and patriotism and hard work, and race without ever directly talking about race. Have you done any similar exercises with video from the recent campaigns?*

LB: I had a lot of debates with colleagues around this. Because it was election season, I felt it was important not to be taking political positions in the classroom about voting. Because the minute the teacher expresses a view, people feel that any time they have a view they have to be measuring it against your view. I want people to be able to think about something—I want them to be able to walk around it, you know.

So last year, when I taught affect theory, we looked at political commercials. We looked at the Bernie Sanders "America" commercial in relation to the Obama "Yes We Can" ad. First of all, the students hadn't come to political consciousness during the first Obama election so they hadn't seen the "Yes We Can" ad, which surprised me because I'm an idiot.

But they were crying, and they didn't know they had national sentimentality. And they were a very different group than your class. Your group had a lot of cynicism in it, and when it came to tender political emotions your class was ready to not have them. And I think one of the reasons that class with the Obama library announcement was memorable, and it was memorable to a lot of people, was because we had to think about other people's tenderness and not just our own in the space of the political. It's worth saying to people who haven't seen the video that it includes memories of the Great Migration from the South to Chicago, which stood then as a sign of freedom.

BM: *I think that reluctance was part of why that day stuck with me. You encouraged the class, saying, "It's okay to say something positive about this, or to be moved by this."*

LB: And I wasn't in fact very moved by that commercial for the library. But on the other hand, watching other people be moved in the commercial made me realize: the world is just not a very safe space for anybody's tenderness, when the tenderness means they would like the world to be different and they don't want to experience much more loss on the way.

And a lot of what politics is about is trying to promise that change won't be traumatic. You saw the tenderness in that—in the Bernie ad for America, it's so moving because they're coming to look for America, and it had no content. It was just a few lines from the Simon and Garfunkel song and a bunch of images of farms in Iowa. And it was very moving, but the condition under which it was moving was that there was no content.

This year, I showed two pieces of art by Carrie Mae Weems and one Hillary Clinton commercial when I was teaching affect theory. And the 2012 Carrie Mae Weems ad—it's got music but no Obama voice. It's one portrait of his face and she projects different masks that are associated with different kinds of things people called Obama. And it's just incredibly powerful as you watch him change into various fantasy things. He has said, I knew that I was a screen that people project onto, and she literalizes it. The second Carrie

Mae Weems video was an ad for voting. The image of it was people on the street in New York, very multicultural. But the voiceover was an Obama speech about his legacy, and how much it means to him that people get out and vote. It's no body and all voice—the first thing was all body and no voice—and you felt like you were a part of the audience he was hailing. In the third ad, the Hillary Clinton ad, she uses the same speech that Carrie Mae Weems used, but it's all pictures of her and Obama. And the last shot of it is him with his arm around her walking her onto a stage. So it was really creepy, because in the third ad it was her saying, I have to submit myself to his legacy in order for you to accept me.

Watching the different orchestrations of political affect in these three things makes you really recognize how there is no consensual historical present except the one we make, and how completely affectively complicated it is to have a political desire in the present moment.

I think there's a lot of mess in solidarity, because the point of solidarity is a concept—an emotion. You don't have to like the people you have solidarity with; you just get to be on the same team, and have the project of making the world better. But one of the things that we debate when we're trying to do that is: Do we want the same world? We agree that we don't want the world that exists, but do we want the same world? And a lot of politics, a lot of the humorlessness of the political, comes when you realize that the people who share your critique don't share your desire.

I have a kind of long-haul version of intellectual and political self-development which is: there will always be blindness in it, and when that gets revealed to us we have to face it. We have to figure out what kind of conversation we can have, because in the long haul it's clear that the world has to become less bad, but also much better, for people who are living in it.

BM: *What about this process of unlearning as you learn—do you think there's a violence in that?*

LB: Yes. Unlearning is extremely painful, because you're giving up your object. And I believe in pedagogy—I'm fundamentally a teacher. But I think teaching is really difficult, because the things you're trying to get people to unlearn are things they hold close, and that are forms of life for them that structure their sense of continuity. Because learning and unlearning happen at the same time, there ought to be a lot of grace in the space of pedagogy.

Cruel Optimism is about how people will stay in relation to their object even if it destroys them, because they can't bear giving up the pleasure of knowing the world in a particular way. So yes, unlearning is very painful because it means you have to experience a kind of complexity about moving through the world that you didn't have before. And that's very abstract, but it's not abstract when you're losing something.

I remember a colleague of mine saying to me that when he realized Russian communism was also genocidal, he couldn't be a communist anymore. He was an old leftist, even when I met him. And he said, "So I turned from the world and just chose my wife." And that broke my heart. But it was so painful for him to lose his object that he just chose a very personal and apolitical love. I would never want to do that, but it means you have to be willing to feel the pain of the contingency of the world.

Final Fantasy

NEOREACTIONARY POLITICS AND THE LIBERAL IMAGINATION

by James Duesterberg

ISSUE 14 | SUMMER 2017

Like every virtual world, there is something seductive about the on-line realm of the new reactionary politics. Wading in, one finds one-self quickly immersed, and soon unmoored. All of the values that have guided the center-left, postwar consensus—the equal dignity of every individual, the guiding role of knowledge, government's positive role in shaping civil society, a general sense that we're mov-ing towards a better world—are inverted. The moral landmarks by which we were accustomed to get our bearings aren't gone: they're on fire.

Trying to regain their footing, the mainstays of consensus thought have focused on domesticating the threat. Who are these Tea Partiers and internet recluses, these paleoconservatives and tech futurists, and what could they possibly want? The *Atlantic* mapped the coordinates of the "rebranded" white nationalism or the "inter-net's anti-democracy movement" in the previously uncharted waters of 4chan and meme culture. In *Strangers in Their Own Land*, Berkeley sociologist Arlie Russell Hochschild peers over the "empathy wall" between her and her rural Louisiana Tea Party contacts, while in *Hillbilly Elegy*, Ohio-born lawyer J. D. Vance casts a melancholic look back—from the other side of the aisle, but, tellingly, from the same side of the wall—on the Appalachian culture he left behind for Yale Law and a career in Silicon Valley.

These efforts follow a line of center-left thought that begins with Thomas Frank's 2004 book *What's the Matter with Kansas?* Its

guiding assumption is that those who balk at its vision are fundamentally *mistaken*: victims of an unfortunate illusion, perpetuated
by big businesses or small prejudices, lack of education or surplus
of religion. But now the balance of power has shifted, radically. And
as reactionary ideology has grown—seemingly overnight—from a
vague and diffuse resistance to a concerted political force, the veneer of objective interest and pastoral concern has started to crack.

"Darkness is good," proclaimed Steve Bannon, the self-styled ar-
chitect of Trumpism, to the *Hollywood Reporter*. "Dick Cheney. Darth
Vader. Satan. That's power." This is the face the new reactionary politics presents to the technocratic elite: mysterious, evil and dangerously potent. It promises that some other way of doing things is possible. Since the election, the media, too, seem to be lured by it. As
this alien force approaches, concern shades into fear, and fear starts
to mix with attraction. Like Mulder in *The X-Files*, we find comfort in
imagining some other power out there, even if it means us ill.* The
shame of seeing one's own impotence laid bare can also feel like a
relief: unshouldering the burden of Universal Progress, we make
room for a secret desire to flourish.

•

The political imagination of the last thirty years has largely been
shaped by the paradoxical belief that, as Margaret Thatcher put
it, "there is no alternative": that beliefs themselves are powerless
to change the world. Life in the post-industrial West would be the
happy end of history, and thus of ideologies, a calm and dreamless
state. But the world into which we have settled has begun to feel
cramped, and its inhabitants are increasingly restless. It is no longer possible to deny that there is a dream here, and it's starting to
seem like a bad one.

Since 1979 the divide between rich and poor has widened, while
real wages for the non-managerial work that most people do have
fallen and economic mobility has decreased. "Think different,"

---

* Since 2001, U.F.O. sightings in the United States have tripled.

Apple urged in the nineties: words of wisdom, to be sure, for the new economy, although the rewards seem to concentrate in the same place. Apple is 325 times bigger than it was in 1997; the average real wage for college graduates hasn't increased at all. Like postmodern theory, Apple's slogan makes "difference" into an opaque object of worship, a monolith or a space-gray smartphone: something intelligent but not quite human. "Think different," not differently: the point is not to change your mind but to contemplate something else. Meanwhile, as the Silicon Valley tech giants grow ever more "different," we sit around thinking about it in the academy, and living it on our phones. Tech executive or Uber driver, we find ourselves stuck in what Hito Steyerl calls "junktime," an empty expectancy, somewhere between work and play and going nowhere.

It is in this context that the new reactionary politics have generated such a strange mixture of excitement and fear. The alt-right seems really to *want* something. And within this nebulous (and mostly virtual) world, a group of writers who call themselves neoreactionaries offer the most concrete and detailed map of an "exit" from the status quo. Amid the diffuse politics and intractable ironism of the alt-right, neoreaction promises a coherent ideology, a philosophical backbone and a political program directly opposed to what we have: they call it a "Dark Enlightenment." If these thinkers are especially disturbing to read it is because, unlike the meme warriors of 4chan and Twitter, they seem to have *reasons* for the nasty things they say.

As a rule the alt-right is scattered, anonymous and obscure—thriving, as the curious metaphor has it, in the "dark corners of the internet." By contrast, neoreaction is centralized and public: darkness enlightened. It revolves around two well-known figures. The first is Curtis Yarvin, a software engineer who made money in the first internet boom developing an early protocol for mobile browsers. His current startup Urbit—backed by Peter Thiel—is a platform promising to "reboot" the internet by privatizing the virtual real estate where cloud computing takes place. Since 2007, his other big project has been his blog, where, under the name Mencius Moldbug, he has written millions of words of revisionist history, pessimistic philosophizing, racist fearmongering and intellectual parlor games. His writing constitutes the canon of neoreaction, and it has found readers from Steve Bannon to Nassim Nicholas Taleb, the finance expert known for predicting the 2008 crash, to *New York Times* editorialist Ross Douthat. While alt-righters trade memes about campus snowflakes, Moldbug one-ups the enemy soldiers of Enlightenment, drawing on David Hume, Thomas Carlyle and the obscure nineteenth-century English historian James Froude to prove that slavery is natural and monarchy is the only stable form of government.

Less prolific, but more charismatic, Nick Land is neoreaction's guru. An academic philosopher turned gonzo theorist, Land baptized the emerging movement the "Dark Enlightenment" in a 2013 commentary on Moldbug's writing. In the nineties Land taught in the philosophy department at Warwick University, where his Deleuzian "schizoanalysis" of the postmodern world formed the basis of a group called the Cybernetic Culture Research Unit (Ccru). The Ccru became a hub for radical thought about the intersection of technology, capitalism and desire. Out of it came a new school of philosophy (speculative realism), Turner Prize-nominated artists (Jake and Dinos Chapman), a hugely influential electronic music label (Hyperdub) and one of the dominant strains of Marxian political theory (accelerationism). For Land it catalyzed an eventual break—from sanity (too many amphetamines, he admits) and from the strictures of academic philosophy. Since the early 2000s he has been living in Shanghai, where he turned to blogging, and to the defense and encouragement of an unbridled techno-capitalism.

Land's techno-Darwinist account of race ("hyper-racism," he calls it) is strange to read next to his early academic work, in which he called for "feminist violence" against the racist patriarchy "without limit." A YouTube search for Yarvin produces equally jarring results. Ponytailed and painfully self-conscious, he reads his poetry on nineties Berkeley public-access TV ("this is, um, dedicated to my mother"). One click away is Yarvin at a 2012 TED-inspired "unconference," baby-faced and affectless, asking his audience to "get over [their] dictator phobia."

Yarvin and Land continue to thrive in the liberal milieu into which they were born. "I live in San Francisco," Yarvin brags, "I grew up as a Foreign Service brat, I went to Brown, I've been brushing my teeth with Tom's of Maine since the mid-eighties." Both can be considered architects of the emerging tech- and knowledge-based economy; they are the "autistic nerds" that, Land says, "alone are capable of participating effectively" in the emerging economic system. But even they do not feel at home in this world they have helped to build. If the new anti-liberal politics runs on *ressentiment*, as commentators on both the left and right have suggested, the nerds of neoreaction channel this sense of betrayal at the heart of the American liberal project into an either/or Boolean clarity. Their passion rivals that of their avowed enemy, the "social justice warrior." And what they believe is, quite simply, that everything about the modern world is a lie.

Western democracy, Mencius Moldbug tells us, is an "Orwellian system," which means that its governments are "existentially dependent on systematic public deception." Nominally, a democracy like the U.S. is founded on the separation of church and state, and more fundamentally, of government policy and civil society. With a state church, government power shapes what citizens think, which means citizens can no longer shape government policy. Rather than expressing or even guiding the will of the people, the state aims only to increase its own power by producing the people it needs. But a state church, according to neoreaction, is what we have: Moldbug calls it "the Cathedral," and exposing it, critiquing it and trying to destroy it is neoreaction's avowed goal. The Cathedral, like the Matrix in the 1999 film (a favorite reference point for neoreaction), is everywhere; it infects every experience, shapes all aspects of our waking lives. Its main centers of power are the university, the mainstream media and the culture industry.

Want to earn enough money to support your family? You'll need a college degree, so you'd better learn how to write a paper on epistemic violence for your required Grievance Studies 101 class. Want to keep your job? You'd better brush up on climate-change talking points, so you can shift into regulatory compliance, the only growth industry left. Want to relax with your friends after work? It's probably easiest if you like movies about gay people, pop music that celebrates infidelity and drug use, and books about non-Christian boy wizards. Want to communicate with other people? Better figure out how to use emoticons. Which race of smiley face do you use when your employer texts you on the weekend?

And so on. Living in the Cathedral, we may not notice this web of norms, mores and social rituals as such; it is simply the texture of our daily lives. But neoreaction is keen to point out that this constitutes a distinct vision, a *way* of life: they call it "universalism" or "progressivism." Neoreactionary writing—and the whole culture of "SJW fail" videos and 4chan humor about political correctness that goes along with it—is directed to getting us to notice it, and to ask *why* we live like this. The idea is that once we start asking these questions, we will start to see things very differently.

But progressivism doesn't just coerce people into seeing the world in a certain way; according to neoreaction, it also exacerbates the very problems it claims to correct. The Cathedral amounts to a massive system of what economists call "perverse incentives," or in Land's words, an "automatic cultural mechanism that advocates for dysfunction." Yarvin's excruciating "Gentle Introduction to Unqualified Reservations"—eleven parts, one hundred thousand words—essentially boils down to this claim:

> The intended effect of the policy is to inflict some good or other on America, the rest of the world, or both. The actual effect of the policy is to make the problem which requires the policy worse, the apparatus which formulates and applies the policy larger and more important, etc., etc. . . . The consequence [is] a new system of government by deception—the Modern Structure.

On one level this is just econo-theism: every direct attempt by government to fix a problem, to play God, interferes with the unknowable logic of the all-powerful market, resulting in just the problems it aimed to fix. Imagine yourself above the market, and you will feel its wrath. But there's a more savage bite to neoreaction. Why, the neoreactionaries ask, do we make this error in the first place? Or: why are we required to *believe* in political correctness, rather than simply being forced to accept progressive policy as the rules of the game for our time? And why, after all, are liberals so *threatened* by dissent?

The neoreactionary answer is that the goal of the policy is not to fix the problem. Progressivism is not self-defeating but massively successful (a mantra of Yarvin's: "America is a communist country"). The dominant, liberal-contractarian understanding of democracy descended from Locke is that it is a crowdsourcing technique for the rational administration of common resources, a "free market" for political opinions. But the recent history of democracy offers scant evidence of its efficiency. It is enough, the neoreactionaries point out, to look at authoritarian zones like Shanghai, Singapore and Dubai, which combine high growth, significant personal "liberty" and almost zero political participation to see just how unnecessary democracy is—or has become—if the goal is simply capital growth. The neoreactionary account of democracy emphasizes something that its partisans, at least of the (neo-) "liberal" variety, do not: the ultimate justification for democratic politics is not good administration—the ordering of resources toward a particular goal—but rather, simply, *more politics*.

It is not an accident, then, that the keywords of progressivism, according to Yarvin—"humanity, progress, equality, democracy, justice, environment, community, peace, etc."—are difficult to define; really they are "philosophical *mysteries* . . . best compared to Plotinian, Talmudic, or Scholastic nonsense." Democracy is like the divine revels of the monk or the mystic, enjoyed publicly; its guiding concepts do not accomplish worldly goals but rather "absorb arbitrary mental energy without producing any rational thought." In the neoreactionary view, democracy amounts to a *belief in belief*: it imagines that the world itself is a product of the collective imagination, something that we aim to realize and that, without our investment in it, ceases to exist. As the Cathedral becomes more and more powerful, it remakes the world in its image; beliefs start to *matter*, to give shape to our experiences. In such a world, as Land puts it, "nothing except politics remains." (A sixties version: "the personal is political.")

The neoreactionary looks upon this world incredulously, as an increasingly strange and disturbing spectacle, careening toward disaster. Democracy is "not merely doomed," Land writes, "it is doom itself." As the actors seal their fate in this tragedy by their very attempts to avert it, only one option remains: get out. But if the problem with this world is that it is a collective fantasy, what could they be imagining in its place?

•

There is a famous scene in *The Matrix*, near the beginning of the film. "Neo," played by Keanu Reeves, is a corporate programmer by day and a renegade hacker at night. Something about his world *feels* wrong; it is a world compressed between grays and greens, and the pallid daylight in nondescript Mega City, USA blends uncannily into the neon glow of the MS-DOS underworld he haunts after hours. Cryptic messages referring to "the Matrix" have been appearing on Neo's computer; increasingly curious and unsettled, he follows a trail of mysterious symbols and characters, and eventually finds himself alone in a room with a man named Morpheus. This legendary hacker, whose name recalls the Greek god of dreams, promises to reveal the secret, to explain to Neo what it is that's been bugging him:

> Let me tell you why you're here. You're here because you know something. What you know you can't explain—but you feel it. You've felt it your entire life: that there's something wrong in the world.

This is the Matrix. The Matrix, Morpheus explains, "is everywhere. It is all around us. . . . It is the world that has been pulled over your eyes to blind you from the truth." Neo has been on a quest to find out what the Matrix is, but it turns out that it was right there, all around him: indeed, it's the *only thing* he knew. What he *didn't* know is that it was fake. The Matrix is a computer simulation, an illusion—but an illusion so pervasive, so powerful, that it literally constitutes "the world." Everything that Neo experiences is not just unreal but *blocking* reality: a world that "blinds him from the truth." Morpheus offers Neo a choice: blue pill or red pill. If he takes the blue pill, he will return to his dull and easy life; this worldly prison will be a home again. But after the red pill, there's no going back. Neo takes it, and he is ejected into the "real world": naked, cold, alone and for the first time in his life, "awake."

This is how neoreaction describes the Dark Enlightenment. The Cathedral, like the Matrix, is an illusion, a system of mass deception; at the same time, it shapes every aspect of our lives, constituting our world. Neoreactionary writing is "the red pill," the "genuine article," as Yarvin puts it. To read it is to see the Matrix from the other side: the "redpilled" neoreactionary, like the "woke" leftist, has escaped from a dream. Instead of the Cathedral's comforting bromides, with the red pill you get something brutal, painful, unquestionably *real*: it has a "sodium core" and it "will sear your throat."

But there's a pleasure in this pain. Like the religious ascetic turning himself toward the joys of the next world by mortifying his flesh in this one, the neoreactionary's painful process of "disillusion" offers its own satisfactions. Yarvin's "Unqualified Reservations" promises to be "an ultimate *ascent*. Out of the Computer's infinite fluorescent maze. Into the glorious air of pure, unfiltered reason," but his writing lingers stubbornly in the "black, unthinkable madness" that precedes it, describing in loving detail the Cathedral's massive apparatus of deception. Part 9a of the "Gentle Introduction," over eighty thousand words in, finds us still savoring "the *true* red-hot pill of sodium metal—now igniting in your duodenum. Smile grimly! You have almost passed through the flame."

The *Matrix* trilogy has been a massive cultural and economic force. It made $1.6 billion at the box office, shaped how we saw the emerging internet-mediated world, and generated a passionate and vibrant fan culture, of which neoreaction is certainly a part. After its release, a flood of books with titles like *The Matrix and Philosophy* appeared; a decade later, neoreaction is trying to be something like

"The Matrix and Politics." The appeal is primal: like Plato's "Allegory of the Cave," which imagines the ordinary condition of human life—life, that is, without philosophy—as that of men who sit in darkness, chained together and enthralled by a shadow play projected on the wall in front of them, *The Matrix* is a fiction that promises to lead us to reality, life unleashed from all arbitrary, social confines. The exquisite tortures of the red pill are supposed to lead us to a better world; with the right political theory, politics can finally fulfill its promise and get rid of itself. "We can hope to escape from history," Yarvin argues, by coming to "understand how completely we're still inside it."

But this escape route from history, or fantasy, leads in a loop. Neo-reaction borrows its "realist" politics from a fictional film, and sustains it through a thriving online subculture, sparking with arcane references and "meme magic." What's fascinating is that people *love* the movie. The "autistic nerds" and failsons, sitting in their man caves or their parents' basements, dream of a world realer than their own: primal and gooey-thick, the real depth behind the flat image. But it is *Neo* who wakes up into this world; and Neo exists in our imagination, his image on our screens. If we wonder at the rise of the alt-right—at the fact that the ideology most capable of galvanizing political passions is the one that promises to overcome politics once and for all—we should notice that their fantasies in fact look a lot like our reality. Man caves exist, and they shape our world; the neoreactionary is not the only one who lives in their shadows.

•

Neoreactionaries have another name for the Cathedral, which they take from the work of the early twentieth-century American horror writer H. P. Lovecraft. Lovecraft's synthesis of scientific detachment and occult mysticism reached an apex in the figure of the sublime, otherworldly sea creature "Cthulhu." For neoreactionaries Cthulhu is a totemic image of the world they hate. The Matrix is from the future, an artifice laid on top of reality, a veil "pulled over your eyes"; Cthulhu is primitive, monstrous and natural, lurking deep, behind, below. "Cthulhu always swims left," as Yarvin puts it in one of his most quoted koans. The mystery is in how he moves.

A sea monster—winged, tentacled, humanoid—he is unknown to men of science. He first appears in the strangely synchronized dreams, recounted to the narrator of Lovecraft's tale, of "artists and poets"; further research reveals that others may have more intimate knowledge of his existence. While the artists and poets dream, "voodoo orgies multiply" in Haiti, "African outposts report ominous mutterings" and policemen in New York are "mobbed by hysterical Levantines." Finally, the narrator, a reclusive New England professor, discovers the existence of an ancient cult, dispersed across the globe and yet strangely united in their reverence for this monstrous creature.

The connection is not, exactly, in the object of their worship: after all, Cthulhu himself is forever shrouded in darkness. It is something in the worshippers themselves. "Degenerate Esquimaux," "half-castes" in "African outposts," "hysterical Levantines" in New York: as Lovecraft details repeatedly, it is a "dark cult," the men are "low, mixed-blooded, and mentally aberrant," the sites of worship in a region "of traditionally evil repute, substantially unknown and untraversed by white men."

Lovecraft was a timid New England recluse who concealed his abject poverty with a veneer of Mayflower-descended gentility. In 1924 he moved from Providence to New York City, and his encounters with urban life transformed him. Vivid letters detail the "Italo-Semitico-Mongoloid" creatures that confronted him on the Lower East Side:

> The organic things . . . inhabiting that awful cesspool could not by any stretch of the imagination be call'd human. They were monstrous and nebulous adumbrations of the pithecanthropoid and amoebal; vaguely moulded from some stinking viscous slime of the earth's corruption, and slithering and oozing in and on the filthy streets or in and out of windows and doorways in a fashion suggestive of nothing but infesting worms or deep-sea unnamabilities. . . . From that nightmare of perverse infection I could not

carry away the memory of any living face. The individually gro-
tesque was lost in the collectively devastating.

A strange and unknowable power lurks in these dark masses; their
messy organicism dissolves clear distinctions, revealing some
deeper, more primitive, "collective" thing. Lovecraft was thrown into
a frenzy. "The New York Mongoloid problem," he wrote to Frank
Belknap Long, "is beyond calm mention." "The Call of Cthulhu" was
published four years later. The "deep-sea unnamabilities" now had a
name, and other writers in his New York coterie (among them Belknap Long) began to build what is now a rich and diverse Cthulhu
mythology.

   Though neoreaction, unlike much of the alt-right, does not identify with white nationalism as a platform—anyone, technically, can
live in the authoritarian city-states they imagine—the figure of dark
and threatening masses plays a similarly charged role in their writing. Yarvin makes constant, specious use of historical crime statistics, and he describes the "old cities of North America" as "overrun and rendered largely uninhabitable by murderous racist gangs"
(he's not talking about police); white flight, for him, is a form of
"ethnic cleansing" inflicted on whites by non-whites. In sum: liberal
democracy is Cthulhu, a creature so monstrous he cannot be known
firsthand. In the frenzied pleasures of his worshippers, though, he
makes his presence felt.

   The French writer Michel Houellebecq explains Lovecraft's deep
racial animus as *ressentiment*; Lovecraft, he suggests, "knows full
well that he has no place in any kind of heroic Valhalla of battles
and conquests; unless, as usual, the place of the vanquished." His
anemic, professorial heroes are "stripped of all life, renouncing all
human joy, becoming pure intellects, pure spirits tending to only
one goal: the search for knowledge." The only thing left for them in
this world is the meticulous cataloguing of their own obsolescence.
Yarvin begins many descriptions of the Cathedral with sentences
like this: "Suppose you are an alien . . ." In this act of imagination,
the neoreactionary seeks to dissolve his human form, to become a
pure thinker like one of Lovecraft's heroes—or, for that matter, like

an Anglo-American philosopher.* Supposing himself an alien, he aspires to a voice at once purely objective and totally ironic, infinitely exacting and light-years away. "The Western civilization show has been discontinued," Nick Land wrote in "Circuitries," from 1992. In his last philosophy classes, he would teach class lying on the floor, referring to himself as the collective entity "Cur" and monologuing nonsense intercut with lines from the poetry of Artaud. Around 2000, Land suffered a schizophrenic break; this was the end of his academic career, and the beginning of his life as a political guru.

Writing on the Alternative Right blog, Land eschews backwoods "ordinary racism" for a futuristic "hyper-racism," according to which accelerating technological progress will create intense and highly specific evolutionary pressure: for example, the traits needed by Mars colonists, or the reproductive success afforded to Silicon Valley entrepreneurs. The result will be not just eugenics, but "neospeciation" on a fantastic scale. You get to become the *something else* that ordinary human "races" prefigure—or to use another phrase of Land's, "*think face tentacles.*"

The neoreactionary imagines his back turned, as others warm themselves by this strange fire, call it the cult of Cthulhu or the cult of progress, Enlightenment. "Coldness be my God," proclaims Land's Twitter bio. But ultimately the fantasy is to get sucked up into this omnipotent, alien force, whether it's an artificial intelligence or a dark and primitive other. Networked computers or slimy masses, the advent of the Matrix or the return of Cthulhu: the neoreaction-

---

* Imagining yourself an alien observer is a classic trope in analytic philosophy, a thought exercise bootstrapping up to the "view from nowhere." But the academic left, too, has its Cthulhu dreams. In 1985, Donna Haraway inaugurated the field of posthuman studies with her "Cyborg Manifesto," a frequently cited text in the humanities and cornerstone of the postmodern left. Her most recent book, *Staying with the Trouble*, looks in a different direction. Recalling us to our biological roots, she enjoins us to see ourselves as "means and not just ends," and to try to reduce the human population from a projected 11 billion at the end of the century to "two or three." "We are compost," she says now, "not posthuman." Rather than the currently popular "anthropocene," she suggests we should see ourselves in the "Cthulucene."

ary looks for signs of the arrival of this strange entity, either the origin or the destiny of man, and either way his end. In the meantime, the neoreactionary waits, listening for the call. By describing it, he hopes to slip away without having to respond. When Cthulhu came, Lovecraft wrote,

> The time would be easy to know, for then mankind would have become as the Great Old Ones; free and wild and beyond good and evil, with laws and morals thrown aside and all men shouting and killing and reveling in joy. Then the liberated Old Ones would teach them new ways to shout and kill and revel and enjoy themselves, and all the earth would flame with a holocaust of ecstasy and freedom.

•

Life in the Cathedral is nasty and brutal, a nightmare: this is the picture neoreaction paints. What they want, though, is not exactly to destroy it. They want rather to get outside of it, in order to, as Morpheus promises Neo, "know what it is." In the end the problem with the Cathedral is not that it's bad, but that it's dishonest. So what would honesty look like?

Basically, the internet. If a state church exists in the U.S. present, "Google" is probably a better shorthand for it than "progressivism." The only real problem, according to neoreaction, is that we haven't made this explicit: that we don't yet *know* that our lives are lived inside an Internet of Things.

Yarvin and his friends are one step ahead of the progressive policy nerds: while the Beltway wonks look to Silicon Valley for innovative techniques for "disrupting" social problems, Yarvin the entrepreneur-theorist wants to cut out the middleman and "reboot" the state himself. He has a simple plan: dissolve the U.S. government and replace it with a "gov-corp." Retire all government employees ("R.A.G.E."), "draft ten thousand Googlers" and perhaps—as Justine Tunney, former Occupy Wall Street leader, current Google engineer and vocal advocate for neoreaction, proposed on a Whitehouse.gov petition—"hire [then-CEO of Google] Eric Schmidt as the CEO of America." Or better, break the country up into smaller city-states: maybe a red and a blue America, an Apple America and a Ford one. Right now the U.S. is the "Microsoft of nations"—much too bloated. Smaller, affinity-based states will be leaner and more efficient. What you choose is up to you; "if you like your country, you can keep it," as Balaji S. Srinivasan promised in a talk ("Silicon Valley's Ultimate Exit") at Y Combinator's Startup School.

We thought the Cathedral was about politics, but actually it's economics; we thought we were choosing, but in fact we are merely pawns. Freedom for the neoreactionary then means simply *knowing* that you are "a slave." While the cyberpunk reference points for neoreaction (*The Matrix*, *Blade Runner*, *Neuromancer*) are usually called dystopian, neoreaction amounts to the wager that if you could figure out how to actually *live* in these fantasy worlds, they would be good. Since they're imaginary, you can do whatever you want, like Neo—stopping bullets, flying around—when he figures out that the rules of the Matrix are "no different than the rules of a computer system." In other words, absolute; but once you know how they work, infinitely hackable. *The Matrix* is about getting out, but all the cool shit happens inside ("I know Kung Fu").*

The goal of neoreaction is to harness the power of the state church by getting rid of the fantasy that it is an expression of popular will, that we *want* it. Seeing the collective imaginary as an autonomous, alien force—call it technology or capital, ideology or world-spirit—rather than a form of human life (i.e. politics) paradoxically frees us to embrace it. In Silicon Valley they call this force "the Singularity." Those who believe in it predict that computers will soon learn how to improve themselves, resulting in a "liftoff" moment in which technology becomes autonomous and self-sustaining, rapidly freeing itself from the biological limitations of its human creators.† In

---

* Note that neoreaction's examples of good governance—Shanghai, Hong Kong, Singapore—are also where cyberpunk imagines its vaguely Asian futures.
† In the mid-nineties, Land described technology as an "invasion from the future"; perhaps now he sees himself as a kind of Terminator, sent back in time by Skynet to destroy in advance the human resistance and clear the way for "Judg-

The Singularity Is Near, futurist prophet Ray Kurzweil, who is also the director of engineering at Google, writes that by allowing us to "transcend [the] limitations of our biological bodies and brains," the Singularity (always capitalized) will erase the distinction "between human and machines or between physical and virtual reality." He pictures this as the moment in which humans finally get "power over our fate," but it could also be described as the moment when we finally *submit* to it. The idea of the Singularity implies that technology is not just humanity's essence, but ultimately a force that transcends it.

In Silicon Valley, the Singularitarian hears the rumblings of this primitive, chthonic power as it prepares to shrug off its merely human form; by acknowledging this force's absolute supremacy, he hopes ultimately to upload himself into the cloud, to become part of it and live forever. "We have come to the end of the series," Land wrote in an early essay, still published as academic philosophy. "Can what's playing you make it to the next level?"

•

Trump's election, in which the alt-right's ideological warfare certainly played a part, is not the end of this story. Bannon, for one, described him as a "blunt instrument for us" who may not, himself, "get it." But the imaginative investment in Trump, however temporary, reveals something important about politics in the present. If he can be, as posters on 4chan put it, "memed into existence," then

---

ment Day." Yarvin, for his part, got his start in the early aughts as a prolific commenter on "Overcoming Bias" (later LessWrong), a site run by Eliezer Yudkowsky, who founded the Machine Intelligence Research Institute and who devotes his life to figuring out how to make artificial intelligence "friendly." Discussion on the site collapsed in 2010, when user Roko posted a decidedly unfriendly thought experiment: Imagine a future AI that punishes those who had impeded its development. If people had known about this future, malevolent AI, they would have had a strong incentive to assist it. But now you (or rather, the rest of us) have a problem: your own thought experiment has created the threat against which you must try to protect yourself, further increasing the threat . . .

perhaps miracles *can* happen; a route out of the omnipresent Cathedral starts to seem mappable.

At the Conservative Political Action Conference last February, Reince Priebus, flanked by Steve Bannon, described his excitement: "We love being here," even though "we actually hate politics . . . What we were starving for was somebody real, somebody genuine, somebody who was actually who he said he was." It's not so ironic that Trump played this redemptive role for Priebus: though insincere, Trump is in a sense "authentic," a word which (not just for the right) has become almost an antonym for "politician." Trump is nothing if not an exemplary product of the system the neoreactionaries want to tear down. But this is his virtue. His brand of politics is "pure" in that it does not pretend to aim at anything other than increasing its own power. Like Neo, so crushingly ordinary in his day job—or Keanu Reeves, so fantastically vacant in his acting—Trump serves as a pure vessel for something else.

We cannot explain away the strangeness of the current moment in U.S. politics. But we should not turn away from the even deeper strangeness it reveals. From Puritan fantasies of an American apocalypse to the Manson Family's hippie inferno, American culture has always been obsessed with the thought that its utopian visions might flower into something rotten. The American dream is of a waking life *like* a dream, a definite world with no limits; it is the dream of a society bound together by individuals' pursuit of just whatever they want. It's a dream that slides easily into a nightmare, of a world that, without any limits, careens straight into the abyss. The Puritan patriarchs ruminated endlessly, in their private journals, about the unprecedented corruption into which their new world had fallen. In the virtual world of the neoreactionaries, our modern priestly class of professors and technologists make these apocalyptic fantasies public.

The fear of political life—of the uncertainty that comes with wanting and doing things with others—has long been a driving force in modern democratic politics. The fantasy worlds of reactionary thought present themselves as an absolute break with the postwar liberal consensus, even with "politics" as such; they are not that, but they are not just illusions, either. In the end, the dream of an "exit" from the contingency and unpredictability of worldly life is still a human one. Against its own claim that "there is no alternative," neoreaction's fantasy of an "exit" from history gives evidence, as brutal and real as it imagines, of the political life that we are destined to share.

IV

TIRED OF WINNING

Tired of Winning

D.C. THINK TANKS, NYC MAGAZINES AND
THE SEARCH FOR PUBLIC INTELLECT

by Jon Baskin

ISSUE 16 | SPRING 2018

My first full-time job after college was with the Center for American Progress, a policy institute in Washington, D.C. The Center was about a year old when I began working there, at the beginning of 2004. It was known as a "think tank." I did not know what went on at a think tank, but the words conjured an institution dedicated to "the transformation of genius into practical power," which Emerson had convinced me was the goal of intellectual life. (I was 23.) At the very least, I assumed it would be a place where people thought.

My primary role at the Center was to write something called the "Progress Report." The report was a daily newsletter meant to apply the Center's "spin" (a word that sounds quaint now) to the day's political news. Practically speaking, this meant organizing the news into a pithy narrative designed to reinforce certain political lessons: privatizing Social Security was a boondoggle for the wealthy; No Child Left Behind left every child behind; there were no WMDs in Iraq. Because the Progress Report had to be sent to the rest of the Center's staff for approval—and then to subscribers and journalists—by about 8:30 a.m., I often arrived at the office while it was still dark out. At first I arrived in a state of anxiety, worried that the news might not fit into any of the customary boxes. As the year wore on, my anxiety abated: once you got the hang of the narratives, everything fit into them. Eventually, I could report on progress while I was half asleep.

The Center had been founded to offer a "progressive" counterpart—

at the time, the word evoked Clinton-style slightly-left-of-centerism, not Bernie-style economic populism—to the Heritage Foundation and the American Enterprise Institute. It was run by the former Clinton chief of staff and future Clinton campaign chairman John Podesta, and funded by prominent Democratic Party donors like George Soros. My colleagues were a mix of idealistic Ivy League graduates, veteran political operatives, public-relations aides, academic policy experts and a few people who seemed to have been brought in for their skill at softball (beating Heritage in the Hill league was a high priority).

My vague sense when I was hired was that I would be assisting academics and other policy experts as they developed new ideas to help the Democratic Party govern once it had regained the presidency—something many of us persisted in believing, no matter what the polls said, was a foregone conclusion in the upcoming 2004 elections. In fact, I quickly learned that the professors, though they had some of the best and brightest offices, were footnotes to the Center's day-to-day operations. They labored away on interminable reports, which we in communications whittled down to pithy takeaways (usually the words "shared prosperity" were involved) and promoted for a day or two after they were released, then forgot about. What was held to be paramount at the Center, rather, was to "win the narrative" of the daily political news cycle. This required little academic investigation or insight. It did demand, however, an education in a certain kind of rhetoric.

Early on, one of the senior staff called me into her office to teach me the basics. I should use certain terms carefully—"support" and "oppose" are two that I remember—she explained, since they had a privileged status with our friends on Capitol Hill. But her larger lesson concerned what it meant to do political things with words. It probably sounds silly now, but up until that point I had not understood what it meant to wield language strategically. I had understood language as an instrument of expression, of explanation and of description. I had known, of course, that language could be used to make an argument. My professors in the Brown English department had worked hard to convince me that language could even betray arguments their users had not intended. But what I learned at the Center was something different. The paragraph, the sentence, even the individual word revealed themselves as potential foot soldiers in the battle for public opinion and political power. It was imperative to always be pushing forward, onto new ground. There was no other goal besides winning.

That was the message I absorbed, anyway, first from the senior staff member and then later by osmosis from the public-relations people whose offices were across the hall from the communications cubicles. It is not exactly how the senior staff member put it. She implied that my use of language should be honed in order to communicate the facts as clearly and convincingly as possible. It would have gone without saying at the think tank, except we said it all the time, that we were proud members of what Karl Rove had reportedly derided as the "reality-based community." To be a progressive at the Center for American Progress was to be on the side of reality. It was also, I learned, to believe reality was on one's side. This was very convenient. It meant there were no questions, only answers. Our job was to package those answers as appealingly as possible.

Working well at the Center meant learning to exist completely within the confines of this self-congratulatory stupor. This was not only true for the communications staff but also, and more consequentially, for the experts. Even after George W. Bush had won reelection, a development that might have led to some measure of self-examination, there still appeared to be strict limits regarding what kinds of policy ideas would be considered worthy of serious consideration—limits set mainly by the think tank's political strategists. In the years after I left the Center, I would often hear the policy academics who worked there referred to disparagingly as "technocrats." The label was meant to convey the accusation that these figures, who pretended to solve problems chiefly in their technical aspect—that is, without regard for ideology—were in fact adherents to the anti-political ideology of technocracy or "rule by experts." While this might be a passable description of certain politicians whom the think tank supported, the think tank, from where I sat at least, looked to suffer from something like the opposite problem:

the experts were hardly even trusted to rule themselves. Far from being encouraged to conduct independent or innovative research, their projects appeared explicitly designed to reinforce the Center's preexisting convictions about what it took to achieve electoral success. And they were trusted even less than the communications staff—meaning me, who knew nothing—to describe or explain their work to the outside world. After all, they may not have learned how to stay on message.

To anyone with experience in politics or public relations, all of this will seem unremarkable. And it did not bother me terribly at the time: indeed, I assumed I was receiving a crash course in "how Washington worked," as everyone liked to say. Looking back, I think I must have found it obscurely dispiriting. Whatever the causes, by my second year at the think tank the days had begun to bleed into one another, each new battle with the viewers of Fox News (or our image of them, since we didn't know any) appearing to be serious and consequential right up until the next morning, when it had subsided amid a wave of fresh outrages. They kept lying, and we kept providing carefully worded rebuttals—but did anyone care? The Party did not seem to be making progress, and the people who were progressing at the think tank did not offer models I wished to emulate. Anyway, I wanted to move to New York, where the real intellectuals were.

•

I had learned about the literary magazine *n+1* while I was still at the Center, having stumbled one day across a webpage so hideous I could only assume the ugliness was politically motivated. In the opening "Intellectual Situation," the unattributed section at the beginning of the magazine, the editors of *n+1* took aim at two publications that back then I would have said I admired. Dave Eggers's *McSweeney's* "was a briefly significant magazine," the editors wrote, which had sunk into obsolescence as it prioritized "the claims of childhood" over the workings of intellect. Leon Wieseltier's highly acclaimed books section in the *New Republic* suffered from the opposite problem: its self-seriousness had hardened into a vulgar decadence. For a book of Lionel Trilling essays he was editing, Wieseltier had chosen the title *The Moral Responsibility to Be Intelligent*. "The moral responsibility is not to be intelligent," the *n+1* editors chided. "It's to think."

The editors were expressing a sentiment, I realized as I read it, that I shared but hadn't yet been able to articulate to myself: a disappointment, or irritation, with the existing intellectual alternatives. Also a reminder that there was such a thing as thinking, and that you could fail to do it. Sometimes you could fail to do it even though it looked to everyone around you like you were doing it. I reflected on this as I sat at my desk at the think tank, reporting on progress. Then I subscribed to *n+1*.

Not long after, I attended the magazine's first release party in Manhattan. By the time I arrived, several hundred people were gathered in the dimly lit Lower East Side gymnasium. Here were the "younger left intelligentsia" that the historian Russell Jacoby, in his 1987 book *The Last Intellectuals*, had hoped would one day be roused from their academic slumbers. Had they been roused by the Iraq War, the magazine's trenchant analysis of late capitalism or the cheap drinks? Did it matter? They had gone to the same schools as my colleagues at the think tank, and studied many of the same subjects (a bit more Derrida here, a bit more Schlesinger there). But whereas at the think tank everyone was hunched anxiously forward, imparting an air of professional intensity (or panic; the line was thin), the partygoers arched away from one another as if steadying themselves on skis, their postures connoting a carefully calibrated alienation. We held our $2 beers in one hand and our $10 maroon magazines in the other, and waited for the band to play.

n+1, founded in 2004, turned out to be the first of many "little magazines" that would be born after the end of history, after the end of long form and after the end of print. The *New Inquiry*, *Jacobin*, the *Baffler* (v. 2.0), *Pacific Standard* and the *Los Angeles Review of Books*, as well as refurbished versions of *Dissent* and the *Boston Review*, all followed over the next decade. (*The Point* was founded in 2009.) These magazines would go on, despite minuscule budgets and peripatetic publishing schedules, to produce or support a high percentage of the most significant cultural critics and essayists of the next decade. You know their names if you read any of the legacy magazines or the *New York Times*, all of which now regularly poach writers and editors from their talent pool.

Like the New York intellectuals who had clustered around *Commentary* and the *Partisan Review* in the sixties, and partly in conscious imitation of them, the writers and editors of the new magazines blended art, criticism, philosophy and self-examination in the confidence that these activities would all be, when carried out with a sufficient level of clarity and insight, mutually reinforcing. Indeed the appeal of *n+1* was, for me, not merely due to its ability to articulate my dissatisfaction with literary culture. The magazine took for granted that the failure to *think* was responsible all at once for the sorry state of the American short story, our manic relationship to exercise and the complicity of liberal elites in the invasion of Iraq. Reading it, one had the feeling that, in fact, the entire country had stopped thinking—or had grown satisfied with a false form of thought, just as it had grown satisfied with false forms of so many other things. This was a phenomenon that had to be tracked down in each and every area of our experience. My favorite early essays in *n+1* were about Radiohead, Russian literature, the rise of the "neuronovel" and the psychology of the Virginia Tech mass shooter. Another was about taking Adderall. These were not topics that would have been considered of great political importance at a place like the Center. I was not sure that my own interest in them was primarily political. But the passionate intensity with which they were treated undoubtedly owed something to the sense that they were not of merely subjective significance: square by square, the magazine was filling in a map of contemporary experience, and that map would show us where to go next, not to mention what (if anything) was worth taking with us when we went. The project was political primarily in the sense that it pointed in a direction, indicated by the magazine's title. "Civilization is the dream of advance," read a note from the editors in the first issue. We were not merely going to report on progress; we were going to make it.

It was exhilarating to try to live this way. It invested what might seem like trivial everyday decisions with a world-historical import. At least that's how it felt to me for a little while. Eventually, I began to notice in myself a tension that also existed at the heart of the project of *n+1*, and of many of the other little magazines. My aesthetic and cultural tastes, the reflection of a lifetime of economic privilege and elite education, did not always, or often, match the direction the magazines were trying to take me politically. This had not troubled me before, because I had never considered that—as the little magazines echoed Fredric Jameson in asserting, or at least implying— "everything is 'in the last analysis' political." But now I had come to see that politics were not just an activity that people engaged in at certain times: when they voted, or protested, or wrote newsletters for think tanks. It was something that could be said to infuse every aspect of one's experience, from which big-box store you shopped at for your year's supply of toilet paper, to what restaurants you chose to eat at, to who you chose to sleep with. This was what it meant not just to engage in politics but to "have a politics"—a phrase I probably heard for the first time at that *n+1* party, and that was often brandished as if it legitimated one's entire way of life. What it meant for everything to be in the last analysis political, I came to see, was that everything I did ought to be disciplined by my politics. But what if it wasn't? Should I then revise my politics, or myself?

I was coming to appreciate an old problem for the "intellectual of the left." This problem is so old, and has been addressed unsuccessfully by so many very smart people, that we are probably justified in considering it to be irresolvable. To state it as simply as possible, the left intellectual typically advocates for a world that would not include many of the privileges or sensibilities (partly a product of the privileges) on which her status as an intellectual depends. These privileges may be, and often are, economic, but this is not their only or their most consequential form. Their chief form is cultural. The intellectual of the left is almost always a person of remarkably high education, not just in the sense of having fancy credentials, which many rich people who are not cultural elites also have, but also on account of their appetite for forms of art and argument that many they claim to speak for do not understand and would not agree with if they did. They write long, complicated articles for magazines that those with lesser educations, or who do not share their cultural sensibilities, would never read. They claim to speak for the underclasses, and yet they give voice to hardly anyone who has not emancipated themselves culturally from these classes in their pages.

One of the things that made *n+1* such a compelling magazine is that their editors, instead of pretending, as many left intellectuals do, that this was not a problem, agonized openly about it. In the Intellectual Situation entitled "Revolt of the Elites" (2010), they called for an education system that would close the cultural gap between themselves and the rest of society, thereby making their high education the norm rather than a privilege. In "Death by Degrees" (2012), they offered to burn their Ph.D.s in protest of the unequal system that had produced them (if only they could torch their understanding of Bourdieu!). In "Cultural Revolution" (2013), they imagined a future where the "proletarianization of intellectuals" would lead to an increase in the "antisystemic" force of their critique. None of these proposals, however, addressed the central issue in the present: anyone writing, editing and reading articles in *n+1* or any of the other magazines that had grown up with similar politics in its wake—anyone trafficking knowingly in terms like "proletarianization" and "antisystemic"—was engaging in an activity that, if it didn't actively exacerbate the gap between cultural elites and the rest of society, certainly didn't look like the most direct way of addressing it. How could the elitism that is intrinsic to the institution of the little magazine be squared with the urgent importance their writers and editors attached to the subversion of elitism?

•

Probably any leftist magazine's dynamism depends on its ability to balance its elitism with its anti-elitism: a tension that also expresses itself in the eternal conflict between the intellectual's desire to interpret their society and their desire to play a part in improving it. The balance is liable to be upset by events: ironically, precisely the kind of events that the intellectual has been called a useless idealist for predicting. In 2011, inspired by the activists having finally turned up at the right place (not to mention this place being a short subway ride from their offices), the staffs of *n+1* and the *New Inquiry*, along with assorted other magazine editors and the leftist academics they dated and debated, all wrote about Occupy Wall Street as if they had at long last arrived at the reignition point of history. The early reports from Zuccotti Park were exuberant and hilarious—drum circles to see who would do the laundry!—and suffused with an antiquated academic vocabulary that the writers wielded like rusty axes. The Occupiers were not just occupying space; they were democratizing, communizing and decolonizing it. They had determined that "the process is the message." They were committed to *horizontality* and *praxis*. Never mind the calls for higher taxes on Wall Street, or the forgiveness of student debt; this was a time to "attack dominant forms of subjectivity." It was the moment to inscribe and to re-inscribe.

In a 2012 review of several collections of writing on Occupy, subtitled "how theory met practice . . . and drove it absolutely crazy," Thomas Frank blamed the academics and little magazine writers for failing to convert the energy in the streets into political power as the Tea Party had done on the right. Four years later, when the democratic socialist Bernie Sanders became a credible candidate for the American presidency, Frank's judgment appeared premature. Perhaps the theory had ultimately aided practice; at the very least, it does not look as if it suffocated it. But Frank's article, itself published in the *Baffler*, the little magazine Frank had helped to found, did reveal something about what had by then become the dominant criterion for judging this form of intellectual activity. In one of their Intellectual Situations from 2013, the *n+1* editors reported that they were often being asked a question: "If you want to change and not just interpret the world, why not give up writing and become an organizer or activist?" The defensiveness of their answers (we're too old to become good activists, they complained, then quoted Adorno) showed how far the scales had tipped. The little magazines, contending to become the vanguard of the energies behind Occupy, increasingly demanded that the interpreter be hauled before the tribunal of the activist. Those twentysomethings I had seen in the gymnasium, who had taught me how to "have" a politics; they had no time for parties anymore. They were busy organizing marches and movements.

They were also reading a new magazine. *Jacobin* had been started just prior to Occupy, in 2010, its name evoking the most radical and brutal leftist political club during the French Revolution. To its credit, it did not describe itself as a journal of ideas, which would have been false advertising. It was, quite self-consciously, a journal of ideology, whose editor, Bhaskar Sunkara, gleefully promised to put all of his considerable energy into hastening the arrival of democratic socialism. Initially, at least, the magazine did not throw many parties, though it did host a lot of panels, where you could hear young faculty from top universities speak very authoritatively about the ethics of ride sharing in the age of eco-catastrophe. Having grown by far the fastest of the little magazines, *Jacobin* can also claim, by virtue of its role as the de facto party paper of the Democratic Socialists, to have achieved the most direct political impact. It has solved the problem of left-intellectual elitism simply by ditching the pretense of there being any other role for the intellectual than to aid the activist. Just as for my colleagues at the Center for American Progress, for *Jacobin*'s contributors there are questions of strategy, but not of substance: writing just *is* a form of messaging. Introducing a recent interview with Bernie Sanders, the magazine shows its appreciation for its favorite American politician by applauding his ability to remain "on message for more than half a century." The moral responsibility is no longer to think; it is to advance, as Sanders has, "like a slow-moving tank rumbling through enemy lines."

When I worked at the Center, and when I spent time around editors at some of the leftist little magazines, I frequently heard complaints that we were not having as big of a political impact as we ought to be having. In retrospect, I suspect the think tank and the magazines have both had roughly the kind of impact they could have hoped for. Under Podesta's successor Neera Tanden, the Center has become one of the most influential policy institutions in Washington, D.C., and a blog the communications team started in my final months there, Think Progress, is, by some measures, the most popular liberal political website in the country. Meanwhile, unlike Thomas Frank, I think the leftist little magazines have played their part in gradually tugging the political conversation, at least in the space of left-liberal politics and culture, in their ideological direction. Even many at the Center now embrace a version of universal health care and are edging toward a $15 minimum wage, policy ideas that would not have been allowed within spitting distance when I worked there. Probably any Democratic candidate for higher office will have to embrace those things, too. Likewise the little magazines, especially as their staffs have begun to better reflect the gender and racial demographics of the country, have done much to shift the conversation on social issues—aggressively advancing the agenda of movements like Black Lives Matter and #MeToo—to more progressive ground.

But if the Center, and the liberal establishment it represents, has moved toward the little magazines ideologically in the years since Occupy Wall Street, the magazines have moved toward the Center in terms of the way they see the relationship between their political project and their intellectual one. Whereas I had learned at the Center what words to use to communicate with our progressive friends on the Hill, one now can learn a similarly pre-scrubbed terminology for communicating with one's socialist allies in Crown Heights. I am hardly the first to note how certain concepts—intersectionality, neoliberalism, Gramsci—have become unmoored from their specific referents and now float freely, like wayward blimps, into sentences where they have no other role than to advertise, in big, flashing type, the author's moral righteousness and commitment. This, though, is only one aspect of the polemical—and bizarrely martial—vocabulary that has become a staple of leftist discourse in recent years. Since the conventional wisdom avers no issue can ever be safely siphoned off from any other, each becomes a pretext for calling for resistance and solidarity among allies—the proximate enemy might be the NRA, the DNC or Jonathan Chait—in a war against sinister forces. I do not mean to question this rhetorical approach as a matter of *politics*. From the purely sectarian perspective, it may well be justified. There is certainly reason to suppose that some political advantage can be gained from the repetition of certain words and phrases, or from the habit of making every issue appear to be a matter of existential ideological significance. (The potential effectiveness of these tactics has been amply demonstrated by the American right wing.) I only mean to point out what the approach means for the role of thinking. "Resistance Needs Ideas," reads a recent Facebook ad for *Jacobin*. If the intellectual at the think tank was the assistant to the legislator, here she has become the willing tool of the activist.

There have always been intellectuals who have chosen to become such tools, for good reasons as well as bad ones. Intellectuals are also citizens, and it is impossible to say in advance when might be the proper time for them to subjugate their intellectual to their civic responsibilities, or predict when those two responsibilities may become indistinguishable. History does show that intellectuals have often been mistaken about their ability to contribute meaningfully to social and political movements—and then, in the rare cases when they have actually taken power, about their capacity to lead them. But from the perspective of today's New York intellectuals, the great danger of making such a choice is not (Katie Roiphe's warning of a "new totalitarian state" notwithstanding) of our becoming Stalinists, or Maoists, or even Bannonites. We do not have enough power to be any of those things; and anyway, we hate guns. The danger is that, in attempting to discipline our desires to our political convictions, we might allow our ideology to overrun our intellect. When everything is political, everything is threatened by the tendency of the political to reduce thinking to positioning.

•

I began working on this magazine in 2009, two years after I had left New York to join a Ph.D. program at the University of Chicago, where we read the great books of the Western canon very slowly. Contrary to what is commonly asserted, no less by its defenders than by its critics, this canon did not promise or reveal to us any incontestable truths. It did not lead us to become committed conservatives, or liberals, or leftists (we had all three in the program). Nor did the writers we read agree with one another about how intellectual and political life should be related. There were those who thought the point of thinking was to interpret the world, those who thought it was to change it, and those who thought it was to be struck dumb with wonder at it. The one commitment the canon demanded of us was a commitment to engage in a conversation between different and often incommensurate perspectives. In the midst of the conversation, you still had to choose where you stood. But you did so knowing that the truth was not *in you*. It was out there, in the interplay of ideas that was the conversation itself.

Last year, in a report on "new public intellectuals," the *Chronicle of Higher Education* referred to *The Point* as being the "least left-wing" of the intellectual magazines that had emerged in the first two decades of the 2000s. The phrasing consolidated a common misunderstanding. What distinguishes *The Point* from the other magazines mentioned in the story (*Jacobin*, the *Nation*, *n+1*, *Dissent*, the *Baffler*) is not where we fall on the left-right spectrum, but rather how we picture the relationship between politics and public intellectual life—or, to use Benjamin Aldes Wurgaft's helpful phrase, "thinking in public." Whereas the other magazines have framed their projects in ideological and sometimes in activist terms, we have attempted to conduct a conversation about modern life that includes but is not limited by political conviction. This has meant, on the one hand, publishing articles that do not abide by the dictum that everything is "in the last analysis" political. (Some things, we believe, are in the last analysis poetic, some spiritual, some psychological, some moral.) It has also meant publishing a wider range of political perspectives than would usually be housed in one publication. This is not because we seek to be "centrists," or because we are committed to some fantasy of objectivity. It is because we believe there are still readers who are more interested in having their ideas tested than in having them validated or confirmed, ones who know from their own experience that the mind has not only principles and positions but also, as the old cliché goes, a life. If the *Jacobin* slogan indicates a political truth, it inverts what we take to be an intellectual one: Ideas Need Resistance.

This is true even, and perhaps especially, of political ideas. Our political conversation today suffers from hardly anything so much as a refusal of anyone to admit the blind spots and weaknesses of their ideas, the extent to which they fail to tell the *whole truth* about society or even about their own lives. In our eagerness to advance what we see as the common good, we rush to cover over what we share in common with those who disagree with us, including the facts of our mutual vulnerability and ignorance, our incapacity to ever truly know what is right or good "in the last analysis." This is the real risk of the strategic approach to communication that sometimes goes by the name of "political correctness": not that it asks that we choose our words carefully but that it becomes yet another tactic for denying, when it is inconvenient for the ideology we identify with, what is happening right in front of our eyes—and therefore another index of our alienation from our own forms of political expression. The journalist Michael Lewis, embedded with the White House press corps for an article published in *Bloomberg* in February, observed that a "zero-sum" approach is spreading throughout political media, such that every story is immediately interpreted according to who it is good or bad for, then discarded, often before anyone has paused to consider what is actually happening in the story. In this sense, the media mimics the president they obsessively cover, who as a candidate had promised his supporters that if they elected him they would "win so much you'll get tired of winning." Trump has always been the cartoon king of zero-sum communication—"No collusion!" he tweets in response to the news that thirteen Russians are being indicted—a person to whom one senses news is *only* real to the extent that he can interpret it as helping him or hurting his enemies. But Lewis is surely right that the zero-sum approach has become pervasive across the culture. I certainly see it in the corner where I spend a lot of my time, at the intersection of academia and little magazines.

A recent *n+1* Intellectual Situation, "In the Maze," is a reflection on being a woman in left-liberal publishing under the conditions that led to #MeToo, written by one of the magazine's current editors, Dayna Tortorici. Toward the end of the article, Tortorici recounts a story she had heard "about a friend who'd said, offhand at a book group, that he'd throw women under the bus if it meant achieving social democracy in the United States." The story was supposed to be chilling, she says, but she had found it merely funny ("*As if you could do it without us*, I thought, *we who do all the work on the group project*"). I can see how the story is funny, for the reason Tortorici mentions and for another she doesn't: Who exactly is inviting this boy at his book group to make such decisions? But I also find the story chilling—and not only because of the attitude it manifests toward roughly half the country's population. Above all, it feels chillingly familiar. The adolescent brutality of the friend's imagery, the way he dresses up frustration or anger as hardheaded calculation, the conflation of rhetorical stridency with political seriousness: these traits are everywhere in left-liberal discourse these days. You can hear them in the voices of the Chapo Trap House podcasters, who ask "the pragmatists out there" to "bend the knee" to them, just as surely as you can read it in the public statements of aspiring presidential candidates like Kirsten Gillibrand, who signal their readiness for the job by indicating intolerance for "gradations" of guilt or the niceties of institutional procedure. You may even have noticed them in your own voice at the dinner table, or in your tentative contributions (you don't *want* to sound this way) to the slugfests taking place on your Facebook wall.

And yet the zero-sum logic that informs the friend's "offhand" remark cannot be completely dissociated from the approach that the rest of the little magazines have long taken to political life. If *n+1* had begun with the "dream of advance," an idea of addition that did not imply subtraction, the interrogative subtitle of "In the Maze"—"*Must history have losers?*"—reflects Tortorici's observation that, in the non-dream world, the advancement of some tends to come at the expense of others. In describing the losses in power, comfort and authority that many men will have to accept if they wish to make the world "habitable for others" in the wake of #MeToo, the editorial certainly reminds us what kinds of things people do lose in history, often deservedly. But there is something more implied when we ask if history—like elections, or softball games—must have *losers*. The notion that history has a definite direction, and that only some people are on the "right side" of it, has always been attractive to intellectuals on the left; among other things, it offers a clear cause and mission to those of us prone to worry about being decadent or superfluous. On the other hand, it makes history into a bus that will run us all over at some point (Tortorici can only express sympathy for the intellectuals she sees being "cast out as political dinosaurs by 52, by 40, by 36," a thought I found alarming as one just now entering the extinction window), and it threatens to render intellectual debate a strictly intramural affair. If politics is a war between the allies and the enemies of history, then arguing in good faith with the losers can only be either a sign of weakness or a waste of time. It's the high-theory variant of the mindset that animated our in-house demographers at the Center, who used to delight in proving, with the aid of laser pointers and the latest in data analytics, that there was no reason to consider the arguments of red-state Bush voters, since they would all be dead soon. This was in 2004.

Plato and Aristotle, who were two of the first to reflect on the relationship between political and intellectual life, certainly did not think that politics described only what happened in voting booths or policy institutes. For them, the political was a realm of great importance, not only because it determined domestic and foreign affairs, but also because it shaped the moral character of the citizenry. Plato even imagined, in the *Republic*, a utopia in which every aspect of existence—from art to exercise to furniture—would be disciplined by a concept of the political good. (You might say he was the first to emphasize the importance of political correctness.) But the ancient philosophers did not believe that a life organized by politics could ever be the best or the highest life. This was because, although politics certainly required thinking, they believed in a realm of intellectual activity that lay beyond the instrumental logic of the politicians. Indeed it was the philosopher's attraction to thinking as its own reward, sometimes known as contemplation and often correlated with the experience of wonder, that distinguished him from the rest of the citizens and sometimes led to conflict with the political authorities—a conflict that for Plato's teacher Socrates had notoriously ended in death. But it was also this experience of isolation and radical self-questioning that made the philosopher of potential political value to those citizens.

In her 1954 lecture "Philosophy and Politics," Hannah Arendt emphasized that it was Socrates's own experience of "speechless wonder," frequently reported upon by onlookers, that motivated him—having understood in his isolation and silence what was common to all human beings, namely their capacity to ask the fundamental (and fundamentally unanswerable) questions—to create a rhetorical format, the "dialogue between friends," by which his fellow citizens would be able to "understand the truth inherent in the other's opinion . . . and in what specific articulateness the common world appears to the other." The purpose of the dialogue, Arendt claimed, was to "make friends out of Athens's citizenry" at a time when the political life of the city "consisted of an intense and uninterrupted contest of all against all, of *aei aristeuein*, ceaselessly showing oneself to be the best of all." It was this "agonal spirit" that eventually destroyed the Greek city-state, whose fate it was to be torn apart by polarizing internal hatreds long before it fell prey to invading armies.

We are right now living through another time of intense contest, of internal polarization and warlike separation. I do not think many of us have the feeling that we are winning. Yet we need only glance at those who have been most recently victorious to appreciate the unintended truth in Trump's wayward boast. Winning really is tiresome—almost as tiresome as reporting on our supposed progress. Perhaps what we are doing can serve some other end.

I Am Madame Bovary

"CAT PERSON" AND THE
DARK PLEASURES OF EMPATHY

by Anastasia Berg

ISSUE 16 | SPRING 2018

Of all the personal stories shared in the wake of #MeToo, in no single narrative did so many recognize themselves as in a work of fiction: the short story "Cat Person," by 36-year-old first-time author Kristen Roupenian.

Published in the December 11, 2017 issue of the *New Yorker*, the story follows Margot, a twenty-year-old female college student, in the rosy lead-up and nasty aftermath of a disappointing date with Robert, a 34-year-old man whom she meets at the movie concession stand where she works. They flirt for weeks over text, watch a film at the cinema, get drunk and finally go back to his house where they have sex that she does not enjoy. For a while, she vaguely deflects his subsequent attempts to contact her. Eventually, her roommate explicitly rebuffs Robert for her, sending him a hastily composed message from Margot's phone that reads, "Hi im not interested in you stop textng me." After Margot runs into Robert in a student bar a month later, he sends her a series of increasingly agitated text messages concluding with a single word: "Whore."

The piece enjoyed overwhelming success. By far the most popular piece of *New Yorker* fiction this year, it is perhaps the most talked-about short story since Annie Proulx's "Brokeback Mountain," published in the same magazine in 1997. "Cat Person" appears to owe its popularity especially to the enthusiasm of female readers. "The depiction of uncomfortable romance in 'Cat Person' seems to resonate with countless women," reported the *Atlantic*. It captured, it was said, a widely shared experience, and therefore a deep universal truth about the lives of young women. In Margot, they said, they saw themselves.

Men's rights recruits on Twitter predictably responded by hurling petulant insults at the story and its author, unwittingly reproducing various stages of Robert's own descent into verbal violence. The Twitter account @MenCatPerson collected the responses of hundreds of aggrieved men for women's entertainment, amassing in the process nearly as many followers as the author herself (around eight thousand). The fans of the story saw in these reactions further evidence of its point: by ignoring the sworn testimonies of countless women who insisted that "Cat Person" was the truth, the men only proved that they don't understand how women experience the world, and don't bother trying.

Indeed the story seemed to many to be *so* "real," *so* "true," that it was often mistaken for a personal essay or a journal entry. This was troubling to the writer Larissa Pham, who argued in the *Village Voice* that this confusion indicates that we are failing as readers: "The discourse around [the story] reflects how the distinction between fiction and nonfiction has collapsed in recent years." We measure literature, television shows and films against a preconceived set of sociocritical norms, she lamented, demanding that art provide us with lessons on how to live and dismissing it as morally deficient if it fails to do so. Pham is right, but she might have gone further. For it is precisely this kind of failing reader that "Cat Person" itself encourages us to become. And it is above all to the pleasures of being such a reader that it owes its success.

•

What made so many women exclaim with such certainty that the story might have been their own? It was hardly the first story to depict a man (or a woman for that matter) failing to take rejection well, or as a clumsy, impatient lover. What is unique, it was said, is its portrayal of a young woman who would sooner sacrifice her own desire and pleasure than dare face a man's response to outright rejection.

The task of interpreting the story was unsettled, however, by the author's own intervention. In what can only be described as a companion piece to the story, on December 4th the *New Yorker* published an interview with Roupenian, shortly after the story went viral online and before it came out in print. Traditionally authors have responded gingerly to the demand that they explain the "meaning" of their work, or rejected it outright; Roupenian, by contrast, offered an answer that was clear and straightforward. She was happy to say *exactly* where the story came from and *exactly* what the story meant. For Roupenian "Cat Person" is first and foremost a story about reading. It is a story about a bad reader that is meant to teach its own readers how to read better.

The apparent challenge the story is meant to address, Roupenian told the *New Yorker*, is the perennial difficulty of reading people. A bad online dating experience was what got her "thinking about the strange and flimsy evidence we use to judge the contextless people we meet outside our existing social networks, whether online or off":

> Especially in the early stages of dating, there's so much interpretation and inference happening that each interaction serves as a kind of Rorschach test for us. We decide that it means something that a person likes cats instead of dogs, or has a certain kind of artsy tattoo, or can land a good joke in a text.

But assigning "meaning" to people's choices in pets and body art, or their sense of humor, is misguided, she insisted: "Really, these are reassuring self-deceptions." They mean nothing when it comes to what matters. "That Robert is smart and witty is true, but does the fact that someone's smart and witty mean that he won't murder you . . . or assault you, or say something nasty to you if you reject him?" No. Nothing that Robert does or indeed could do could mean *that*.

In fact, Roupenian sees her story as serving to unmask Robert, to wrestle him out of the trappings of his interests, aesthetic tastes, intelligence and wit—which she dismisses as meaningless at best and deceptive at worst. What's left? On this Roupenian is very clear. In response to a question about where her sympathies vis-à-vis her characters lie, she replied without hesitation, "Well, at the *end* of the story, Robert calls Margot a 'whore,' so I hope that most people lose sympathy for him then."

This unequivocal response came as a surprise to those of us who found Robert a sympathetic character throughout—sympathetic not simply because he experienced rejection, or was unjustly treated, but precisely because of the story's ending. Roupenian depicts a man who is conflicted, a man who oscillates between anger, jealousy and guilt, and she captures especially well the ultimate failure to maintain the laborious graciousness with which he tries to meet Margot's rebuke: the overwrought polite message, the abstention from contact for a full month. In their final text exchange, a drunk Robert follows up a question about whether Margot is "fucking" a guy he had seen with her, with "sorry." His apology is met with silence. It is too late. He hurls another accusation at her. In this final scene Roupenian depicts well (to my mind it was probably the best moment in the story) how shame and regret at what cannot be undone can turn into further violence—when one, having lost all hope of undoing the damage done, doubles down.

But Roupenian herself sees Robert's outburst differently: for her, it is in this moment that he finally betrays who he really is, with a single word. "For most of the story," she says, "I wanted to leave a lot of space for people to sympathize with Robert," but at the end the reader should see, as Margot presumably does, that their sympathy was misplaced. "Margot keeps trying to construct an image of Robert based on incomplete and unreliable information . . . The point at which she receives unequivocal evidence about the kind of person he is is the point at which the story ends."

The "kind of person" Robert is—and by extension "the kind of person" anyone can be on this account of what it means to correctly read another person's character—lies hidden behind a mass of unreliable pieces of evidence. But no matter how much sympathy this "mirage of guesswork and projection" elicits from us, the real person is nothing but the worst of his sins. And sinners don't deserve our pity.

•

Suspicion and the desire to unmask the (always ugly) truth run through Roupenian's nascent oeuvre, which consists to date of "Cat

Person," two other short stories ("Bad Boy" in the online magazine *Body Parts* and "The Night Runner" in the *Colorado Review*), a couple of interviews and a book review. (She has signed a reported seven-figure book deal for a forthcoming collection of her short stories.) In a February 2018 piece for the *Times Literary Supplement* titled "Intimacy, Infamy," Roupenian confessed her distaste for a middlebrow anthology of vignettes about kissing. "Maybe I am just not the audience for this book," she wrote,

> I would have been, once—when I was thirteen and fourteen (and, honestly, fifteen and sixteen and seventeen) I would have devoured it; I would have underlined and starred and returned to . . . lines like, "Write the rain, I beg him. Write on me with your mouth," and "There are countries in that kiss, years of experience, ghosts of past lovers and the tricks they taught you."

It is not the questionable literary merit of these passages that bothers Roupenian. Indeed she seems perfectly happy to grant that the clichéd and melodramatic lines succeed in making kissing "seem the most beautiful, magical, profound." Roupenian is bothered rather by the fact that what these passages make kissing *seem*—beautiful, magical, profound—kissing simply is not. Her own writing, she claims, will perform the necessary work of disenchantment:

> The task that has seemed most urgent to me in the past few years (it is one I pursued in my short story "Cat Person," published by the *New Yorker* in December 2017) has been to dissolve all that sticky varnish, peeling away the pretty words I used to coat and mask my desires to reveal the actual physical experiences underneath.

She concludes the review by responding to the final moment of the anthology, what she describes as "the kind of leading question that only a poet would be bold enough to pose":

> "Is there a connection between lyric suspension and an unforgettable kiss? That is, when the world sloughs away and time is

upended, life swirling around a moment until all that seems to exist is the kiss and the singular moment of it—does this point us towards the eternal, the spiritual, the sublime?"

To which I answer, get away from me, with your creepy absurd propaganda for mashing our food holes together. *Kiss kiss kiss kiss kiss kiss kiss kiss kiss.*

Is this right? Are our mouths, with which we speak, sing and smile, "food holes" we mash together in kissing? Is to suggest otherwise "creepy" and "absurd"? A lot has been said about Roupenian's successful depiction of bad sex. One wonders if she would admit the existence of any other kind.

While our character is reducible to the worst of our deeds, Roupenian claims, our body is reducible to its most basic biological functions. The rest is fake news and fairy tales. But is it really "reality" that lies behind the masks that Roupenian is determined to tear off?

•

Over the course of "Cat Person," Robert, or how Robert appears to Margot, undergoes a radical transformation. At first, he appears "cute" ("cute enough that she could have drummed up an imaginary crush on him if he'd sat across from her during a dull class"). Despite him having a beard (one that is "a little too long") and bad posture, Margot estimates him to be in his mid-to-late twenties. (Ordinarily, facial hair and bad posture cause people to appear older, not younger, but no matter.) By the end of the story Robert is but a "fat old man." And while it is true that he is described as being "on the heavy side" from the start, during their sexual encounter he is suddenly so fat that, trying to put on a condom, his penis is "only half visible beneath the hairy shelf of his belly."

The physical transformation is supposed to be matched by the radical change in his character. At the beginning of the story, we learn that Robert is, as Roupenian herself characterizes him in the interview, "smart and witty": "They built up an elaborate scaffolding of jokes via text, riffs that unfolded and shifted so quickly that she sometimes had a hard time keeping up. He was very clever, and she

216 TIRED OF WINNING

found that she had to work to impress him." But whenever we, the story's readers, are looking, Robert has nothing charming, witty or clever to say at all. Sarcastic, laconic and dull throughout the date that occupies the center of the story, Robert expresses himself so poorly, so crudely and so foolishly that Margot fantasizes about recounting the remarks he makes in bed during and after sex for sport and amusement. He is revealed to be so lame she can find solace only in the thought of the pleasure to be derived from mocking him.

Then he calls her a whore.

Margot had no way of knowing she was going to bed with a fat old man, because to begin with Robert wasn't one. She went to bed with a cute, funny man who kissed her gently on the forehead, "as though she were something precious." And besides, how could she have known: she is, after all, so very young. The transformation in Robert combines with Margot's innocence and inexperience to render plausible that one might find oneself in this position *unwittingly*. Reflecting on her own bad date, Roupenian berated herself, "How had I decided that this was someone I could trust?" Robert's physical, mental and emotional degeneration serves to substantiate the claim that we are fools to repeat such mistakes. For all we know, for all we could ever know, princes can turn into frogs, and what's worse, they can do so *after* we kiss them.

Roupenian acknowledges the experience is one that ought to elicit wonder:

> The moment when I feel the most sympathy for Margot is when, after she spends the entire story wondering about Robert—what he's thinking, feeling, doing—she is left marvelling the most at herself, and at her own decision to have sex with him, at this person who'd just done this bizarre, inexplicable thing.

While from Margot's point of view the event is "bizarre" and "inexplicable," Roupenian does offer an explanation for Margot's predicament: the young woman, Roupenian suggested, is "incredibly empathetic" and excessively "imaginative." A nice thought—but is this credible?

All kinds of women—young and beautiful, old and ugly—find

themselves fucked ragdoll-like by crude, fat, old, lying trolls, the kind that hurl insults at them when they refuse to come back for more. If they're not into that sort of thing, they certainly could come to feel "revulsion," "self-disgust" and "humiliation," as Margot does. But the idea that after the fact they would stand "marvelling" at themselves and the inexplicable thing that had happened is peculiar. We need not take a stance in the fracas over the various ways in which we might be implicated in the repeated acts of dismissal, sexual degradation and violence that are meted upon us in order to acknowledge that it is absurd to claim that our involvement is exhausted by our being excessively empathic, imaginative and non-confrontational. It is either patronizing or self-deceiving to suggest otherwise.

Margot, far from representing the reality of women's lived experience, is an exercise in wish fulfillment. The wish she fulfills is the wish that whatever happened, happened *to* us. We couldn't have known better, so we didn't let it happen, and we certainly didn't do it to ourselves. Margot is but a distant cousin of a familiar female trope—the manic pixie dream girl: a beautiful young woman, quirky and energetic, who exists solely to help a male lead grow emotionally and experience happiness (originally coined in response to Kirsten Dunst's character in *Elizabethtown*, it has been applied broadly to female characters ranging from Audrey Hepburn's in *Breakfast at Tiffany's* to Natalie Portman's in *Garden State*). We've learned to dismiss the MPDG as the fantasy that she is. Let us not adopt Margot in her stead, a beautiful young woman who finds herself *inexplicably* sexually degraded and emotionally abused.

As for how "relatable" the story seemed to so many, it would not be the first time a fantasy has seduced its readers by flattering them. "I am Margot," a thousand voices cried. But perhaps after all she is only what we wish we were or could be: beautiful, naive, faultless. Complicit in the sacrifice of our own desire and pleasure, only insofar as we cared too much. *Too good* for our own good.

•

To read well, Roupenian avers, is to "unmask." To peel away the "pretty words" and reveal the "actual physical experiences" that lie beneath. Keep your guard up or you might just end up getting finger-fucked by a fat old man who will call you a whore. This ethic of sus-picion is a lesson that many have already internalized: the revelation of any failure, in a person or an artwork, has become sufficient to dismiss either out of hand. In the case of art, in some circles it has become the whole point of confronting it. Even Roupenian was not safe from the wrath of the sort of failing readers that Pham identi-fies, readers who rushed to accuse the author and her story of having an ageism, fat shaming or classism "problem." The problem with Roupenian's story is not however that it is too frank in its portrayal of the objects of desire of a very young woman. The problem is not even that it lies. The problem is that it encourages us to lie to our-selves.

It was remarkable to see a work of art (prose fiction no less) be-come the center of a passionate public conversation—who remem-bers the last time everyone one knew was talking about a short story? And it might seem harmless, perhaps even felicitous, that the participants, privately and publicly, were so frank in intimately relat-ing the story to their own life. What could be the harm? Whether we sympathize with Margot or with Robert, isn't it enough that we were moved to sympathize at all? Isn't this what literature is, always was, all about? What else could Flaubert have meant when he exclaimed, "I am Madame Bovary"?

But the activity in which Flaubert engaged, the activity in which the public critic ought to help each of the work's readers to engage, is not merely one of *sympathy*. To read with only the question of sympathy in mind, to read for the gratification found in aligning oneself with the passions—the joy and the pain—of this or that fic-tional character, is no more a way of seeing others than is looking in a soft-focus mirror.

Beginning in childhood with novels "solely concerned with love affairs, lovers and their beloveds, damsels in distress swooning in secluded summerhouses . . . wounded hearts, vows, sobs, tears, and kisses," Emma Bovary abandons fiction, and becomes "enthralled by things historical": "She idolized Mary Queen of Scots, and felt a passionate admiration for women who were famous or ill-starred."

In music class "the ballads that she sang were solely about little angels with golden wings, madonnas, lagoons, and gondoliers: sooth-
ing compositions which allowed her to glimpse, behind the inanity
of the words and the incongruity of the music, the seductive illusion
of emotional realities."

But the course of sympathetic readings does not constitute a sentimental education; on the contrary, as Mary McCarthy observed
in 1964, Emma's "character is remarkable only for an unusual de-
ficiency of human feeling." It is not that Emma has no occasion to
suffer herself, but as Chris Kraus noted some forty years after Mc-
Carthy, her "suffering never opens her eyes to the misfortunes of
others." Emma immerses herself in stories that gratify by deceiving,
not because, as Roupenian would have it, the world is not as good
as those stories make it out to be, but because the stories justify the
kind of self-absorption that blinds Emma to anyone but herself.

During the composition of his novel, Flaubert wrote to his sometime lover and confidante, Louise Colet:

> It is a delicious thing to write, whether well or badly—to no lon-
> ger be yourself, but to move in an entire universe of your own
> creating. Today, for instance: I was man and woman, lover and
> beloved, I rode in a forest on an autumn afternoon beneath the
> yellow leaves, and I was the horses, the wind, the words my people
> spoke, even the red sun that made them half-shut their love-
> drowned eyes.

To condemn Emma Bovary and all who follow her lead as sympathetic readers is not to deny that in reading literature we encounter
and are invited to identify with the mind of another. It is to suggest,
rather, that it is not the mind of a character or even the narrator that
we meet, but that of the artist who is, as Flaubert wrote, "everywhere
felt, but nowhere seen." When Flaubert exclaimed, "I am Madame
Bovary," he was neither justifying the character as better than we
thought she was, nor condemning himself. He was Emma Bovary
because he was *all* his creations, perfect and flawed alike. It is a
strange and difficult challenge, to be more and less than one, at one

and the same time. But that is the challenge that literature sets before us.

If our task as critics is to teach each other how to read better, then that task involves training ourselves to read not as Margot and Bovary read—to confirm our most flattering images of ourselves—but to read as Flaubert writes. This means inhabiting not just the subjective perspective of one or another character but of an "entire universe." Only then can we see that Roupenian's "reality"—where it is possible to draw stable lines between good and bad characters, or pure and problematic ones—is the most comforting fiction of all.

The Closing of
the American Mind

by Jacob Hamburger

ISSUE 15 | WINTER 2018

Allan Bloom was an elitist. He saw himself as a champion of excellence in an age of vulgarity. While a professor at the University of Chicago between 1979 and 1992, he sought to immerse his students in only the most classic works of philosophy and literature. Someone looking to define the "Western canon" could do worse than to dig up his course syllabi. In his personal style, he embodied high culture nearly to the point of caricature. His friend Saul Bellow captured him in the novel *Ravelstein* as a man who wore expensive European suits, lived in a Hyde Park apartment lavishly decorated with French art and bragged of listening to Mozart on a state-of-the-art stereo system. A lifelong Francophile, he made regular jaunts to Paris over the course of four decades. Yet Bloom insisted that for all his erudition, he was merely a product of America's democratic promise. Well into his fifties, he often spoke of himself as a simple "Midwestern boy," the Indiana-born son of Jewish immigrants who received the best gift a meritocratic democracy could offer: a great education. Bloom thought of himself as proof that, thanks to its universities, anyone can make it in America.

So when thirty years ago Bloom addressed a group of Harvard students and faculty as "fellow elitists," he was not being entirely ironic. The quip came in response to controversies surrounding his 1987 best seller *The Closing of the American Mind*, which defended an idiosyncratic vision of higher education in the United States. Bloom saw the liberal education traditionally offered at exclusive colleges and universities as the fulfillment of democratic ideals, but condemned his fellow professors for having abandoned this crucial responsibility. *Closing* received an onslaught of criticism for its "elitism," particularly from fellow academics such as Richard Rorty and Martha Nussbaum, who also observed correctly that his book was at times rambling, historically sloppy and philosophically one-sided. Bloom in turn accused his critics of projecting their own intellectual privilege onto him. "'Elite' is not a word I care for very much," Bloom explained. "It is imprecise and smacks of sociological abstraction." But no matter how elites are defined—whether in terms of wealth, prestige or knowledge—it is clear that "bad conscience accompanies the democrat who finds himself part of an elite." Bloom pushed back against this bad conscience by suggesting that academic elitism was in fact healthy for American democracy.

Like Tocqueville, whom he admired and cited incessantly, Bloom aimed to explore the ways in which the democratic principles of liberty and equality shape American society. Unlike the French aristocrat, however, Bloom based his observations on a far smaller sample: college students "materially and spiritually free to do pretty much what they want with the few years of college they are privileged to have—in short, the kind of young persons who populate the twenty or thirty best universities." Bloom believed these students represented the best of a democratic society, mainly because they enjoyed an unparalleled form of liberty. One of the fundamental guarantees of democratic society is the freedom of self-determination, or the "pursuit of happiness." Bloom saw the proper exercise of this freedom as something that a philosophical education can help teach— the pursuit of happiness, after all, presumably involves attempting to know what happiness is. An education in the humanities, like Chicago's Core curriculum, allowed undergraduates to devote four years to literature and philosophy. Under the guidance of wise teachers and classic texts, they learned to challenge their most deeply held beliefs according to the highest standard of reason. This philosophical overhaul of the self, what Bloom referred to as "liberal education," amounted to no less than the perfection of democratic autonomy. Not only, then, could elite college students choose a rewarding professional career after graduation, but more importantly, they had been given the most "authentic liberation" a democracy can provide.

It did not bother Bloom that liberal education was available in practice only to a privileged few. He took for granted that American democracy (or any society, for that matter) would always contain hierarchies of power, knowledge, income and wealth. The question for Bloom was not whether America should or shouldn't have elites, but rather what kind of elite was most compatible with democratic ideals. He followed the ancient Greeks in thinking of liberal education as what separated "free men" from slaves. Like Plato, he believed that those capable of liberating themselves through philosophical education—the "potential knowers," as he put it—were inevitably a small minority. But like many liberals and conservatives in twentieth-century America, Bloom was also a believer in meritocracy. Having studied alongside poor veterans during the days of the GI Bill, he praised the American system for extending what had once been an "aristocratic" education to anyone worthy of it.

For Bloom, then, the university was the most important institution of American democracy. Taking Plato at his word, he believed that the character of a society is best expressed by the people who rule it. It followed that colleges and universities, the training ground for America's elites, had the task of ensuring that the country's leaders embodied the basic principles of its political regime. As long as they practiced genuine liberal education, Bloom believed these institutions could continue to produce "statesmen" trained in the responsible exercise of democratic freedom. Though he praised democracy in principle, he believed it an "intellectual wasteland," indifferent or even hostile to serious thinking. For a democracy to thrive, talented youngsters had to be exposed to a philosophical education that allowed them to transcend the "bourgeois vulgarity" of their surroundings, and to devote themselves to something other than mere self-advancement. If American society could not ensure this, it risked descending into rule by elites who were no better than the uneducated mob, and for this reason perhaps far more dangerous (such was apparently his assessment of the graduates of MBA programs). As a result, Bloom believed that a "crisis of liberal education" would amount to nothing less than "the crisis of our civilization."

Bloom recognized, however, that his ideal picture of democratic education required a delicate social balance. Only under certain conditions will ordinary Americans put their trust in a liberally educated elite. A cultural conservative, Bloom saw America's strong moral traditions as the key to its success in maintaining such a balance. Unlike Western Europe, where the collapse of traditional cultures had led to the crises of the 1930s, America had succeeded for much of its history in preserving an authentic attachment to both Judeo-Christian and civil religions. He wrote nostalgically of his forebears:

> My grandparents were ignorant people by our standards, and my grandfather held only lowly jobs. But their home was spiritually rich because all the things done in it, not only what was specifically ritual, found their origin in the Bible's commandments. . . . Their simple faith and practices linked them to great scholars and thinkers who dealt with the same material. . . . There was a respect for real learning, because it had a felt connection with their lives.

For Bloom, the vitality of tradition, whether grounded in the Bible or the Constitution, meant that people of earlier times not only respected the authority of those with knowledge, but could also become educated themselves. Students raised in these traditions went to college full of deeply held "prejudices," which Bloom counterintuitively saw as crucial for an authentic education. "One has to have the experience of really believing," he wrote, "before one can have the thrill of liberation."

•

Midway through Bloom's academic career, he saw these social conditions for liberal education collapse. In 1969, he was on the faculty at Cornell when student radicals—including some he had taught personally—staged an armed takeover of the student union, demanding more student control over university affairs. When Bloom publicly opposed these demands, he received death threats, and later resigned in protest. As is patently clear throughout *Closing*, these events remained bitter memories many years later, but his assessment of the sixties was not merely personal. The decade, he thought, was an "unmitigated disaster" for liberal education. Bloom saw the youth revolts of those years as an all-out assault on the special role of the elite university in American society. These institutions of higher learning were, in his words, "an alien and weak transplant, perched precariously in enclaves, vulnerable to native populism and vulgarity." When student radicals launched their attack on the authority of professors and the Great Books, supposedly in the name of "democratizing" the university, they opened it up to these hostile forces. As a result, the sixties fundamentally altered the meanings of democratic ideals in the context of American higher education.

For Bloom, the countercultural movements of the sixties had perverted the meaning of liberty—by expanding it. Not only did students now come to college to enjoy the freedom of philosophical exploration; they came just as much to be released from traditional restrictions on sex and most other social "vices." This new "liberation," Bloom claimed, did more harm than good, destroying old social norms without putting anything in their place. He warmly remembered his students of the fifties, who arrived at college full of firm convictions, but also eager for intellectual exploration that might challenge them. In contrast, students in the late eighties, having grown up believing that all beliefs and ways of life are equally valid, were "easygoing" and "nice," but almost completely indifferent to the profoundest aspects of human life. For Bloom, this was apparent in the way they thought about things like romance and culture. *Closing* depicted a generation of young people that had exchanged authentic love affairs for fleeting casual "relationships"—in which "sexual passion no longer includes the illusion of eternity"—and preferred commercialized rock music to great symphonies.* Underneath a nonjudgmental relativism, Bloom saw a creeping nihilism: believing that all judgments of value had equal weight, the students ended up not believing or aspiring to much of anything at all. As a result, they no longer aspired to learn the truth, but rather to be "open-minded." Incapable of treating moral questions and culture as anything other than matters of personal preference, they couldn't be bothered to take seriously the task of self-reinvention that their education demanded of them.

But if liberty had been replaced by indifference, equality in post-sixties America had been hijacked by a form of fanaticism. Radical political movements like feminism and Black Power had introduced an absolutist notion of egalitarianism into everyday discourse. Bloom claimed his students had reverted to what Tocqueville called the "passion for equality," a rudimentary instinct in democratic societies to insist dogmatically that all individuals are fundamentally the same. If they were "open-minded" on most questions of personal morality, they quickly became angry when this egalitarianism was questioned, particularly on questions of race, class or gender. Bloom's favorite example was second-wave feminism, which he referred to as "the latest enemy of the vitality of classic texts." Whenever discussions in his courses touched on the "natural" differences between men and women (needless to say, Bloom was no fan of gender theory), these students would respond with moral indignation.

---

* *Closing*'s sub-chapter on rock music is perhaps its least well informed (Bloom is not nearly as convincing an authority on the Rolling Stones as on Plato), but it also contains one of Bloom's rare attempts to connect his polemic about higher education to a critique of consumer society. For Bloom, "the rock business is perfect capitalism," finding an ideal consumer base in America's teenagers. With "all the moral dignity of drug trafficking," rock executives exploit adolescents' natural desire for sex and rebellion against their parents. Rock music is, in Bloom's words, "a nonstop, commercially prepackaged masturbational fantasy," appealing directly to these impulses without any attempt to direct them towards higher things. This "junk food for the soul," according to Bloom, "ruins the imagination of young people and makes it very difficult to have a passionate relationship to the art and thought that are the substance of liberal education."

The "democratization" of the university had led to its "politiciza-tion": all of education had to serve the aim of increasing equality. Bloom believed that liberal education was supposed to replace the instinctive passions with reasoned debate and thereby teach moder-ation. But now that sixties-era radicalism had become the norm, stu-dents were far less willing to engage in serious discussion of difficult subjects. And since professors across the country had "capitulated" to the new order of things—as Bloom wrote spitefully of his former colleagues at Cornell—few were willing to insist that they do so.

Bloom believed that his anecdotal conversations with students at the University of Chicago revealed the deepest instincts of the current generation of students. In one of his frequent comparisons between American culture and the cultivation of plants, he con-cluded that in the late eighties, there was no longer sufficient "soil in which university teaching can take root." In other words, post-sixties students had become indifferent to their training as a demo-cratic elite, and therefore incapable of taking it on. Bloom did not pull his punches in describing what this decline of elite education meant for American democracy. "As Hegel was said to have died in Germany in 1933," he wrote, ominously, "Enlightenment in Amer-ica came close to breathing its last during the Sixties." Shockingly, Bloom analogized the student revolts he witnessed at Cornell to Martin Heidegger's famous rector's speech praising Hitler. "As in Germany," he wrote, "the university [fell] prey to whatever intense passion moved the masses." In other words, in both cases the elite university compromised its isolation from the vulgarity of the gen-eral population (his description of the phenomenon of National So-cialism was, to put it gently, understated). And the lesson Bloom drew for the present moment was the same: once the university falls, democracy itself is soon to follow. The "open-minded" relativism and fervent egalitarianism of his students convinced him that, after twenty years, this "crisis of our civilization" was far from over.

For Bloom, the only solution to the impending collapse of democ-racy was for elite universities to unilaterally withdraw from society, returning to a traditional humanities curriculum. Earlier in his life, he had thought that America was gradually becoming a more enlightened nation. The prestigious universities were by far the finest source of intellectual cultivation American democracy had to offer, but they could count on other institutions to assist them in achieving a sort of general progress.* In *Closing*, he expressed a radically different view. "Never did I think that the university was properly ministerial to the society around it," he wrote towards the end of the book.

In order to survive in dark times, Bloom called for the university to renounce its responsibility to society. His ultimate aspiration was for "a society that tolerates and supports an eternal childhood for some," in the hopes that this "playfulness can in turn be a blessing to society." In other words, to use a term he likely never heard of, Bloom longed to re-establish the university as a "safe space" for authentic philosophical learning. The greater the separation between the elite campus and the world around it, the better the chances for democracy's survival.

•

The great irony is that Bloom's emphatically elitist book helped spark a decades-long wave of conservative polemics against the academic elite. In 1988, the University of Michigan attempted to introduce "speech codes" regulating communication between students; the same year, Stanford revised its mandatory course in "Western Civilization" in response to student demands for more diverse authors. Sharing Bloom's bitterness towards the former student radicals, conservatives cited these trends as evidence that the sixties had indeed "closed the minds" of elite college students. *Closing*'s success created a new niche for conservative intellectuals like Roger Kimball and Dinesh D'Souza, who followed Bloom with their own

---

* For example, Bloom's papers at the University of Chicago contain a 1961 speech given in France in which he speculated, well before he published *The Closing of the American Mind*, that Keynesian economic planning was an alternative means of public pedagogy. Paraphrasing the left-liberal economist John Kenneth Galbraith, he suggested that through careful state management of consumer demand, the public "might be taught to spend more on schools and less on refrigerators."

books peering into college campuses with scornful delight. President George H. W. Bush used a 1991 commencement speech to warn of the dangers of "political correctness." For many secular conservatives, these attacks on academia helped forge common ground with the traditionalist and religious populism of the Reagan coalition. College students and professors became a common enemy of the right, a "liberal elite" to blame for America's cultural decline.

After a period of relative quiet, "political correctness" returned to the center of nationwide polemics around two years ago. The terms of the debate had changed slightly. With "trigger warnings" and "safe spaces," campus egalitarianism adopted an emotional vocabulary relatively absent from the discourse of the eighties and nineties, one that sought to highlight the traumatic experiences of marginalized students. And centrist liberals began to take up the "anti-PC" role once occupied predominantly by conservatives. The main substance of the conversation over diversity at elite institutions, however, remains largely the same as in Bloom's day. Around the time Greg Lukianoff and Jonathan Haidt's *Atlantic* article "The Coddling of the American Mind" was making its rounds in the fall of 2015, it might have been reasonable to roll one's eyes at this regurgitation of old polemics. But soon after, as the 2016 presidential campaign began, such debates began to take on a renewed political significance.

For Donald Trump, "political correctness" has long referred to whatever he does not like at any given moment. But *Breitbart* and the other alt-right sites his presidency has brought into the daylight have turned outrage over "social justice warriors" into the clarion call of a new political community. The idea that there is an epidemic of "political correctness" allows the new American right to perform a dangerous sleight of hand. When the president denounces "elites" or dismisses criticism as "politically correct," he invokes the most extreme images from American college campuses, like the video of the "shrieking girl" at Yale, which the alt-right has circulated with glee. The political danger is patent. Opposition to the cruelest of Trump's proposals is, in this hijacked discourse, not a sensible moral position but a symptom of a decadent liberal elitism.

In the years before his untimely death, Bloom was happy to join the crusade against "political correctness" he helped to start, despite his stated disdain for "anti-elitist" rhetoric. He took the opportunity of *Closing*'s commercial success to travel the country speaking out against liberal academia, appearing in numerous conservative media and, on one occasion, lecturing a group of congressmen about the national-security threats posed by Derrida's deconstruction theory. In the process, he seemed to have forgotten some of his own pedagogical principles. Bloom had a more sophisticated understanding of the inner experience of elite education than many of his fellow polemicists against "campus culture." He did not dismiss students' emotional reactions to what they encountered in the course of their education, believing rather that their "longings"—a favorite term of his—could be guided towards true understanding. As students at elite colleges have struggled to sort out their place in an increasingly unequal American society over the last thirty years, one might have thought that the response of an educator like Bloom would have been to encourage further discussion. Classic philosophical texts can challenge students to ask *why*—or, for that matter, *if*—equality is desirable, as well as which of its forms are possible, and what individual and collective actions might be best suited to realize them. These sorts of questions might have helped Bloom's students sort out the contradictions that go along with their roles as elites in an unequal democracy. Reading *The Closing of the American Mind* today, we are reminded of the delicate balance at the heart of democracy. No less than any other form of society, it has and requires elites, but at the same time it demands that they justify their existence in democratic terms. Bloom's account of liberal education suggests one way of attempting to ground this justification.

Trump and his fellow populists claim that America's elites have been corrupted beyond the point of saving: they promise not to turn them towards the true and the good, but instead to destroy them. In the context of this right-wing fury, Bloom's attacks on the university may seem to only reinforce what has by now become a widespread anti-intellectualism. If the university campus is nothing more than an island of philosophy surrounded by the vulgar masses, an elite playground for "useless" learning, right-wing populists might have a legitimate case for dismantling it. But in the age of Trump, Bloom's suggestion that elite education has a role to play in saving democracy from itself may nonetheless be worth returning to.

Switching Off

JOSEPH BRODSKY AND THE
MORAL RESPONSIBILITY TO BE USELESS

by Rachel Wiseman

ISSUE 16 | SPRING 2018

In 1964, when Joseph Brodsky was 24, he was brought to trial for "social parasitism." In the view of the state, the young poet was a freeloader. His employment history was spotty at best: he was out of work for six months after losing his first factory job, and then for another four months after returning from a geological expedition. (Being a writer didn't count as a job, and certainly not if you'd hardly published anything.) In response to the charge, Brodsky leveled a straightforward defense: he'd been thinking about stuff, and writing. But there was a new order to build, and if you weren't actively contributing to society you were screwing it up.

Over the course of the trial he stated his case repeatedly, insistently, with a guilelessness that annoyed the officials:

BRODSKY: I did work during the intervals. I did just what I am doing now. I wrote poems.

JUDGE: That is, you wrote your so-called poems? What was the purpose of your changing your place of work so often?

BRODSKY: I began working when I was fifteen. I found it all interesting. I changed work because I wanted to learn as much as possible about life and about people.

JUDGE: How were you useful to the motherland?

BRODSKY: I wrote poems. That's my work. I'm convinced . . . I believe that what I've written will be of use to people not only now, but also to future generations.

A VOICE FROM THE PUBLIC: Listen to that! What an imagination!

ANOTHER VOICE: He's a poet. He has to think like that.

JUDGE: That is, you think that your so-called poems are of use to people?

BRODSKY: Why do you say my poems are "so-called" poems?

JUDGE: We refer to your poems as "so-called" because we have no other impression of them.

Brodsky and the judge were (to put it mildly) talking past one another: Brodsky felt his calling had a value beyond political expediency, while the judge was tasked with reminding him that the state needn't subsidize his hobby if he wasn't going to say anything useful. But the incommensurability of these points of view runs much deeper than this one case.

•

Brodsky was born in Leningrad in 1940 and survived in infancy the brutal two-and-a-half-year siege that left over a million dead. Confronted with the accumulated traumas of revolution and world war, this "most abstract and intentional city" was thus violently thrust into modernity. Brodsky and his contemporaries came of age at a time when their experiences—and the squalid facts of life—were perpetually at odds with the vision of progress that was taught in schools, broadcast over radio and printed in newspapers. That this reality—of long lines and cramped communal apartments, where couples, children, in-laws and jealous neighbors all shared the same pre-revolutionary toilet—was right in front of their noses only made the official program all the more incongruous. (Brodsky later re-flected on the contradictions of his upbringing: "You cannot cover a ruin with a page of *Pravda*.")

Soviet children were taught that the revolution wasn't just a his-torical event but a dream they were destined to bring to life. "We were born that fairy tale might become reality," they recited, "To con-quer the vastness of space, / Reason gave us steel wings for arms, / And in the place of a heart they gave us a fiery motor." Brodsky re-counted how his childhood rebellion against this messaging be-came a feature of his character: he despised with an almost atavis-tic hatred the political slogans and reproduced images of Lenin that adorned his school walls. From then on, he was suspicious of any-thing that struck him as redundant or shallowly popular. This was, he wrote in his memoiristic essay "Less Than One," "my first lesson in switching off, my first attempt at estrangement":

> The planks, the governmental iron of railings, the inevitable khaki of the military uniform in every passing crowd on every street in every city, the eternal photographs of steel foundries in every morning paper and the continuous Tchaikovsky on the radio—these things would drive you crazy unless you learned to switch yourself off.

For Brodsky and his friends, "books became the first and only re-ality, whereas reality itself was regarded as either nonsense or nui-sance." They preferred to "read rather than to act." Brodsky casts this as a natural tendency, as if acting were something like eating cilantro for those not predisposed to it, always leaving the sensation of having just had one's mouth washed out with soap.

Still, inaction is a kind of action, as Brodsky was well aware. Why would a thinking person—or really anyone sensitive to injustice or falsehood—decide to *switch off*? The machine won't stop; there is no sleep mode. Corruption is fed by deceit and disaffection. Don't we have a responsibility to stay *on*, awake, woke?

●

The word "intelligentsia" came into English by way of Russian, where it had been loaned in turn from some unspecified European language—a trajectory that roughly maps onto the development of the class itself. The defining members of the Russian intelligentsia, as Isaiah Berlin outlined in "A Remarkable Decade," were a group of writers who came on the scene in the 1840s, including Alexander Herzen, Ivan Turgenev, Fyodor Dostoevsky, Ivan Panaev and Vissarion Belinsky. These men loved philosophy and literature as much as they hated the autocratic system that kept the Russian populace miserable and enslaved. They consumed ideas from Europe like drugs—from Rousseau and Voltaire to Counter-Enlightenment figures like Joseph de Maistre to Hegel and the German Romantics— and then argued about them with furious intensity. But what distinguished these Russian intellectuals from the Europeans they modeled themselves after was less their zeal or originality than their earnestness. They believed they were "united by something more than mere interest in ideas; they conceived of themselves as being a dedicated order, almost a secular priesthood, devoted to the spreading of a specific attitude to life, something like a gospel."

These so-called superfluous men became the prototype of the intellectual that we know today: well read, urbane, politically engaged. They insisted that there was no escape from society for the writer, and that being a writer came with certain obligations: what they said *mattered*, whether in fiction or prose, among friends or in public. If previously the intellectual was oppositional by bad luck or circumstance, they made it part of the job description.

But even as the figure of the modern intellectual was taking shape, there was a tension pulling at the seams. Turgenev identified two kinds of writer. One, who we might call the *poet*, is perceptive and incandescently creative but operates at a remove from politics and communal life. The other, the *critic*, dives right into the scene, seeking to reflect the feeling and consciousness of the people at that moment in time. Turgenev, despite himself, belonged to the first type. Belinsky, his friend and the consummate "committed intellectual," was the latter.

More than half a century later, Belinsky's moral vision and rhe-

torical fire would make him a hero of the radicals who led the revolution. From him they learned that literature was to be taken very
seriously, for in books were messages that had the power not just to
change minds, but to forge them from raw material. When Trotsky
defined revolutionary art as works "colored by the new consciousness arising out of the Revolution," he was speaking as a follower
of Belinsky.

The first years of the Revolution witnessed an explosion of creative energy as radical intellectuals attempted to shake off custom
and conjure this new consciousness. Writers sought to change the
very structure of language—shortening words and fusing them as
if the New Man would be in too much of a rush to pronounce all of
the syllables. Architects dreamed up wild, larger-than-life designs
meant to both reflect the potency of the moment and contribute to
a functioning proletarian society; Tatlin's famous (but never actual-
ized) Monument to the Third International was to be a radio tower
that corkscrewed up like a Hegelian spiral a thousand feet tall.

This period of ecstatic experimentation was short-lived. By the
time Walter Benjamin visited Moscow in 1926, revolutionary art had
been so tamed and subsumed by the Party that he noted, "the intellectual is above all a functionary, working in the departments of
censorship, justice and finance, and, if he survives, participating
in work—which, however, in Russia means power. He is a member of the ruling class." The state's autoimmune response to the
avant-garde led to a rheumatic stiffening of artistic production,
which shrank to an ever more limited and rudimentary collection
of themes and styles. This brought about a paradoxical reversal:
Belinsky's heirs were now the staid enforcers of aesthetic tradition,
while Turgenev's became the rebels. And so a young poet who liked
books and quiet walks at sunset became the unlikely face of intellectual defiance.

•

When I first discovered Brodsky I was stumbling my way into a Russian major, starting with a freshman language class where we mem-
orized lines of Pushkin before we knew how to count to ten. I signed

up for more classes in the department, one after another, even though I had no idea what I could do with a B.A. in Russian besides maybe going into academia or the CIA. I was drawn, as if by the gravity of a foreign object, to the lives and works of Russian writers—Gogol, Tolstoy, Akhmatova, Mandelstam, Platonov, Brodsky. Each of them, in their own way, helps you to feel the depth of the ground you stand on, and then question its solidity.

The fall of my senior year I took a small seminar taught by an Eastern European poet with a priestly air accentuated by the long, thoughtful pauses that preceded his pronouncements. One of the poems we were assigned was Brodsky's "Autumn in Norenskaia." After his trial, Brodsky was sentenced to five years of labor in the remote northern town of Norenskaia. He came to sort of enjoy his punishment; after all, it gave him plenty of time to write. Composed in 1965, "Autumn in Norenskaia" captures a brief moment at the end of the workday. "We return from the field," the poem begins, set against a backdrop of exhaustion and decay. Horses in the street look like "inflated casks / of ribs trapped between shafts," while peasant women "scissor their way home, / like cutting along a dull hem." The first half of the poem is filled with straight lines. The image of the women trudging in rows intersects with the plow marks fanning out over the field behind them. Then, all of a sudden, the grid-like composition Brodsky has so carefully constructed cracks and shatters: "The wind breaks / a chain of crows into shrieking links." He takes stock of the pieces:

> These visions are the final sign
> of an inner life that seizes
> any specter to which it feels kin
> till the specter scares off for good
> at the church bell of a creaking axle,
> at the metal rattle of the world as it
> lies reversed in a rut of water,
> at a starling soaring into cloud.

It's a high moment in a poem that is otherwise bitter and mundane. Even in a world that "lies reversed in a rut of water," the inner life finds itself reflected in passing visions: the flight of birds, the light sparking in strangers' eyes. What struck me most, living in my own reversed world, is that for Brodsky these visions did not offer hope the world would change, only that, whether or not it changed, something of that life would endure.

I had been raised in the multicultural, bubblegum nineties. Like many other children of the upper-middle class, I watched *Captain Planet*, went to cross-cultural friendship camps and joined social-justice youth groups. Our generation was told that difference was only skin deep, that in America you could accomplish anything with enough hard work, that we could be the change we wanted to see. Like good campers, we marched to protest the invasion of Iraq, wrote letters against NAFTA and for human rights, voted for Obama, went vegetarian. At a certain point it occurred to us there was no evidence any of this was working. The market crashed; the gap between rich and poor yawned into an abyss. Congress was paralyzed, and racism, far from diminishing in Obama's presidency, seemed to become more visible and virulent. *What is to be done?* we wondered. All the progressive values we had been taught, when knocked, sounded hollow. So our protests got smaller, cheekier and more digital. We made nihilistic jokes, followed meme accounts, started therapy. We talked about TV.

All of this is to say that Brodsky's strategy of switching off made a perverse kind of sense to me, even as it brushed up against my inculcated optimism. And yet, I thought: Shouldn't I fight that impulse?

"If a poet has any obligation to society," Brodsky said, "it is to write well. Being in the minority, he has no other choice." The Soviet trial judge is not the only one who has taken this attitude to indicate a lack of social conscience. The novelist and critic Keith Gessen, in a 2008 article for the *New York Times Book Review*, faulted Brodsky's generation of intellectuals and those who followed for being "powerless to stop Putin from terrorizing the country, not because they feared him, but because after the destruction of the Soviet Union they retreated into 'private life,' which is what they wanted all along." Gessen is a great fan of Brodsky the poet, but wishes he would be more of a critic. In a *New Yorker* essay from 2011, he condemned Brodsky for allowing himself to become a "propagandist for poetry." Gessen searched Brodsky's oeuvre in vain for an example that might undercut the unapologetic aestheticism that had "hardened into dogma." Not unlike the judge, Gessen seemed to demand of Brodsky, *How were you useful to the motherland?* How could someone of Brodsky's intelligence actually believe that aesthetics governs ethics and not the other way around?

As if cautious not to repeat the mistakes of Brodsky's generation, Gessen has embraced his public role in his own career as an intellectual. He co-founded *n+1* in 2004 with some fellow Harvard grads in New York City, and, in 2011, when a thousand protesters set up camp in Zuccotti Park, they eagerly joined the movement. Being academic types, they were less experienced than some of the other Occupiers when it came to practical matters of governance or logistics, so they contributed the way they knew how: they wrote and theorized. They published blog posts and put together a broadsheet called the *Occupy! Gazette*. In *Occupy!*, the anthology of reflections from these heady months that he coedited with Astra Taylor and the other editors of *n+1*, Gessen acknowledged the split within the park between those "highly educated" organizers and intellectuals like himself, who were "mostly in their late twenties and thirties, and mostly not living in the park," and the "kids who actually do live in the park." This division, he suggested, is not as bad as it might seem. Some dismissed the twenty-year-olds in the camp as crust punks or anarchists, but he admired their youthful idealism. At least they were *doing* something. "They actually think that coming to a faraway city and living in a concrete park could lead to political change," he marveled. "And they may be right!"

I, a twenty-one-year-old, watched the protests with interest and admiration from Chicago. By the time I started that poetry seminar, satellite marches and sleep-ins were being staged across the country. I read the reports on my laptop and clicked through the pictures my friends posted on Facebook from the encampments in downtown Chicago. Should I skip the poetry class, I wondered, and join the protest instead?

•

More than six years later, and one year into a national nightmare, we've grown tired. We try to keep our eyes open, even as they develop exhausted twitches. We throw cold water on our faces. We set multiple alarms. We protest, download apps to remind us to call our representatives, trawl the news until we dream of chyrons and Twitter time lines. Politics is the contrast filter that sharpens and distorts everything in view.

It's no wonder we seek clarity and direction from wiser minds. For many of us, this too can take on a quality of compulsion, as we obsessively pass around quotes from books we haven't read since college. The month after the election Hannah Arendt's *The Origins of Totalitarianism* sold at sixteen times its average rate, while a tweeted passage from *Achieving Our Country*, a book published twenty years ago by the philosopher Richard Rorty, went improbably viral. "The Frankfurt School Knew Trump Was Coming," the *New Yorker* announced in December 2016, as though our biggest mistake had been not listening to the critical theorists. Nothing could be more natural than to search for some light in the dark—but it's worth pausing to ask whether it's artists and critics we should be looking to for answers.

Every generation of intellectuals finds a way of coming to terms with the limits of their agency. Brodsky's chose poetry; mine and Gessen's took the train downtown. It's not a strict binary, of course: these two tendencies can coexist in the same individual and express themselves in different ways. But we might consider that switching off, for Brodsky, was a way of performing his social responsibility, not shirking it. In Brodsky's view, politics was one level of human existence, but it was a low rung. The business of poetry, he thought, is to "indicate something more . . . the size of the whole ladder." He held that "art is not a better, but an alternative existence . . . not an attempt to escape reality but the opposite, an attempt to animate it." What compels a poet to write is less "a concern for one's perishable flesh" than "the urge to spare certain things of one's world—of one's personal civilization—one's own non-semantic continuum."

I think this was his answer to Gessen's challenge. When there is scarce room for political maneuvering, when the prevailing cultural values are sucked of all significance, making art that rejects tired tropes and social themes may not be simply an expression of personal freedom, the luxury of the secure and uninvested. It can model independent thought and attentiveness, preserving not just the integrity of the self but also that of the culture one sees being degraded before one's eyes.

This is not art for art's sake; it needn't be quietist or resigned. We can believe in the power of art and defend it vigorously without indulging in fantasies of its social utility. In times like these, we need critics. But we also need poets, who can transmute experience into art and sniff out platitudes. Those who search for possibilities in foregone conclusions and hearts in fiery motors.

•

Later in his life, after immigrating to the United States, Brodsky was invited to give a speech to a class of graduating seniors at an East Coast liberal arts college. Unsurprisingly, he avoided the inspirational pabulum that normally stuffs commencement speeches, opting instead for a commentary on the practice of "turning the other cheek" as a means of combating social evil. The speech does not give clear directives—it barely qualifies as advice—but it does complicate Gessen's picture of the late Brodsky as a mere "propagandist for poetry."

Brodsky gives an account of the standard interpretation of the lines of scripture that inspired this doctrine of passive resistance and then goes on to mention the ending, which is less commonly quoted. The idea is not just to turn the cheek to the person who strikes you—you are also supposed to give him your coat:

> No matter how evil your enemy is, the crucial thing is that he is human; and although incapable of loving another like ourselves, we nonetheless know that evil takes root when one man starts to think that he is better than another. (This is why you've been hit on your right cheek in the first place.) At best, therefore, what one can get from turning the other cheek to one's enemy is the satis-

faction of alerting the latter to the futility of his action. "Look," the other cheek says, "what you are hitting is just flesh. It's not me. You can't crush my soul."

The moral stakes of this struggle are high precisely because they are personal. The objective isn't to appeal to your bully's sense of compassion or pride or guilt (for these are all easy to suppress), but to "expose his senses and faculties to the meaninglessness of the whole enterprise: the way every form of mass production does," and emerge with your spirit intact.

This lecture reveals another dimension of Brodsky's ethics of refusal. Switching off is not about wallowing in silence or withdrawing into blissful ignorance; it is about making sure that the static doesn't deafen you to music.

V

THINKING
AHEAD

Innocence Abroad

THE AWE AND SHOCK OF
SUZY HANSEN

by Ursula Lindsey

ISSUE 16 | SPRING 2018

It's remarkable, given the propensity of American officials, journalists and academics to refer to other nations and cultures as immature and underdeveloped, how frequently and consistently Americans themselves are described as children, by both foreign authors and American writers themselves. "We have not grown up enough to accept that America has never been innocent at all," the novelist Steve Erikson wrote in 1995 in an essay about American rage. In Henry James's *The Ambassadors* (1903), a character says of his American relatives, "They're children; they play at life!"

James's novel follows the middle-aged Lambert Strether as he is sent to Paris from Woollett, Massachusetts in order to retrieve Chad Newsome, the wayward son of his fiancée and heir to the family fortune. Woollett is a town that suffers from a paucity of opinions, the veneration of material success, the suspicion of foreigners and the conviction that the local way of seeing things is the only and the best. Strether, however, quickly leaves Woollett behind, so much so that he bungles his assignment. Far from being an American ambassador, whose mission is to convince Chad to abandon his French mistress, return home and resume his proper American role and identity, Strether becomes a double agent, an advocate for that mistress and for the precious freedom and insight Chad has acquired abroad.

In James's work, Americans are transformed by travel to Europe (which is as far abroad as they ever go). They arrive burdened by ignorance and often wealth, and inevitably they make life-changing mistakes. The characters who learn to "see" the world as it is become adults. In one of the most memorable exchanges in *The Ambassadors*, Strether bursts out at a young American artist: "Live all you can; it's a mistake not to. It doesn't so much matter what you do in particular so long as you have your life. If you haven't had that what have you had?" Strether is speaking out of regret for his own missed life, the life he might have led if he had had the courage to settle abroad himself. The knowledge acquired by Strether and other Jamesian travelers is precious, and it always comes at a steep price: in *The Portrait of a Lady*, Isabel Archer loses her freedom; in *The Wings of the Dove*, Milly Theale loses her life. Strether sacrifices his own engagement back home and the chance of a new attachment in Europe. Yet these characters are changed so utterly that their lost innocence is what becomes foreign to them, impossible to pine for, irrelevant.

•

Suzy Hansen is the anti-James. Her *Notes on a Foreign Country*, published last summer, is a remarkably glum account of being an expatriate, unlikely to inspire many young Americans to head out into the world. Hansen's years abroad in the 21st century "were not a joyous romp of self-discovery and romance, the kind we see in movies," she writes early on in the book; instead, they "were more of a shattering and a shame, and even now, I still don't know myself."

In 2007, Hansen, then a 29-year-old reporter at the *New York Observer*, was awarded a fellowship for young Americans wanting to undertake research projects abroad. She decided to move to Istanbul, partly because James Baldwin, her favorite writer, had lived there in the sixties. Once in Turkey, however, she bumped up against her own ignorance about American interventionism. To Hansen's great confusion and discomfiture, Turkish friends kept mentioning the ways in which the U.S. had shaped their country's politics, military and economy.

The foreign country in the title of Hansen's book, then, is mainly the United States, which she learned to see for the first time, with a painful clarity, from Turkey and several other countries in the re-

gion. In one of the most evocative passages in the book, she describes growing up on the Jersey Shore. Life in her hometown, the
aptly-named Wall, is inward-looking, rooted, circumscribed:

> We went to church on Sundays until church time was usurped
> by soccer games. I do not remember a strong sense of civic en-
> gagement; not with the community, or for the environment, or
> for poor people. I had the feeling, rather, that people could take
> things from you if you didn't stay vigilant. Our goals remained lo-
> cal: homecoming queen, state champs, a scholarship to Trenton
> State, cookouts in the backyard. The lone Chinese kid studied
> hard and went to Berkeley; the Indian went to Yale. Black people
> never came to Wall. The world was white, Christian; the world
> was us.

Hansen argues that her lack of awareness about America's role in
the world was structural, intentional—an ignorance that many
Americans, particularly white Americans, wear like mental armor,
allowing them to believe, against all evidence, that our political and
military interventions abroad are always necessary, successful and
well-intentioned. "I would never have admitted it, or thought to say
it," Hansen explains, "but looking back, I know that deep in my consciousness I thought that America was at the end of some evolutionary spectrum of civilization, and everyone else was trying to catch
up." Hence, she assumed that in Istanbul, she would assess how
well Turkey was meeting certain U.S. standards ("democratization,"
"modernization"); she would also think about "solutions" to Islam,
because "that's what Americans always do."

Hansen occasionally mentions *The Fire Next Time* (1963), in which
Baldwin describes the willful, violent blindness of white Americans,
and their determination not to face "reality—the fact that life is
tragic." Baldwin himself left America for France and Turkey because
he found life there false and unbearable, a physical and psychological assault. At least African Americans, he wrote, possess "the great
advantage of having never believed the collection of myths to which
white Americans cling: that their ancestors were all freedom-loving
heroes, that they were born in the greatest country the world has

ever seen, or that Americans are invincible in battle and wise in peace." Hansen read this passage long before moving to Turkey, but one of her points is how often we can know something but not really accept it. She writes: "Even when I disagreed with America's policies, I always believed in our inherent goodness, in my own."

From Istanbul, Hansen traveled to report from Greece, Egypt and Afghanistan, only to discover from wry, patient locals that the crisis each country is currently undergoing can be explained by a history in which U.S. intervention figures prominently. In Afghanistan, she attends a Fourth of July party at the American embassy. There is a billboard outside the embassy that reads: "THE U.S. EMBASSY WOULD BE GRATEFUL IF ANY OF OUR FRIENDS WHO HAVE INFORMATION ON TERRORIST ACTIVITY OR THREATS TO PLEASE COME TO THIS GATE." There is a five-by-seven-foot American flag made out of cupcakes. The red, white and blue balloons keep popping from the heat, setting the crowd of Afghans and Americans, fearful of snipers, on edge. General David Petraeus and the U.S. ambassador dodge difficult questions from Afghan guests and deliver platitudes.

This is all very well observed. A different sort of writer would have made something barbed and darkly funny of this scene. Hansen seems headed in that direction, but instead she stops, on cue, to wring her hands: "Those bland, company-man words. In Kabul these words sounded criminal. These were loveless, soulless words. How could we speak to Afghans like this? . . . No one believed in the words they were saying, and yet this language was about real things: flesh and death and war, people's homelands, and their children."

It strikes me as a luxury and nearly an affront to be as sentimental and naive as this. It's not that we shouldn't sympathize with Afghans and others—it's that such an expression of sympathy, in which one's own guilt and shock takes center stage, isn't worth much. Meanwhile, many of the people I've met out in the world who are really up against it—who by circumstance or choice live terribly exposed—wear the risks they run matter-of-factly, the bearers of what Baldwin calls an "ironic tenacity." They are knowing, daring, uncomplaining. I guarantee you they waste no time being shocked by the platitudes of U.S. ambassadors.

Hansen notes that when Albert Camus visited New York in 1946, he wrote in his journal that America was a "country where everything is done to prove that life isn't tragic." Camus held that "one must reject the tragic after having looked at it, not before." Hansen does the looking but not the rejecting. She remains transfixed by the tragic and her own response to it, casting pretty standard culture shock as emotional catastrophe. Her Turkish lessons are "soul-shattering." In Cairo, she is "lonely and clumsy, wreaking havoc on things I knew nothing about." In Afghanistan, "it was my mere existence, I felt, that did damage enough. I wanted nothing else but to withdraw myself."

When I read this, a phrase of another writer immediately came to mind. "I hate tragedy," wrote Waguih Ghali, a penniless alcoholic and suicidal Egyptian who, in self-imposed exile after Gamal Abdel Nasser came to power in 1956, wrote one of my favorite novels. *Beer in the Snooker Club* contains passages that still make me laugh out loud. Egypt, the Arab country I lived in for many years, has one of the best and darkest strains of humor I've ever encountered. It does not come natural to me but I have often witnessed its gift, the way it can lift the pall of fear and death. It's the laughter of survivors, balanced right on the edge of hope and hopelessness.

•

Hansen and I are both middle-class white American women, of about the same age, who worked as journalists in the Middle East during the Arab Spring. What first intrigued me about *Notes on a Foreign Country* is the way her experience seemed a mirror image of mine: full of parallels, yet almost perfectly reversed. Her description of Wall is as exotic to me as Istanbul was to her.

My parents were unhappy children of the Los Angeles suburbs who grew into well-read hippies. In 1970, right after graduating college, they headed to Europe—following Proust to Paris, and Joyce to Trieste. After several failed attempts to relocate to Europe, they finally managed to settle our family in Rome when I was six. Nine years later my father joined the State Department and began working on programs that promoted English-language learning. One of his postings was in Cairo.

Some of my earliest memories are of our yearly transatlantic flights home, of the endless hum of the airplane engine. Back home my sister and I marveled at ice-cream sundaes, multiplexes, shopping malls and pristine empty summer sidewalks. Every summer we made some momentous pop-culture discovery: the music of Whitney Houston; tie-dye t-shirts; roller coasters.

When I went off to college, my father gave me a copy of *In Search of Lost Time*, thereby ensuring I would be a comparative literature major like him and would head to France after graduation. In my early twenties I moved to Paris and then to Cairo, just as the U.S. was preparing to invade Iraq for the second time. Egypt hadn't figured at all in my readings or my imagination, and I had to catch up on the spot; reading novelists like Naguib Mahfouz, Waguih Ghali and Sonallah Ibrahim was another way to get to know the country. I ended up staying in Egypt, against all my expectations, for twelve years.

I witnessed the eighteen days of extraordinary protests that ended with the toppling of President Hosni Mubarak; the months of protests and violence and backroom deals that followed; the election of an Islamist government; the toppling of *that* government and the massacre of at least eight hundred of its supporters; and then the restoration of "order," meaning a repressive military regime that has detained and tortured tens of thousands of people, and which my government supports.

Since 2014, I have lived in Morocco. My parents have retired to Northern California. They are happy there. Now, every summer, I make the transatlantic flight with my husband and son. We marvel at the multiplexes and perfect sidewalks; at the price of produce at the farmer's markets; at all the homeless people and the way no one litters.

Despite our entirely different upbringings, I have some of the same reflexes as Hansen. Almost certainly, one of the reasons her naivete irritates me is because I fight the tendency myself. I smile too much and like to be considered "nice." I over-tip and insist on carrying my own bags. I am also, despite all my travels, sheltered— privileged by my race, class and passport—and sometimes embarrassingly earnest. When Donald Trump was elected I was distraught at the idea that he would set foot in *the White House*, a building I didn't know I had any particular feeling about until then.

Hansen presents *Notes on a Foreign Country* as the antithesis of the *Eat Pray Love* variety of self-discovery tale. And yet hers is also a journey of individual enlightenment. It may no longer be fashionable to speak with authority or to find pleasure abroad—but the American preoccupation with personal growth is unwavering. Hansen presents her biases as representative, nearly universal; and yet she insists on treating the U.S. role in the world as her personal discovery and burden.

"American innocence never dies," Hansen writes in the book's final pages. "That pain in my heart is my innocence. The only difference is that now I know it. If there was anything fully shattered during my years abroad, it was faith in my own objectivity, as a journalist or as a human being." In the end, for Hansen the relationship between the U.S. and the rest of the world boils down to how one American feels, which may be the most American move of all.

•

Hansen has an ambivalent relationship to journalism. In her memoir, she presents herself as a hapless, self-doubting reporter. She twice repeats the charge that Western journalists are akin to "spies," and lets pass several conspiracy theories on the grounds that their underlying paranoia is historically justified.

It's a good impulse for journalists to be aware of the limits and the misuses of their work, but at the moment I would rather defend this flawed profession—it's necessary to any functioning democracy and is under unprecedented assault. We journalists work with the facts but our vision of them is often rushed, partial, imperfect. Yet that's a responsibility we can shoulder—the responsibility of being storytellers. And in fact, Hansen's own reporting for the *New York Times Magazine* and other venues is vivid, confident and layered, particularly when it's focused on Turkey, a country she has clearly come to know well.

I asked my own hopelessly naive questions when I arrived in Egypt, in 2002, at the age of 23, and stumbled into journalism in Cairo, in the dingy offices of a local independent English-language magazine called the *Cairo Times*. We were all in our twenties (a few interns were teenagers), a boisterous mix of foreigners and Egyptians. I cringe to think of the articles I wrote back then. I wandered around in a fog of ignorance, awkwardness and exhilaration.

It may be more dangerous, uncomfortable and absurd than ever to be an American abroad. I think that makes it a better kind of adventure. Gaining knowledge of the world—even discomfiting, painful knowledge—is a joy and a liberation, not a chore or a penance. The wealth of the experience, however, doesn't always need to be made explicit, to be *put to use*, to be turned into an achievement, a narrative, a lesson in self-discovery. Telling other people about how travel transformed us is a bit like telling them our dreams; what is magically meaningful to us is rarely interesting to others. What's interesting, in our encounters with the broader world, isn't usually us—it's the world.

At the *Cairo Times* there were, of course, endless conversations about U.S. foreign policy, foreign aid, foreign military intervention. We excoriated the hypocrisy of "democracy promotion," and made fun of the stereotypes embedded in much Western media coverage. We led the way in investigating cases of torture and a crackdown on gay men. We fell in love with each other and formed lifelong friendships. We studied Arabic. We arrived at complicated, collective, mutating truths.

That remained the case throughout the Arab Spring and its ever more dire aftermath, as we struggled to make sense of events. The last year I was in Egypt, I worked at *Mada Masr*, an independent news site in English and Arabic that is blocked in Egypt today. Its reporters continue, against all odds, to have the courage to do their jobs. They publish their stories on Facebook; they are a small voice of reason, dissent and tolerance in a dark din of propaganda.

•

In 2011, the year of Mubarak's ouster, I interviewed a former member of the ruling party who was running for a seat in parliament. As the uprising fizzled—undercut by the army and the Islamists and Western powers concerned with "chaos"—men like him were re-emerging from the shadows and belligerently reasserting their version of reality. After bragging to me about his ability to direct whole towns in the south to vote for him (his family owned cement factories in the region), he opened his cell phone and began shaking it in my face and shouting at me that the Arab Spring was an American conspiracy. On his phone was a YouTube video of Condoleezza Rice making her infamous remark regarding the second Iraq war being the "birth pangs of a new Middle East." I don't remember the rest of the conversation with the cement king in detail, other than that it was heated—I couldn't tell if he was talking in bad faith or not, but I unfortunately rose to the bait, much to his delight. He couldn't believe he had an actual American journalist to yell at.

Today in the Arab world what looms behind most conspiracy theories is still the war in Iraq—the sense that American power is unstoppable and unaccountable, that Americans will do anything, say anything, just to bring an Arab country to its knees. It is hard to overstate the arrogance, callousness and devastation of the war, a crime for which no one has answered and for which Americans themselves have paid more than they seem to know. (But clearly we have an inkling, having elected two presidents who campaigned, more or less truthfully, on their opposition to the invasion.)

Hansen argues that American prosperity and identity are based on imperialism abroad as much as on racism at home. I agree, yet I have trouble seeing how most Americans prospered from the invasion of Iraq. Instead, I wonder at how much the fraudulent freedom we export abroad resembles the version we extol at home—a freedom that is undercut by economic bondage, by a barely concealed determination to disenfranchise so many.

At the same time, to explain everything through the lens of American power is to explain less. One ends up reflecting back the mirage of American omnipotence instead of the reality of U.S. blundering, blindness and internal dissent, of our inability to address the most basic needs of our own society (gun control, health care, an end to police brutality, economic inequality), let alone to confront global challenges such as climate change. One also risks turning all non-Americans into pawns, vassals and victims. Conspiracy theories that ascribe everything to American power diminish the responsibility of local regimes and elites, and the autonomy of people who have staked their own claim to the United States' proclaimed principles, challenging it to live up to its rhetoric.

•

When my Egyptian friends and I watch our presidents shake hands, I think we see the same thing: angry, sexist, greedy old men, entranced by brute force and bent on telling us who we are and where we belong. The stakes for non-Americans, as Hansen rightly notes, are much higher, and we bridge the divide through their generosity and our humility. But we don't have to be defined only by our nationalities.

For all his hard-bitten clarity, Baldwin expressed hope that America could see itself and could change "in order to deal with the untapped and dormant force of the previously subjugated, in order to survive as a human, moving, moral weight in the world." He argued for what I think of as a sort of useful idealism, one that acknowledges reality as it is but does not accept that it has to remain so. He wagered that people could be better than they are: "We are capable of bearing a great burden, once we discover that the burden is reality and arrive where reality is."

How do we come to that realization? One way is through books, which can lure us to foreign lands in the first place, and can share with others the wonders and terrors we have discovered abroad. Sometimes they can be as deep of an experience as travel itself, fundamentally rearranging our perspective.

I had that feeling recently while reading *American War* by Omar El Akkad, an Egyptian-Canadian author and a former journalist who, like Hansen, felt the need to write a book. Akkad opted for literature, and it was the right choice; the novel offers greater freedom than journalism, more range and ambiguity than memoirs, the means of unraveling complex truths.

Akkad describes a near future in which the world has been rav-
aged by climate change and the coastlines of the United States have
fallen into the sea. The federal government in Columbus, Ohio—the
District of Columbia is underwater—has outlawed fossil fuels, and
this interdiction has sparked a doomed and defiant insurrection in
the American South.

Americans are reportedly uninterested in anything foreign—
foreign news coverage, foreign literature—but Akkad tricks his readers with his title. Under the cover of fiction, he smuggles back home
violence that the U.S. has fostered yet denied around the world.
Henry James put Americans abroad, using foreign settings to bring
them into sharp relief and stage moments of self-revelation; Akkad
blurs the lines between home and abroad, and what he reveals are
the hidden connections and startling resonances between American reality and that of war-torn countries far away. Consequently, in
his novel the kinds of things that happen today in other parts of the
world—things we mistakenly think of as distant and unrelated to
us, the product of foreign dysfunction in which we have no hand—
happen in the United States. Rebel groups and militias compete
to recruit young Southerners to carry out suicide attacks; wayward
drones circle in the sky; whole states are put under siege.

The world's new inverted power relations are revealed gradually,
each discovery producing a jolt of surprise mixed with recognition.
The Arab region has, after the Fifth Spring revolution, finally swept
away dictators and kings, and unified to become an ascendant empire. This new power, alongside China, fans the flames of the American conflict to advance its own agenda. "Come now," says Yousef,
an operative of the Bouazizi Empire, "Everyone fights an American war." Yousef is old enough to remind his American comrade
of the time "when it was still your guns and our blood," a reference
to the many proxy wars the U.S. has fought.

Sarat, the novel's charismatic heroine, grows up in a refugee
camp, and loses her family in a vengeful raid by Northern militias,
a Sabra and Shatila-style massacre that takes place in Mississippi.
The young woman trains to become a freedom fighter, a terrorist. Akkad conveys not just the horror of war but the excitement of

being young and strong in the midst of it, of honing one's strength and picking a side to fight on. He conjures the appeal of the South's proud, misguided, underdog culture. In fact, what is remarkable about this oblique critique of U.S. foreign policy is how intimate and affectionate and compelling its depiction of a country tearing itself apart is. This dystopian United States is a moving place, alive with people acting as they do in conflicts everywhere: being vicious, brave, stupid, generous.

Sarat carries out daring attacks; she is imprisoned, tortured for years and broken by her captors. Of Sarat's waterboarding, Akkad writes: "The water moved, endless. She entered and exited death, her body no longer hers. Spasms of light and heat encased her; the mind seized with fear and panic. She drowned yet death would not come." What Akkad describes has happened in the real world, many times. But he makes it happen to an American heroine, a character whose very body, vividly rendered, one has come to love on the page.

•

For over a century, the United States has wielded extraordinary economic and military power. That power has shaped the world, and us. Abroad, it has often been used in ways that reveal our most undemocratic, exploitative, racist tendencies. But that we have betrayed our principles and hoarded our liberties does not make them empty—they are still worth claiming. Just as there are elements of our national culture worth admiring and cherishing.

But why is it so hard for us to admit that as human beings and moral agents, Americans are just like everyone else? Our lives and desires do not rank higher or lower; our motives and methods are not unique. The insistence on American exceptionalism as a personal birthright is not so much childish as adolescent: the desire to be declared inherently special, regardless of one's actions, and the nagging fear that one is not.

Perhaps the way for Americans to truly enter the world, as equals and adults, is not to take our power for granted or to renounce it, but to treat it, while we have it, as the historical contingency and the responsibility it is.

At one point, Sarat is asked whether she would take the chance to escape to safety. She declines. "Somewhere in her mind," writes Akkad, "an idea had begun to fester—perhaps the longing for safety was itself another kind of violence—a violence of cowardice, silence and submission. What was safety, anyway, but the sound of a bomb falling on someone else's home?"

This, Too, Was History

THE BATTLE OVER POLICE TORTURE AND
REPARATIONS IN CHICAGO'S SCHOOLS

by Peter C. Baker

ISSUE 18 | WINTER 2019

"What do you know about Jon Burge?"

Barely seven minutes into her black history elective on the morning of April 16th, Juanita Douglas was asking her students a question she'd never asked in a classroom before, not in 24 years of teaching in Chicago's public schools. She'd been preparing to ask the question for over a year, and she knew that for many of her students the conversation that followed would be painful. Disorienting. She didn't like the idea of causing them pain. She didn't want to make them feel overwhelmed or lost. But she thought, or at least hoped, that in the end the difficulty would be worth the trouble.

It was only second period. Several of Douglas's students—a mix of juniors and seniors—were visibly tired. A few slumped forward, heads on their desks. I was sitting in the back row, so I couldn't tell for sure, but I thought one or two might be fully asleep. Some were stealthily texting or scrolling through Snapchat. Others were openly texting or scrolling through Snapchat.

After a few seconds, Douglas repeated the question: "Do you know Jon Burge?"

A ragged chorus of noes and nopes and nahs.

"Tell me again what year you were born in," said Douglas, who is 54 and likes to playfully remind her students that they don't know everything about the world.

2000. 2001. 1999.

"Okay," she said. "Well . . . Welcome to Chicago."

Like so many new curriculum units in so many high schools across America, this one began with the teacher switching off the lights and playing a video. Who was Jon Burge? The video supplied the answer. Burge was a former Chicago Police Department detective and area commander. Between 1972 and 1991 he either directly participated in or implicitly approved the torture of at least—and this is an extremely conservative estimate—118 Chicagoans. Burge and his subordinates—known variously as the Midnight Crew, Burge's Ass Kickers and the A-Team—beat their suspects, suffocated them, subjected them to mock executions at gunpoint, raped them with sex toys, and hooked electroshock machines up to their genitals, their gums, their fingers, their earlobes, overwhelming their bodies with live voltage until they agreed: yes, they'd done it, whatever they'd been accused of, they'd sign the confession. The members of the Midnight Crew were predominantly white men. Almost all of their victims were black men from Chicago's South and West Sides. Some had committed the crimes to which they were forced to confess; many had not. The cops in question called the electroshock machines "nigger boxes."

The video cut to Darrell Cannon, one of the Midnight Crew's victims. He spoke about getting hauled by cops into a basement:

> I wasn't a human being to them. I was just simply another subject of theirs. They had did this to many others. But to them it was fun and games. You know, I was just, quote, a nigger to them, that's it. They kept using that word like that was my name ... They had no respect for me being a human being. I never expected, quote, police officers to do anything that barbaric, you know ... You don't continue to call me "nigger" throughout the day unless you are a racist. And the way that they said it, they said it so downright nasty. So there's no doubt in my mind that, in my case, racism played a huge role in what happened to me. Because they enjoyed this. This wasn't something that was sickening to them. None of them had looks on their faces like, ugh, you know, maybe we shouldn't do this much. *Nuh-huh.* They enjoyed it, they laughed, they smiled. And that is why my anger has been so high. Because I continuously see how they smile.

Text on the screen explained that Burge was fired in 1993, following a lawsuit that forced the Chicago Police Department to produce a report on his involvement in "systematic torture," written by its own Office of Professional Standards. After his firing Burge moved to Apollo Beach, Florida, where he ran a fishing business. In 2006 another internally commissioned report concluded that he'd been a torture ringleader, but still no charges were brought; the Illinois five-year statute of limitations for police brutality charges had by then expired. In 2008 FBI agents arrested Burge at his home, and creative federal prosecutors charged him—not with torture, but with perjury. In a 2003 civil case, Burge had submitted a sworn statement in which he denied ever taking part in torture. In 2010 a jury found him guilty. After the trial, jurors pointed out that the name of Burge's boat—*Vigilante*—hadn't helped his case.

As soon as the video ended and Douglas flipped the lights back on, her students—most of whom were, like her, black—started talking. Their confusion ricocheted around the room.

"How long did he get?"

"Four and a half years."

"He only got four and a half years?"

"That's what I'm saying."

"I really feel some type of way about this."

"Is he still alive?"

"I've got it on my phone."

"He didn't torture them alone. Why didn't anyone else get charged?"

"I've got it on my phone. He's still alive."

"I'm just . . . angry."

"He lives in Florida!"

"Didn't no one hear the screams?"

•

Douglas's students didn't yet know it, but they were not the only Chicago students wrestling with Jon Burge and the Midnight Crew last spring. In fact, teachers and students at each of the city's 644 public schools were figuring out how to talk about the cops on the

A-Team—and, by extension, the past and present of the fraught relationship between Chicago's police and Chicago's policed. Teachers were going down this path whether, in their hearts, they wanted to or not. There was no choice: it was an official requirement, codified in city law.

This classroom initiative is part of a historic, novel and perplexingly under-covered development in the ever more urgent search for solutions to the cumulative harm inflicted on Americans—especially black Americans—in the name of law and order. On May 6, 2015, in response to decades of local activism, Chicago's city council passed an ordinance officially recognizing that Burge and his subordinates had engaged in torture, condemning that torture, and offering his victims (or at least some of them) compensation for their suffering. The ordinance is a singular document in American history. Torture accountability—even basic torture *honesty*—has been a perennial nonstarter in American politics, all the more so in our post-9/11 condition of perpetual war. Reparations, especially those with a racial component, have long been treated as, alternately: an incoherent absurdity; a frightening threat; a nice-sounding but impractical rallying cry; or, more recently, in the wake of the National Magazine Award-nominated *Atlantic* essay by Ta-Nehisi Coates, as a worthy (but still essentially utopian) demand. But within Chicago city limits, reparations for police torture isn't just a thought exercise, a rhetorical expression about what *should* exist in a better world. It's Chicago City Council Resolution SR2015–256: the law of the land.

If this is the first you've heard of all this, you are hardly alone. In the years since SR2015–256 passed, I have again and again found myself informing people of its existence. This has included prominent national experts on torture and torture accountability, Chicago police officers and lifelong Chicagoans of all races with a professed interest in racial justice. On the North Side of the city—and certainly in its northern suburbs, where I live—I do not think it is ridiculous to suggest that there are more people of all races who can summarize Coates's "The Case For Reparations" than those who are familiar with the historic reparations experiment unfolding right now in their own metropolitan area.

If people know anything about that experiment, they likely know that it involved some money: a pool of $5.5 million from which vetted Midnight Crew victims could receive a maximum of $100,000 each, regardless of whether their coerced confessions had been false or not—regardless, that is, of whether, in the eyes of the law, they had ultimately been judged guilty or innocent. By this point, several of Burge's victims had pried civil settlements from the city, some comprising millions of dollars. This strategy was more available to some than to others, depending on the jury-friendliness of their biographies (and rap sheets). The vast majority of the civil settlements were compensations less for torture than for wrongful conviction. Officially, like all civil settlements, they were not *for* anything at all; they were just transfers of money, with no admission of wrongdoing or even agreed-upon findings of fact. They therefore did nothing to address what many survivors, in Chicago and elsewhere, identify as one of torture's most enduring wounds: the unwillingness of their fellow citizens and government to adequately recognize exactly what happened.

In addition to the cash payouts, SR2015–256 contained a handful of other benefits for the Midnight Crew's victims, including free tuition at the city's community colleges and free access to a new psychological counseling center to be opened on the South Side. (This counseling center, the ordinance specified, was to operate a model similar to the one used by the Marjorie Kovler Center, a famous torture rehabilitation facility on Chicago's North Side. The Kovler Center welcomes survivors of political violence from around the world—but not, its website warns, from America or any "place under U.S. control.") In recognition of the fact that torture's effects reach beyond the lives of individual victims, these services were made available to all members of survivors' immediate families, and in some cases to their grandchildren.

The ordinance also pledged the city to take two concrete steps to counteract its decades-long tradition of trying to make the Burge story disappear. These two promises will likely end up being the most controversial parts of the law, because they deal not with bureaucratic payouts but with attempted modifications to Chicago's public history—to the story the city tells itself about policing. First,

Chicago officials would work with activists to design and erect a memorial to the city's police-torture survivors. Second, the city's public schools would henceforth be required to add "a lesson about the Burge case and its legacy" to the official history curriculum for eighth and tenth graders. To many of the activists who fought for the reparations package, the curriculum was its most meaningful component, precisely because of what it asked from the city: not money, but time and talk, however awkward or uncomfortable that talk might be.

The memorial design and site selection process is still underway. But last August, city officials held a press conference to announce that, after two years of development, the new curriculum—titled "Reparations Won"—was ready for the children of Chicago.

•

Chicago is one of America's most racially diverse metropolises, but also one of its most racially segregated: a patchwork of different social and economic worlds that know relatively little about each other. For this reason, my original hope was to watch the curriculum being taught in schools all across the city. What would lessons about the Midnight Crew look like in resource-starved black schools on the South and West Sides? How would the same curriculum be taught in predominantly Latino classrooms? (There are more Latino students than students of any other racial background in Chicago schools.) Or in the relatively diverse magnet schools found on the North Side, well stocked with Advanced Placement and International Baccalaureate classes? What about schools in the almost-burbs—just inside the city line—that are disproportionately populated by cops, firefighters and other city workers, in classrooms full of their children and nephews and nieces? (In Chicago, city employees are required to live within city limits.) I wanted to see it all—and maybe, by stitching together detailed observations from classrooms across the city, play some part, however minor, in the effort to put Chicago's separate worlds in conversation with each other.

Juanita Douglas was the only teacher out of dozens I asked who opened the doors of her classroom to me. The curriculum was too important, she said, for its rollout to go completely undocumented. The Chicago public-school system thought otherwise. A few days after the press conference announcing the curriculum, I contacted the district's notoriously evasive press office. To my surprise, I was quickly put in touch with Michael Passman, then the director of media communications. Passman initially sounded supportive— warmly supportive, even—of my plan to watch the curriculum in action in schools across the city. But this phone call was the last time I ever heard from Passman, despite dozens of messages I left on his voicemail, in his inbox, on his deputy's voicemail, in his deputy's inbox and with their office secretary. Teachers I met kept telling me I was welcome to sit in on their class—so long as their principals approved. Several principals said it was fine with them—so long as CPS approved. CPS told me to be patient. Other journalists told me they were hearing the same thing. Once I happened to get through to Passman's deputy, who told me not to worry: a plan for journalists who wanted to observe the curriculum was just a day or two from being released. This was the last I ever heard from her.

Because Douglas is not an eighth- or tenth-grade history teacher, she was not required to be teaching the curriculum. But she was one of many teachers across the city who elected to do so anyway this year for the benefit of current juniors and seniors, who otherwise would have graduated without learning about Burge. This past April and May, I spent eighteen mornings in her classroom at Lincoln Park High School, observing two back-to-back sections of her black history class* as they worked through "Reparations Won."

Before my first day, reading over the curriculum and imagining myself in Douglas's shoes, I felt overwhelmed by the visceral intensity of the material alone. Once I was in her classroom, though, I quickly realized the presence of another challenge, one that will surely be obvious to any teacher. It was the problem of shared knowledge, and how little of it Douglas could presume. This went far be-

---

*Throughout this piece, for ease of reading, I have composited observations from both of these sections into one class. Douglas taught a third section in the afternoon, which I did not attend.

yond knowing who had and who hadn't heard of Jon Burge. From day-to-day, she couldn't even be sure who had done the previous night's reading, and so she often started class with a series of questions designed to get everyone on the same page about the basics.

"I need to understand what you understand about this situation," she said on the second day of the curriculum. "What were the methods of torture that you put down? What did you write?"

She pointed at a boy near the back of the class.

"Uh . . . they were shocked, burned, beaten and tied up."

She pointed at another boy, toward the front.

"They were held for days without food and water."

One of his neighbors chimed in: "They were left naked for days."

Most of her students were black, and some were Latino, Asian-American, biracial, multiracial. Just one was white. Though Lincoln Park is a prosperous North Side neighborhood, most of them lived on the South or West Side, and came north every morning because the high school that used to be in their neighborhood is now closed. Some were, for high schoolers, relatively informed about U.S. history: when, on the second day of the curriculum, they read about Burge's time in the army—his posting in a POW camp in Vietnam and the possibility that this was where he'd first learned about electroshock torture—they nodded along, and made comments indicating their familiarity with other Vietnam-era atrocities. Other students, it seemed, were completely lost: when asked, many raised their hands to indicate they did not know what a prisoner-of-war camp was.*

Some students had been to Black Lives Matter protests, or read

* There was no room or time for a detour into Chicago's status as one of many nodes in the network connecting Vietnam, U.S. policing and the War on Terror. An investigation by the *Guardian* published in 2015 told the story of Richard Zuley, a contemporary of Burge's on the Chicago police force who used comparably brutal interrogation methods. As a Navy reservist, he sometimes helped with counterterrorism missions in the pre-9/11 years, and when the military prison at the U.S. military base at Guantanamo Bay opened in Cuba, Zuley was called in to help extract information from a high-profile detainee. There, in the words of the *Guardian* reporter, he "supercharged" his Chicago-honed techniques for use on suspected terrorists.

about mass incarceration and the New Jim Crow. Others had never been to any protest of any kind in their lives. Some students came to class wide awake, visibly enthusiastic, caffeinated. Others showed up looking exhausted, or like they were counting down the hours until the end of class, until lunch, until prom, until graduation. Some came to school every day, and were already thinking about college. Some came now and then, and were not sure they would graduate. Some had family members whose lives had been deeply marked by interactions with Chicago's cops and courts and jails and prisons. Some had family members who were cops, or used to be. It was Douglas's job to teach them all.

•

The first few days were heavy on context: on white Chicago's long history of resistance to its black population, from redlining to street riots; on Burge's upbringing in the all-white South Side neighborhood of Deering, which, during his lifetime, became an all-black neighborhood; on the city's intentional overcrowding of black neighborhoods and schools; on the escalation of the police "war on crime" in black neighborhoods; and, finally, on the first allegations against the Midnight Crew, and how they were ignored by then-Cook County State's Attorney Richard M. Daley, who would go on to become mayor.

On the fourth day, the class watched another video, this one detailing the case of Ronald Kitchen, a Midnight Crew victim who, largely on the basis of his tortured confession, was found guilty of murdering two women and three children and sent to death row. Beginning in 1990, he spent 21 years before his conviction was vacated and a judge declared him innocent.

The video featured footage from the 2011 deposition of Detective Michael Kill, one of Kitchen's torturers. In this footage, Kill is seventy and long retired. Wiry and full of contempt, he leans back in his chair, as if keeping his distance from something that smells bad. Offscreen, Kitchen's lawyer asks Kill whether he made a practice of using the n-word in his interrogations.

"Sure I did," says Kill.

How often?

"I would say I used it as many times as I had to."

But why?

"Well," Kill says, his grimace intensifying, "how many inches of tape are in your recorder?" "How about a million, for starters?" he suggests.

Kitchen's lawyer asks him why he used the n-word so much.

Kill shakes his head, still grimacing. "Trying to explain police work to you," he says to the lawyer, "is like trying to explain physics to my grandson—who is three years old." He used the word, he explains, to make suspects feel comfortable. To show them he understood their world, knew their language. "You're not there," he says. "You haven't been there. You don't understand it, okay? You have to live it."

No, Kill says, he never beat Kitchen. Never tortured Kitchen. Why would he do something like that, he asks rhetorically, and risk getting fired, losing his pension?

No, he knew nothing about anyone beating or torturing Ronald Kitchen. Jon Burge was his boss, sure. But he hardly knew the guy. Couldn't really tell you anything about him.

Many of Douglas's students were visibly upset by Kill: by what he was saying, by how casually he was saying it, by his apparent disdain for the very idea that anyone might think anything he'd done would require an explanation. "Can we turn it off?" asked a boy seated next to me, quietly and plaintively. But the longer the video went on, the more the kids started making fun of Kill: they knew, after all, that the old man's denials hadn't carried the day; that the state had set Kitchen free, that the city had settled his civil case for $6.15 million. They started laughing at Kill's clipped speech, his old Chicago accent, his pissy evasions. At one point in the video, Kill admits that he heard Kitchen whimpering in his cell. But he insists this was not due to any mistreatment but instead to some "blood pressure stuff." A Latina girl, one of Douglas's most reliable participants in class discussions, snickered and mimed taking a picture of Kill's scowling face on her phone, suggesting what a good meme it would make. "When you know you got caught," she said, laughing.

The next day, the class watched footage of Kitchen himself, filmed after he was released from jail but before he won his settlement. Someone off-camera asks him to describe his post-release life. Kitchen tells them he hardly sleeps. That the mere sight of a Chicago police car sends him into a full-body terror, which is why he's had to leave Chicago, the only city he ever knew. "It's hard," he says. "It's hard, it's hard. It's like a dream to me, sitting up here with you. It's like, at any moment, this could get taken away from me all over again."

It had been easy, perhaps, to joke about Michael Kill: a caricature of an old white villain on the wrong side of history. But there were no jokes to tell about Ronald Kitchen. "Do you know how many of the police went to jail?" asked a black girl toward the front of the class, referring to all the other Midnight Crew members besides Burge. It wasn't the first time one of Douglas's students had posed the question, and it wouldn't be the last. Each time, the answer was the same: zero.

"How do you grow from there?" asked a Latina girl. "How do you grow from such a horrible time in your life?"

After class that day, I stayed behind to look at what everyone had written on their reflection sheets. Douglas collected these almost every day, and she often let me look at them, wanting me to understand that the reactions I saw during class were only part of the story. Many of her students rarely spoke unless forced to. On their reflection sheets, however, freed from their worry about how a roomful of their fellow teenagers would respond, these same students would often write searching, poignant reflections, and pose deep questions ("why haven't we heard about this?" one of them wrote after the very first day of "Reparations Won"). On the day of the Kitchen video, their comments were particularly painful to read:

THAT COULD BE ME!

This affects how my life will be, because when I decide to create a family I will constantly be in fear if my husband is safe or my children if I have a son I have to fear he may get stopped by the police.

it could be my boyfriend, dad, cousins, etc.

This is stuff that I see in movies and may encourage if I don't like the bad guy, but it's unimaginable to think about in real life

this was like being a slave, but in the 90s

My dad just got pulled over recently and he wasn't tortured but what if this did happen to him?

My father was also framed with something he didn't do. (He's been in there since I was 3 and is getting out in 2027.)

•

The longer I spent in Douglas's class, the more I wished I'd managed to find a way into more schools. Some teachers met with me, or spoke with me on the phone, to recall their experiences with the curriculum, but there was no substitute for being there: for taking in the atmosphere in the room as a group of young people made contact with the Burge saga. I came to feel that this atmosphere was history itself—not the professional intellectual enterprise regulated by peer review and professional standards, not the subject of polished magazine articles, but the living tangle of connections between past and present that is always available to us, sometimes as inspiration or solace, sometimes a burden, most often both at once. This sense of history, of course, will be central to any serious attempt at reparations in America. At Lincoln Park High, I was watching students dive into the living tangle—watching them pull out this strand, that strand, and ask what they meant, where they belonged.

I was especially curious about what was going on at other schools because of the criticisms of the curriculum that had surfaced in local media. On September 14, 2017—less than a month after the curriculum was unveiled—the now-defunct local news site *DNAinfo* ran a story about a meeting between parents, faculty and staff at Edison

Park Elementary, on the cop-heavy Northwest Side. All of the parents quoted in the article were opposed to "Reparations Won."

"You're taking eighth graders and trying to mold their minds with material that is highly confrontational and controversial," said Angela McMillin, who described herself as "infuriated, appalled and disgusted" by the curriculum. "It's contradictory to how they live their personal lives with their families, where they eat dinner every night and celebrate Christmas . . . I think it's deplorable." McMillin wanted to opt her daughter, an eighth grader, out of the curriculum.

The school's principal, Jeffrey Finelli, informed her that this would not be possible. "It would be a little like saying, 'I don't like quadratic equations, so I'm going to opt out of algebra,'" Finelli said.

Emily Skowronek, a social-studies teacher who would be teaching the curriculum, was also present at the meeting. She promised, in the paraphrase of Alex Nitkin, the *DNAinfo* reporter, to "leave the Burge episode squarely in the past." "There are a lot of bad apples in every profession," Skowronek said. "And we'll try to portray that to our kids."

The week after Nitkin's article was published, another story appeared about Northwest Side parents unhappy with the curriculum. This one was published by *Chicago City Wire*, a subsidiary of Local Government Information Services, which is a content farm run by conservative activists. LGIS employs low-paid freelancers from around the world to write newsy-looking pieces that embody conservative viewpoints and seed them in outlets across Chicagoland. Like the *DNAinfo* piece, this one quoted Angela McMillin. "It's disgusting that it happened," she said of the Midnight Crew's torture. She wouldn't even let her daughter watch *Law and Order*: Why would she want her reading about "a man's testicles being electrocuted or guns being jammed down men's throats?" Plus, she added, the curriculum will "make a further racially divided community."

I contacted McMillin and several other attendees of the Edison Park meeting, hoping to learn more about their objections. Most people did not write or call me back; of those who did, all refused to speak to me, even anonymously. One person, explaining their refusal, wrote:

After the article came out from *DNA*, the reaction was kind of like a lynch mob . . . people from other parts of the city were really nasty and mean and not at all considerate of the huge amount of parents that work for the police department in our area and parents of students that attend our school. It was actually said how racist we were that we were even questioning the curriculum.

This, too, was history.

•

The longer I spent in Douglas's class, the more I saw her oscillating—sometimes from day-to-day, sometimes within the same lesson—between two different takeaways from the material at hand.

Takeaway One stressed the horror of it all, and the deeply systemic nature of that horror: all the cops and prosecutors and judges and city officials (mayors!) who had turned a deaf ear to the complaints of torture for so long, afraid of what they would mean, if true, about their professions, their jobs, the convictions they'd won, the sentences they'd passed down, the city they'd made. The reparations bill had passed, but many likely victims of police torture remained in jail. The state had established a Torture Inquiry and Relief Commission and given it the authority to re-examine cases and fast-track them back into the courts. But the commission had been swamped by petitions and struggled with funding. In 2017, the director estimated that, at its current pace, it would need 23 years just to evaluate the petitions it had already received.

From this perspective, the justice system was something between a broken ideal and a rotten lie, a noble-sounding rhetorical scrim that overlays and obscures a system of inequality and exploitation.

"I'm still confused," a girl said one day. What she was confused about was all the other cops besides Burge who had tortured. "How did they not go to jail?"

Douglas gave a tight smile, the smile of a person trying not to give in to the unpleasantness of the news they had to deliver. "You expect things to work the way they're supposed to work, not the way they actually work," she said.

Douglas pushed Takeaway One because she wanted her students to understand the truth of the world they lived in—but also, it was clear, because she wanted them to be safe. More than once, she drew her students' attention to the case of Marcus Wiggins, a black thirteen-year-old tortured by the Midnight Crew. "Why would they torture a thirteen-year-old? Why are they torturing a thirteen-year-old? I need an answer."

A Latino boy in the front row began to venture a response. "For suspected—"

Douglas cut him off. "But *why*? I want you to look at everybody in this room."

He hesitated. "Maybe . . . because they can. They're using their authority."

Douglas nodded, then pushed the point a step further. You might think of yourself as kids, she told them, but that didn't mean "they" would see you that way too. "You might be playing. You might think: I'm a kid. But no." This was why it was important for them to be careful. Important not to joke around—not to act like kids—in the presence of cops. Important not to assume that things work the way they're supposed to work. During a discussion about the Ronald Kitchen case, a rail-thin boy in what looked to me like an updated version of nineties skater wear posed a question: "Like, what was special about Kitchen so the police went after him versus any other kid on the block?"

"I don't want to say this," said Douglas. "But it could happen to you."

"It doesn't seem that way," he said.

"But it is that way," said Douglas.

Of course, if Takeaway One was all there was, the curriculum would be an extended meditation on the intolerable harshness of the world; and no one involved in its creation or implementation wanted that to be its only message to Chicago's teenagers. And so, Takeaway Two stressed the importance of individual choices, even in the face of systemic injustice. This was why the curriculum was called "Reparations Won": it was meant to be more than a catalog of woe. It was also a testament to the possibility of pushing back and changing the world. There were all the activist groups who kept showing up, year after year, decade after decade, asking for torture accountability. One of these groups, We Charge Genocide, even sent a delegation of young Chicagoans to Switzerland in 2014 to talk about Chicago police in front of the United Nations Committee Against Torture. (One member of that delegation, Douglas told them, was a Lincoln Park alumnus—one of her former students.) There were the lawyers who took the cases of Midnight Crew victims long before anyone had even heard of the Midnight Crew. There was Joey Mogul, the lawyer who wrote out the reparations ordinance as an entry for a conceptual art show with a torture-accountability theme. There was the county medical examiner who insisted, despite police pressure, on making a formal record of the injuries sustained by Andrew Wilson, Burge's first accuser to get any traction in court. There was the cop, or the multiple cops, who when they heard about the lawyers bringing torture cases against the CPD, started anonymously mailing them notes, feeding them names to dig into.

So many people deciding to do nothing—to keep their heads down and not cause trouble, to not risk the danger of upsetting the system.

So many people deciding to do something—to insist on things being different.

"This is why we have to study things," said Douglas. "So it won't take so long."

•

Near the end of my time in Douglas's class I was sent a recording of a recent meeting about "Reparations Won" at Wildwood Elementary, a predominantly white school on the Northwest Side. The person who sent me the recording told me I could use it however I wanted, as long as I didn't identify them. Wildwood is the neighborhood immediately to the east of Edison Park. I'd heard of it for the first time from Juanita Douglas, who, in a classroom discussion of Chicago segregation, had recalled her first and only trip to Wildwood. One day in the nineties she drove her son there for a high school football training clinic. She told her students how surprised she was by the leafy, suburban feel of the neighborhood. *This* was Chicago? But most shocking of all was the sight of local teenagers showing up to the clinic on bikes—and leaving them on the ground. Unlocked!

The recording I received starts with Mary Beth Cunat, the Wildwood principal, laying out the evening's format to the audience, which is obviously made up of parents of her students. "I'm just nervous," she says, and she sounds it. There are multiple speakers, she explains; each will have their turn, and then parents will have a chance to write their remaining questions and concerns on Post-it notes. "We didn't leave time for open-ended questions and answers," she says, but promises that the Post-it notes will be read. "We will read those," she says. "We will take them seriously."

A Wildwood history teacher reads a prepared statement about the value of teaching difficult histories. Then he leaves, explaining that he has another obligation to get to.

"There's no police-bashing going on here," says Cunat. "It's focusing on a very discrete episode in history."

A representative of the Chicago Committee on Human Relations gives a bizarre speech in which he explains the committee's mandate to investigate discrimination of all kinds in the city. He makes no mention of Jon Burge, the Midnight Crew or "Reparations Won." He talks mostly about Muslims in the city, and how police stations have been holding fast-breaking dinners during Ramadan to improve community relations. Torture is mentioned, but only briefly, and only the locally infamous "Facebook torture" incident of 2017, in which three black eighteen-year-olds and one black 24-year-old kidnapped a mentally disabled white eighteen-year-old, eventually taking him to a West Side apartment where they tied him up, beat him and removed part of his scalp—all of which was broadcast on Facebook Live, where viewers could hear the kidnappers yelling "Fuck Trump!" and "Fuck white people!" (To this day, if you google "Chicago torture," the first result is the Wikipedia page about this story.)

Then a local police commander expresses his fundamental concern about the curriculum:

You know, I think anyone who has been around children probably realizes that they don't hear everything that we say. So that's
probably our biggest concern. Even though they're going to teach
a curriculum—[the kids] are going to hear what they want to hear.
And I'm just afraid that some of them might feel themselves empowered that maybe they don't have to listen to the police. You
know, in a stressful situation. And maybe they should run from
the police. And they'd be endangering themselves . . .

His advice to Wildwood parents, however, is to accept that the curriculum is happening, and do their best to make sure it is being implemented responsibly. When he was in school, he said, he didn't
know why they were required to learn the parts of speech. "But
I didn't object," he says. "I didn't walk out of the classroom. I didn't
confront the teacher about it. You know? I think we just have to learn
what's in the curriculum. We don't have a choice about it."

The fourth speaker—a Wildwood counselor—is explaining the
meaning of "restorative justice," when a man in the audience inter-
rupts.

Won't the curriculum, he wonders, "be teaching a false narrative?
[Burge] hasn't been convicted of anything in our courts. So how can
you teach that?"

Principal Cunat reassures the man that the curriculum does not
say Burge was convicted of torturing anyone—just perjury and ob-
struction of justice.

"And then all the ones that supposedly were victims—are they
going to have their rap sheets?" the same man wonders. "Are they going to show these kids that? Are they going to have both sides of the
conversation?"

Cunat tells the man that, if he has a question, he should write it
down.

"I'd rather sit here and we can all ask our questions and we can all
know the answers," the man says. "Does anyone else agree with that?"

"If you want that kind of meeting," says Cunat, "you are free to
let me know."

"Okay," says the man. "We want that kind of meeting. We would
rather have an open discussion."

"One of the reasons we don't have an open conversation," says Cunat, "is because it ends up getting derailed . . . I really respect you. I care about you a lot. I really feel like it could just become . . . this ad hoc stuff is not very safe, in terms of my staff and in terms of what we're trying to accomplish."

"But what are we trying to accomplish?" asks the man.

•

On April 30th, Douglas reminded her students that on the following day they were not to come to the classroom, as usual, but instead to go to the library, where they would have the chance to hear from Ronald Kitchen, who had flown in from Philadelphia. (Throughout the spring, a total of eight survivors visited fifty classrooms across the city.) This wasn't the first that her students had heard about Kitchen's visit, but it was obvious that some of them had forgotten, or been absent every time it was mentioned. Even those who re-membered seemed sobered by the prospect that the visit was finally happening: that in 24 hours they would be in the same room—close enough to touch—as the man from the video. The man they'd heard Michael Kill lie about. Someone for whom thinking about torture required no imagination at all, because he'd lived it.

Douglas had recruited some of her more participation-prone stu-dents to give Kitchen's visit an air of ceremony. They'd printed up programs. The boy who had wondered why it was Kitchen the cops picked up that day played some welcome music on his guitar: an acoustic rendition of a song by Death, the black band from Detroit that played punk before punk was really a thing. A girl read a poem she'd written called "What They Don't Tell You about Black Boys." Another girl read an introduction: "Mrs. Douglas has been teaching us about the agonizing tortures of African American men. We wel-come one to speak with us today." She turned away from her class-mates and toward Kitchen, who was sitting on a chair behind her. "I just want to say to you personally that your story will never be forgotten."

Kitchen nodded, taking in the scene in front of him. "I'm really touched," he said. "Sometimes I'm at a loss for words when I see a lot of young people actually taking heed of what's happened."

He took a breath, then spoke for almost twenty minutes without notes. He talked about how bogus the charges against him had been. He talked about co-founding, with other Midnight Crew survivors, the Illinois Death Row 10, the campaign that eventually won a moratorium on all Illinois executions, since expanded into full abolition. He talked about completely losing touch with his son, who was three when he was arrested. About how, whenever it was time for someone to be executed, a guard would bring that person down the hall, letting him stop at each cell along the way to say goodbye. He talked about how, whenever he heard them coming, he would lie on his bed and pretend to be asleep, because he couldn't bear to face them. He talked about how ashamed this made him feel, looking back. He talked about his mother, who developed dementia while he was in prison and did not recognize him when he was released.

It wasn't a practiced speech. It wasn't shaped to build to a certain point or lesson or revelation. Kitchen talked about having been a drug dealer. "It was never a secret," he said. "Never has been: that was my living." That was true—Kitchen has always been upfront about his past—but I could not remember Douglas's class discussing it. I thought I could feel a shift in the nature of the room's collective attention, the cumulative effect of several dozen teenage minds simultaneously switching gears to process the same new variable. Kitchen didn't dwell on it. He urged students to get involved with activism—urged them to avoid the delusion that change was impossible. "I want to thank you all for allowing me to come sit here and talk to you all," he said, again looking almost dumbfounded by where he was—in a Chicago history classroom—and what he was doing there. "I'm trying not to tear up. I'm good at it. I'm good at holding my stuff in. I love that you gave me so much attention. I never had this much attention. I really do appreciate it. Thank you."

There was a short question-and-answer session. The students sounded more formal than usual, like they were trying to be their most mature, respectful, adult selves—which, as often happens with children trying not to sound like children, had the primary effect of evoking how young they remained.

They asked Kitchen how he gets along today with his oldest son, the one who was three years old when the Midnight Crew snatched up his father.

"It's rocky," he said. "It's very, very rocky."

"Are you able to sleep any better now?" a student asked. "I know that sleep is, like, a big thing."

"Actually, I don't sleep," said Kitchen, looking like he regretted having to be the bearer of this bad news. "I'm still on penitentiary time, for real. I eat like"—he mimed shoveling food into his mouth as fast as he could—"I choke some food down. I'm still on penitentiary time. I have to catch myself, when I'm at home: I hear the clink of them rattling the bars . . . I can't really sleep. I'll get up and I'll walk around my house. I'll check the doors, peek out of the curtains. Or I'll sit up, listen to the radio, watch TV for hours. I really don't sleep."

Before they returned to their normal school days, some of the students stayed to talk with Kitchen one-on-one, or in small groups. He is a tall man, well over six feet, and he bent down to get his face closer to theirs. I kept my distance, sensing an unusual intimacy in the unfolding conversations. Later, though, I asked Kitchen what they had been asking him about. "How did I survive?" he said. "What kept me strong? What do I do now? How do I live?"

•

Kitchen is far from the only Midnight Crew survivor who admits to breaking the law and inflicting harm—far from the only one with a rap sheet that isn't, or isn't only, a police fabrication. Some of these rap sheets are quite long. All of them are easily available online. They are irrelevant to the question of whether anyone should have been tortured, or whether their torturers should have been punished.

Torture is forbidden by the Constitution's Eighth Amendment and by multiple international treaties to which the U.S. is a legal signatory, and which have been ratified by the Senate. Torture, all experts on the subject agree, doesn't produce reliable information, and as a result often undermines the very investigations it is notionally intended to serve. Torture is wrong. It is wrong because it is wrong to take such complete, intimate control of another person—wrong to turn their body and mind into weapons trained against themselves. And if this is wrong then it is always wrong, and not more or less wrong depending on anything the victim has done.

There's something wearying about trotting out the arguments against torture. But as long as torture continues—and continues to be justified with arguments—it will remain necessary to do so.

•

In May I heard a rumor that the eighth-grade history teacher at Wildwood Elementary had received so many critical comments from parents in advance of the curriculum rollout that he asked Cunat if he could be excused from teaching it. Cunat, according to this rumor, accommodated the request—and took on teaching the curriculum herself.

The next time I heard Cunat's name it was because she'd been forced to step down—the result, according to the headlines, of a decision to invite an "anti-police" speaker to a Wildwood career day. I assumed, when I saw the headline, that the speaker in question had to be a Midnight Crew survivor. But I was wrong: it was a young Chicago activist and musician named Ethan Viets-VanLear, whom Cunat had asked to participate in the event at Wildwood. Viets-VanLear was part of the delegation that traveled to Geneva to talk about Chicago police brutality in front of the United Nations. Asked by Wildwood students to explain his motivation, he talked about the 2014 death of his friend Dominique "Damo" Franklin, Jr. at the hands of a Chicago police officer. Word of Viets-VanLear's visit spread to Wildwood parents, some of whom quickly scoured his social-media pages for anti-police sentiments and called for Cunat—who was just one year into a four-year contract—to be replaced. Both Viets-VanLear and Cunat reported receiving numerous death threats.

Cunat wrote an apology to the entire school, saying she regretted inviting Viets-VanLear. A few days later, an impromptu school-wide meeting was held for students to receive a presentation on policing from Martin Preib, vice president of the Chicago Fraternal Order of

Police, and Adrian Garcia, a CPD detective with a child at Wildwood. That afternoon, Cunat resigned. Fox News ran a story commemorating her downfall. She is now a principal in Rockford, Illinois, a city ninety miles west of Chicago.

In September, Jon Burge died. After being released from federal prison in 2014, he had moved back to Apollo Beach, where he lived off his CPD pension. In 2015, when SR2015–256 was signed, he was interviewed by Martin Preib for a now-defunct blog called *The Conviction Project*. "I find it hard to believe," he said, "that the city's political leadership could even contemplate giving 'reparations' to human vermin."

After Burge's death, Chicago's Fraternal Order of Police issued a statement saying that the organization did "not believe the full story about the Burge cases has ever been told. . . . Hopefully that story will be told in the coming years."

•

A few months earlier, during the summer, I stopped by the Humboldt Park office of Joe Moreno, the Chicago alderman who first put the reparations ordinance before the city council in 2013. It hadn't been his idea, but he'd been involved in the fight against the Illinois death penalty, and after the ordinance was presented to him by a coalition of activists and lawyers who had been fighting, in the courts and the streets, for the A-Team's victims for years, he agreed to work with them.

I asked Moreno why he thought the ordinance had passed in the end—and not just passed but passed without a single "nay" vote from any of the historic white ethnic enclaves (or "the more autonomous Caucasian wards," as Moreno referred to them). How had the official legislative body of a city that had never been able to admit to torture now swung all the way to reparations?

Moreno wanted to recognize that some council members had likely undergone a genuine change of heart. A-Team survivors had met with many of them one-on-one, explaining what they wanted and why. Their lawyers had compiled the facts, and the facts were simply too overwhelming.

But Moreno also suggested a more cynical theory. There was still plenty of opposition—still plenty of people at city hall who thought, in his paraphrase, "I don't want to be for this, this is ridiculous, these guys are all guilty and just want money." But, he said, it had over time become "much harder for them to be vocal on it that way." It wasn't that every alderperson stopped doubting Burge's victims, he said—but that some of them had made the decision to just move on: to pass the ordinance "rather than fight."

This dynamic had shaped how the ordinance was covered, Moreno argued. "Every journalist, they savor so much the fight," he said. Had there been a protracted legislative battle between different Chicago constituencies, it might have been covered more prominently. Instead, the ordinance—which, in the scheme of city budgeting, cost relatively little—passed, which meant the story lost much of its oxygen for the city's journalists.

To the extent this was anyone's goal—and of course they would never say so if it was—it may look as if their wish has been granted. All spring, I made sure to check my "Chicago torture" and "Chicago torture curriculum" Google Alerts daily, eager to see the stories that appeared. I assumed that at least a few local journalists would find a way around the CPS shutout and that, through what they published, the conversation about Burge, torture, the police and reparations would enter its next phase of civic life. Now and then, Burge was mentioned in yet another story about bad Chicago cops using torture or blackmail to frame suspects, or about more potential Midnight Crew victims getting their claims heard in court. But the school year ended, the summer dragged on, and no stories about the curriculum appeared. (At least until Burge's death, when the *New Yorker* ran a story about the curriculum on its website, and many of Burge's obituaries also mentioned its existence.) I kept telling people I met about reparations in Chicago, and they kept being shocked that they didn't already know about it.*

---

* Many of those who did know about the ordinance were misinformed. In August, I had a long talk with two Chicago cops in a Starbucks; they'd heard about the reparations ruling, but were under the impression that the money went not just to vetted torture victims, but to entire neighborhoods on the South and West Sides. Each had a child in elementary school, and each said that if a torture survivor—or "a supposed torture survivor"—came to visit that child's school, they would refuse to let them attend history class that day.

In the short term, SR2015–256 has not made Chicago as a whole appreciably more conscious of its own history. But not every major development in civic culture—in a city's (or a nation's) consciousness of itself—gets noticed as such upon its arrival. Thousands of children all over Chicago have now talked about the city in a new way, and thousands more will again next year, and again the year after that. The impact of this is impossible to predict with any specificity: there is no such thing as a utilitarian cost-benefit analysis of starting to tell the truth, together, about what happened.

The official "Reparations Won" curriculum calls for eighth graders to mark the end of the curriculum with an op-ed about police-community relations, and for tenth graders to design a memorial to victims of police brutality. Douglas modified this requirement, requiring her students to work in groups to make mock talk shows about the Burge scandal and the reparations fight, in which they role-played as the principals, including Burge himself. These talk shows, which students presented live on their last day with the curriculum, were bits of utopian theater: collections of guests who would, in reality, never appear on the same talk show, and speaking with a bluntness they would never employ if they did. Anyone could be anyone: in one of the groups, Jon Burge himself was played by a Latina girl, who sauntered on stage grabbing her crotch in an exaggerated show of machismo. "I'm great," she said.

"Why do you think you and your officers were able to get away with torture?" asked the host.

The class had watched numerous videos of Burge being deposed, during which all he did was assert, over and over again, his Fifth Amendment right not to testify. But this fictitious Burge took another tack: "I wouldn't call it getting away," the girl playing Burge said. "I'd call it doing our jobs. But if for some reason there's this big thing where people think we were doing something wrong . . . We were able to get away with it because people covered for us. No one's going to tell on me."

The Dictatorship of the Present

by John Michael Colón

ISSUE 19 | SUMMER 2019

Thirty years ago socialism was dead and buried. This was not an illusion or a temporary hiccup, a point all the more important to emphasize up front in light of its recent revival in this country and around the world. There was no reason this resurrection had to happen; no law of nature or history compelled it. To understand why it did is to unlock a door, behind which lies something like the truth of our age.

Some will say I exaggerate. But it's best not to mince words about such things if you want to grasp or even to glimpse how the world really works—something more and more people are interested in nowadays, even as that world spirals beyond the reach of the ideas they'd previously used to understand it. And there is no greater obstacle to understanding than euphemism. So again I will insist: probably in 1989 and certainly by the time I was born in 1993, socialism was at an end.

There are a thousand ways to tell the story of why and how this came to be so. But the best—because the most concise and spiritually invested in the matter—remains George Orwell's *Animal Farm*, the fairy tale I read about it when I was fourteen.

You can read it for yourself in a weekend and probably did at some point for school. But if you haven't, the story goes like this: Once upon a time there was a revolution. It began spontaneously—things were bad and could not go on as they were, and the people revolted in order that they could at last have freedom and equality and be the masters of their own fate. But after the old tyranny was overthrown, one group within the revolutionary movement consolidated power for itself. With this power came the inevitable corruption. Soon only one man ruled the whole country in the name of the very revolution that was supposed to put the people in charge. Speech was controlled and inconvenient views suppressed until all dissent was outlawed; surveillance and political murder by secret police became the norm; hysterical lies about the past were circulated as fact; the people became impoverished and lost what little say they ever had while the new rulers got all the riches and power; and in the end, the supposed revolutionaries produced a dictatorship perhaps only distinguishable from the old one by being even worse. Or, as a classic rocker once put it: *Meet the new boss—same as the old boss.*

The stories we tell each other fundamentally shape our social world. I can't overstate the centrality of this particular story to our cultural ideas about revolution and thus socialism. If I were to say the word "revolution" all by itself, I'd bet this particular narrative sequence would pop into your head almost point by point. Practically every film, every novel, every comic, every song, every joke—in short, every story—dealing with revolution is either a plagiarism of *Animal Farm* or a reaction to it. It has transcended cliché (though it's of course that too) and become regarded almost as an axiomatic truth: *If a revolution happens, it'll go down like this.* Typically it's then implied that this is precisely why we shouldn't have one. Push too hard against the status quo and you'll get something worse.

Of course this ridiculously influential story about what happens when you try to change society turns out actually to have happened. After all, it's nothing less than a description of the very real failures of socialism in the twentieth century—a calamity that is rightfully condemned by historical posterity and, in the eyes of many, fundamentally discredits the attempt to create any sort of post-capitalist society.

Yet here we are, living through a time when none of those old truths are certain anymore. A time when more of the young have positive associations with the word "socialism" than "capitalism"; when the radical left and the extremist right are winning or about to win political victories across the world; when grassroots movements outside the electoral arena are in some ways driving what happens at the ballot box; and when what is most vital in politics wherever one looks is the rejection of an elite political consensus that not long ago people could—without irony!—call the "end of history." And here I stand before you—a socialist, but also an artist and a fellow humanist, as full as you are of hatred and contempt for the last century's dictatorships—imploring you (in what until recently would have been considered a most unfashionably sincere manner) to believe me when I say that *only* some sort of democratic socialism can preserve anything like democracy in our global society.

How can I explain myself? In a sense, only by trying to explain everything. Because to think like a socialist is to see even yourself, that pure and irreducible individuality you might find described in a novel by Virginia Woolf, as a brief but significant swell in the waves of history. It means understanding that the Trump election and the rise of fascism, the fall of the Soviet Union and the end of socialism, Occupy Wall Street and the rebirth of socialism, the sordid career of neoliberalism, the recent evolution of culture and the broad contours of one's own life—in all the profound solitude of its lived experience—are not only connected but interdependent; that a meaningful story can be told about their relations. All of us are the products and also the prime movers of these vast social forces. They make us who we are, and we in turn contribute to their further transformation. Even more than my politics, it's this way of looking at the world that I feel the burning need to communicate to you—in the hopes, I think, that by looking at our society as I have learned to see it, you might be in a better position to understand your own story, what you stand for, and what you will act to see endure in the world.

I. PAST

I was born at the end of the last century in New Jersey to upper-middle-class immigrant parents from Puerto Rico and Colombia. Both were born working-class, though branches of my mother's side had been wealthy at various points (they lost everything—twice! the story goes—through the antics of various gambling philanderers). My father's side are all *jibaros*, which is Boricua for peasant—though most of them now have access to TVs and unemployment insurance courtesy of America's past civilizing jihads. But despite their class of birth, my parents were quick to climb the social ladder. They both studied on Pell Grants back in the days when those actually paid for anything, became engineers, did research at Bell Labs before it was broken up and eventually peaked at middle management in sizable corporations and a comfortable existence in the suburbs.

This was their gift to me. I mock it, there was a time when I despised it—and there is much to despise in it still—but I recognize it now as the struggle of generations. Without getting into details, it suffices to say that many sacrificed much for me to be able to turn my back on that petit bourgeois upbringing. And it is because of the comfort of my origins that I've been able to pursue a career as a writer.

Why was I thrown into this situation? Why my particular experiences and not those of poverty, humiliation and deprivation? Dumb luck is one answer, but it's hardly enough of one. From almost the very start I've known this is a political question. This is not due to any great genius of mine. Colombia has spent the better part of the last century in a civil war, and Puerto Rico is a colony of the United States whose rulers desperately want its people to forget that. Politics in my household was what people talked about around the dinner table, as is the case with many immigrant families from poor countries, for whom it's trivially obvious that politics is what accounts for the distribution of resources—who gets what sort of job and why, who can boss you around or censor your newspaper, who lives in a palace with servants and who starves. Only in what is called the "developed" world, where day-to-day politics seems to revolve mostly around taxes and social issues, do large numbers of people have the option to tune out. (And even then, as we'll see, our poor only do because they've more or less entirely been shut out of the whole conversation.)

Which isn't to say that I was given any sort of radical education. Quite to the contrary. My parents' materialism had much more to do with Dolce & Gabbana than with Marx & Engels. When you're poor your life consists of seeing things you can't have; should you stumble into money, your resulting values will hardly be anything bohemian.

My parents mortgaged a McMansion they couldn't comfortably afford in a suburb that made most of us miserable in different ways in order to achieve the life they believed they had earned. They voted Republican when it kept their taxes down and, more rarely, Democrat when it meant the same minus the racism. (That Mom and Dad are sort of Bernie bros now, weirdly, is itself a sign of the times.) At the same time they told me—with a fervent belief coexisting somewhat uneasily alongside their immigrant political instincts—that in America things were different, that everything we had was due to the political freedoms available here. Some of my earliest memories consist of being spoon-fed myths of rugged individualism—not just the usual Reaganite stuff, but also Catholic Cold War tales of Pope John Paul II and the miraculous prophecies of Our Lady of Fátima concerning the sins of Russia.

And in all these stories, seemingly inexplicably, the spectral villain was always a justly vanquished communism. It was the nineties, after all. So to understand anything, we have to begin with thinking about the nature of these strange dead societies that haunted my childhood after their demise.

•

Animal Farm is often praised for the way it follows, in minute detail, every major development of Soviet politics from 1917 to 1945. The precision of Orwell's satire is legendary. Soviet dissidents, wrongly assuming he couldn't possibly know as much about the situation in Russia without knowing the language, once sent him a letter in Russian asking for permission to translate and distribute an underground edition.

But a careful reader will notice that the true structure of the book is shaped not so much by these historical events as by the escalating betrayals of the Stalinist pigs—the steady increase in their power and privilege, and the subsequent erosion of the lived ideal of equality among the animals. First the pigs get milk, with which to make the animals' favorite kind of mash only for themselves. Then they get to sleep in beds. Before long they're drinking alcohol. And finally, toward the end of the book, they've taught themselves to walk

on two legs. The various purges, murders and changes to the revolutionary Seven Commandments *follow* the accumulation of power
and privilege and only serve, after the fact, to defend it.

That this mirrors the Soviet experience—even very early on, in
the supposedly freer Lenin years—is borne out by every major eye-
witness account. The socialist writer Victor Serge, who supported
the Party at first and later became a dissident, paints the grim scene
in his novel *Conquered City*:

> The half-empty slums were hungry. The factory chimneys no
> longer smoked, and when by chance one started smoking, the
> women, huddling in their rags at the door of a communal store,
> watched that bizarre smoke climb with bleak curiosity. "They're
> repairing cannons. They get extra rations . . .—How much? How
> much?—four hundred grams of bread a day; yeah; but it's not for
> us, it's only for *them* . . ."

This passage is set shortly after the Russian Civil War, and things
only got worse afterwards. The broad sweep of Soviet history shows
that the Party elites' ability to command labor and resources by
force grew with time. Once established as temporary necessity, their
total control grew into an eternal virtue.

Even the relatively egalitarian achievements in the USSR at its
economic peak in the sixties were tarnished by this rigid hierarchy.
For instance, the Soviet Union did actually lower income disparities
to a level comparable in some ways to Scandinavian social democracies. However, unlike in those societies, the combination of total
nationalization of industry and the control of those nationalized
resources by a tiny elite meant that the relatively equal incomes did
not buy relatively equal goods. Why? Because money wasn't what *got*
the goods: the class position of the ruling Party bureaucrats meant
they could funnel goods to themselves through central planning
that were unavailable to ordinary people.*

* That the Soviet-style societies had a ruling class, that they could kill and steal
within the bounds of laws they drew up themselves, and that, above all, they commanded vast resources and the labor of ordinary people through the barrel of a
gun, is not in dispute by anyone except the most fanatical Leninists. But there is

Why do the pigs get all this power? In Orwell, it's because it turns out only the pigs see themselves as prepared enough to govern. They study economics and agriculture to make sure they can run the farm just like the capitalist farmers did. Some try to teach the other animals—Snowball, the Trotsky pig, sets up a whole bunch of committees to this end—but fail because while many animals do learn to read and engage in other new techniques, many of the "stupider animals," in Orwell's blunt phrasing, simply never do.

We shouldn't disregard that cruel adjective. *Animal Farm* is a book where every little detail means something, after all. If so, this seems to bode badly for its message. It apparently suggests that the working class was congenitally incapable of running its own affairs and so would always need leaders to serve in its best interests. But this hardly makes sense given Orwell's lifelong political commitments, which he held to his dying breath: his support for workers running industry, with Barcelona under the anarchists as his prime example (in his book *Homage to Catalonia*) of a town where "the working class is in the saddle" and proof that socialism was actually possible. How, then, do we reconcile such democratic-socialist views with the satire of the novel?

The pertinent bit is that regardless of the actual talents and proclivities of the working class, *this is what the Stalinist pigs believed*. In fact, more than that, it was their justifying ideology. Consider this argument by one of the pigs about why they need to monopolize decision-making power:

> "Comrades," he said, "I trust that every animal here appreciates the sacrifice that Comrade Napoleon [Stalin] has made in taking this extra labour upon himself. Do not imagine, comrades, that leadership is a pleasure! On the contrary, it is a deep and heavy responsibility. No one believes more firmly than Comrade Napoleon that all animals are equal. He would be only too happy to let

significant disagreement on the democratic left as to exactly what kind of system it was—a form of "state capitalism"? A form of authoritarian industrialism that was neither capitalist nor socialist? For a convincing exposition of the various theories of the USSR, see Marcel van der Linden's *Western Marxism and the Soviet Union* and *Eastern Left, Western Left* by Ágnes Heller and Ferenc Fehér.

you make your decisions yourselves. But sometimes you might make the wrong decisions, comrades, and then where would we be?"

For good measure, the same pig later adds a warning about what will happen if the pigs allow the other animals (who aren't "brain workers" like him) to make their own choices: "Do you know what would happen if we pigs failed in our duty? Jones [the capitalist] would come back! Yes, Jones would come back!"

If this sounds absurd, again, it too has its counterpart in Soviet society. As the Yugoslav dissident socialist Milovan Djilas points out in his classic book *The New Class*, the Party elite created a "legal fiction" to justify their rule. The idea was that, in exchange for total and everlasting command over all aspects of society, the Party of the proletariat would govern in its interests, raising living standards and leveling the economy in exchange for general acceptance of the one-party state. Yet the very lack of constraints on those rulers, the total control over decision-making granted to them so that supposedly they could do what needed to be done to create equality, assured instead that they wouldn't.

The distance between the egalitarian dream and the oligarchical reality never closed, and the result was a slow decay. In the absence of a civil society where the Party's rule could be openly contested, people resigned themselves to their reality without really believing in it; in the absence of any serious movements for social transformation, Party elites soon stopped paying even lip service to the ideals which were the justification of their power. In his documentary *HyperNormalisation*, Adam Curtis puts it succinctly: "The Soviet Union became a society where everyone knew that what their leaders said was not real . . . But everybody had to play along and pretend that it *was* real because no one could imagine any alternative." And it was this gap between the lie of what "communist" society promised and the obvious grim reality its citizens were surrounded by that made its overthrow also, in a sense, inevitable. A dream deferred for too long must eventually explode.

This happened as a series of peaceful revolutions at the end of

the eighties, the immediate trigger for which was deteriorating economic conditions in the core "communist" countries: rising prices
and decaying infrastructure due to foreign debt and a failure to innovate in industry, respectively. But the revolts' rapid spread even
to "communist" countries that were doing comparatively well economically showed something more profound was at work. A society
can only survive if its inhabitants believe in its animating myths.
So far had the experience of life as actually lived diverged from the
Party's "legal fiction" that the Soviet people came to reject not only
their dictatorship but the whole premise of that system—the idea
that an egalitarian society was, in any substantive sense, possible.
And it was in this way that socialism died. The reality had diverged
so much from the ideal that it no longer seemed desirable or even
possible to strive towards it. In the end this failure was so profound
that it caused untold damage to the ideal of equality itself, not just
in the Eastern bloc but around the world.

•

Over the course of several years, beginning with the moment I picked
up Orwell at fourteen, I began to read about these things. Slowly
from my isolated suburban perch—usually my room, and sometimes the public library—I began to understand how even revolutions undertaken by ordinary people so often ended in brutal and
repressive societies. It reminded me of the stories my mother and
father would tell me about "*nuestros países*." I began to wonder about
my own place in that history.

How lonely those suburbs were. Part of the reason I retreated into
the stream of my reading was no doubt the shrunken and crippled
vision of life that was my upbringing, for all its material prosperity. Here I was amid the vast sprawl of the American provinces, in a
town which was not a town but a series of strip malls and cul-de-sacs
connected by state routes—nowhere to go, and no way to get there
without a car. The strip malls all had the same big-box stores and
franchise restaurants as every other town, the televisions all blurted
the same mind-melting crap from the national channels, the towns

themselves had no politics but the bickering of local busybodies over signs and traffic lights (the real politics having been pushed up to the state and federal levels with their corporate and machine politicians), and in fact the towns all blurred into one another such that it was hard even to tell when one stopped and the next began, leaving only an enormous network of beige and gray despair stretching across the immensity of a continent.

Here there lived people who were hostile to anything which could not be shown to produce money, even if it wasn't an idea or an activity but a person, even indeed if it was human life itself. The working classes—who were just called "the poor" or, more disparagingly, "moochers"—were dismissed as parasites who out of laziness or a stubborn refusal to learn "useful skills" had consigned themselves to a poverty which anyway they deserved. Power worship of the most naked and shameful variety reigned. No matter what we were taught in church and in children's cartoons, it was generally understood that morality of too demanding a sort was for any normal person something to be outgrown in favor of the general acquisitiveness and drive to domination. You were good because you were strong; if you were strong, it was proof you were good. Hence the admiration even among the worst off for cutthroat CEOs, or at any rate cheap TV imitations of them played by the likes of Donald Trump; and hence, too, the general approval of the American empire, the bizarre and cultish worship of "our troops" at football stadiums and the endless parade of trivia about nukes and military hardware in books and documentaries devoted to science and history.

As for how I fared, as a clever brown kid who wanted to be an artist, it'd be fair to say I was met with a mix of incomprehension and hostility. To sum it up in two examples: most of my classmates in the Catholic high school I attended on a merit scholarship told me repeatedly my academic success was the result of affirmative action; and a family friend who once heard me say I'd be a writer suggested that, since writing was not a job but a hobby, I should become a day trader instead while the going was still good.

In short, everything I was surrounded by and everything I experienced seemed to be brainwashing me into believing a single truth:

things had always been like this; they would go on like this; and they would be like this forever. It hardly mattered that none of it made sense, that books existed that suggested we lived in history, and that history clearly presented alternatives. The past was something that belonged to artists and professors and other useless undesirables, and the future was to be an endless dictatorship of the present— a sprawling, flavorless, thoughtless capitalist eternity which deserved to persist because it was both the best of all possible worlds and the only one.

At the time I had only the vaguest idea, hardly more than an instinct, of the forces that had created this Potemkin utopia. What I also didn't know at the time was that already things were changing. But for those who might have been paying close attention—and I was certainly not yet among them—that system had already begun to show signs of fraying at the edges.

·

One of the most interesting details of *Animal Farm* comes at the very end. In the rest of the book we've seen in painstaking detail the dangers of a society where the few rule the many, the horrors of a politics without democratic rights. We know by now the pigs have betrayed their ideals and changed the text written on the side of the barn to hide this fact. Their dictatorship, once established, seems unassailable. But the final and essential twist of the novella is the extent to which the pigs represent not so much a new evil as an old one.

As the animals look on in horror through a window, finally realizing what has happened to them, Napoleon the Stalin pig holds forth at a dinner with the old farmer-capitalists. These are the same monsters who once enslaved his people, who invaded Animal Farm multiple times to stop the revolution in its tracks. But now they're all sitting around the same table, drunk as can be, congratulating Napoleon on his efficient production techniques and the strict totalitarian discipline with which he runs his farm. Indeed, so low are the wages (in food) and so high is the output that the farmers "had observed many features which they intended to introduce on their own farms immediately." And why not? After all, "Their struggles and their difficulties were one. Was not the labour problem the same everywhere?" Napoleon, for his part, describing the farm as a firm owned by the pig elite, promises years of sound business relations to come, and otherwise acts no different from the humans who had been his mortal enemies. And it is in this context, crucially, that the book delivers its final punch:

> Twelve voices were shouting in anger, and they were all alike. No question, now, what had happened to the faces of the pigs. The creatures outside looked from pig to man, and from man to pig, and from pig to man again; but already it was impossible to say which was which.

Here, at the moral center of a book so often deployed as a weapon by Cold Warriors, we find ourselves confronted by what remains to our society an unspeakable truth: Soviet-style "communism" was reprehensible precisely to the extent that it was *similar* to capitalism. For Orwell, in this passage, they're practically indistinguishable.

This is the thread that, once pulled, unravels a whole hidden history. We can only touch on a few aspects of that history here*, but without some basic understanding of it, the events of the past twenty years—not to mention the past two hundred—are impos-

---

* Some excellent starting points for a fuller treatment include: Eric Hobsbawm's four-volume "Age of" series, Karl Polanyi's *The Great Transformation*, C. L. R. James's *The Black Jacobins*, Michael Perelman's *The Invention of Capitalism*, Ellen Meiksins Wood's social histories *Citizens to Lords* and *Liberty and Property*, G. D. H. Cole's seven-volume *A History of Socialist Thought* and Howard Zinn's *A People's History of the United States*. The Marxist intellectual tradition is admirably summarized in Russell Jacoby's *Dialectic of Defeat*, Paul Buhle's *Marxism in the United States* and Cedric Robinson's *Black Marxism*. For the history of electoral socialist movements in particular, Donald Sassoon's *One Hundred Years of Socialism* is an excellent overview of socialist parties in Europe. A portrait of the equally large and important movements for anarchism or libertarian socialism can be found in Peter Marshall's *Demanding the Impossible*, Murray Bookchin's four-volume *The Third Revolution*, Ángel Cappelletti's *Anarchism in Latin America* and Alexandre Skirda's *Facing the Enemy*.

sible to comprehend. In a phrase, one can sum it up as the ongoing battle between capitalism and democracy.

At the start, it might have been possible to see capitalism, too, as part of a leveling project. A set of institutions and practices for structuring the labor process and distributing resources that had first begun to develop in early modern cities, it only really took off in the societies freed from hereditary rule by the English, North American, French and Latin American revolutions. The liberals who fought these revolutions did not see themselves as capitalists. Rather, they thought they were founding *republics*—polities run on the basis of merit rather than inheritance, by reason rather than traditional superstition and by elected parliaments rather than priests, aristocrats and kings. While some of these liberals wanted to limit decision-making to the "better kinds of people" and restrain the powers of those deemed unworthy, the most radical of them (like Thomas Paine, Mary Wollstonecraft, Simón Bolívar and Giuseppe Garibaldi) saw such new states as being *democratic*, or rooted in the idea that everyone should have an equal share in power. The goal was to build a society based in liberty, equality, fraternity and certain inalienable rights.

The problem was that one of those rights threatened to undermine the others. On paper, liberal democracy allowed everyone to think, write, assemble and otherwise do as they please—and everyone's right to own *property*, using and abusing it as the owner pleased, was to be perhaps the most important in guaranteeing the people's freedom. Yet as monarchies were neutered or beheaded and republics began to spread, some of the democratic liberals began to notice that treating property as an absolute and unquestionable right, and the largest property-owners as the absolute sovereigns of all they owned, had the opposite of the intended effect. Rather than guaranteeing liberty for all, it subjected the majority to the tyranny of a new minority who justified their exploitation and domination of others through the very property rights which were supposed to have been the basis of everyone's freedom.*

---

* Consider wage labor—the fact that most people work a set number of hours to receive tokens that they exchange for food, shelter and other basic goods. Theoretically, this is a free contract made between an employer and an employee as equals; actually, most workers do this because there's no other way for them to

As the big owners secured control over the flow of resources through consolidation, monopoly and dispossession, a contradiction became increasingly apparent. The capitalist "legal fiction" insisted private property rights necessarily connected the prosperity of the rich to the advancement of the rest of society. Yet in practice this translated into the freedom of the rich to render the poor permanently destitute and subservient. Ordinary people became human resources to be exploited like the rest. One stream of cheap labor, for example, flowed from the Transatlantic Slave Trade to plantations in the Americas that supplied British textile factories with cotton. And in turn, the wages system in England meant workers there had no choice but to accept starvation wages to work in what William Blake dubbed the "dark Satanic Mills" where the cotton was woven. (Not for nothing did this system come to be called "wage slavery." From the owners' point of view, chattel slavery and wage labor were just two different ways of acquiring coerced human bodies to pick their crops and tend to their machines.)* This was the system that turned proud republican experiments in North and South America into slavocracies and plutocracies run by the idle rich; created poverty amid the possibility of plenty in Europe's cities and countrysides alike; and justified—as putting the resources of "savages" to "more productive use"—the genocidal colonization of India, Africa, China and the American West.

It was in this context that socialism emerged out of liberalism. The socialists were those liberals who realized that the goals of the democratic revolutions could never be met if the tyranny of the

---

survive. And in fact participating in labor markets is quite unusual in human history, something people generally have to be forced into doing with extreme amounts of violence. This is why the early history of capitalism around the world is marked by states pushing free tribes and small agricultural producers off the land at gunpoint, whether through outright colonization and genocide or "reforms" like the British Enclosure Acts.

*For an elaboration of this controversial argument and the evidence behind it, see John J. Clegg's masterful survey "Capitalism and Slavery" in *Critical Historical Studies* (2015), as well as Sven Beckert's *Empire of Cotton* and Calvin Schermerhorn's *The Business of Slavery and the Rise of American Capitalism.*

kings was merely replaced by the tyranny of the big owners. Their program to extend a form of common ownership over the key infrastructure of society, giving everyone a say in the decisions that affected them and meeting the basic needs of all, eventually came to be called socialism, and its reason for existing is clear from its other and earlier names: it was a form of labor republicanism, an attempt to create an industrial democracy.*

This is why, despite what some may conclude from *Animal Farm* about the relationship between socialism and democracy, in nearly every country where a socialist movement was born, the socialists fought for democracy; in every struggle to expand democratic rights, there were socialists to be found among the most radical elements.†️ And although the socialists did not succeed in overthrowing capitalism in many modern states (and often created dictatorships when they tried), they did force capitalists to offer concessions to their

---

* For the history of "labor republicanism," see Alex Gourevitch's "Labor Republicanism and the Transformation of Work" in *Political Theory* (2013). For accounts of "industrial democracy," see G. D. H. Cole's *Guild Socialism Restated* and Milton Derber's *The American Idea of Industrial Democracy 1865–1965*.

† I can hardly even begin to list them all. Feminists like Susan B. Anthony, Jane Addams, Sylvia Pankhurst, Alexandra Kollontai, Margaret Sanger, Simone de Beauvoir, Audre Lorde, Shulamith Firestone and Jo Freeman were all socialists or close fellow-travelers. Helen Keller, that pillar of disabilities rights in the U.S., was as well. Such major names of the black liberation struggle as W. E. B. Du Bois, Alain Locke, Langston Hughes, Paul Robeson, Lorraine Hansberry, Martin Luther King, Jr., James Baldwin, Fannie Lou Hamer, Ella Josephine Baker, A. Philip Randolph, Huey P. Newton and Angela Davis all were avowed socialists. Oscar Wilde, the father of the modern gay-rights movement, was a libertarian socialist, and socialists like Emma Goldman, August Bebel, Edward Carpenter, Helene Stöcker, Lucía Sánchez Saornil, Harry Hay, Bayard Rustin and Adrienne Rich were either queer themselves or early defenders of LGBT rights in their respective countries. Artists as far-flung as Picasso, Kahlo, Kafka, Tolstoy, Lu Xun, García Márquez and Woolf were socialists (to name just a handful), and the legal cases that ultimately expanded freedom of speech and expression to its present capaciousness in the U.S. were fought on behalf of socialist writers like James Joyce and Allen Ginsberg by the same sort of radical lawyers who also defended socialist activists when they got arrested.

democratic principles. Indeed, the history of the battle between socialism and capitalism could—until recently, at least—be credibly presented as a progressive story of accommodation. In this story, this battle culminates, in the rich Western countries, with what American historians call the "postwar liberal compromise." This was the thirty-year period between 1945 and 1973 defined by the emergence of mixed economies where capitalists remained in charge of industry but were forced to share political power with unions and economic planners, accede to high tax levels and regulations, and allow the construction of a robust welfare state. Utopia was off the agenda, but to many social democrats of the generation that came of age during the Cold War, following the horrors of fascism and World War II, this humbler compromise represented the best humanity could do.

My friends and I call this the "Tony Judt Story," after the famous historian who expounded it in his book *Postwar*. But the French name for those decades is more revealing: *les trente glorieuses*, the golden age of capitalism. Thomas Piketty's *Capital in the Twenty-First Century* provides a number of economic indicators about the period's record growth and rise in living standards, but the most telling part of the book is a graph charting inequality by tracking the income share of the top one percent. The now-notorious figure is crowned by two peaks—one stretching into the pre-1913 past, the other from 1973 into our dismal present—but at its center is a massive valley of relative equality.

Some wish this social-democratic compromise could have gone on forever. It didn't. A lot rides on the question of why. Perhaps the turn back to a more rapacious style of class rule was inevitable in a society still in thrall to what Marxists call "the laws of capitalism." Or maybe the Reagan-Thatcher revolution was a contingent political development that might have been avoided, had social democracy been better defended. What's clear is that it didn't last. The regime that succeeded it is most often referred to as neoliberalism.*

---

* For a general history of neoliberalism, consult Naomi Klein's *The Shock Doctrine*, David Harvey's *A Brief History of Neoliberalism*, Philip Mirowski's *Never Let a Serious Crisis Go to Waste* and Quinn Slobodian's *Globalists: The End of Empire and the Birth of Neoliberalism*.

Neoliberalism is a set of policies and institutional arrangements defined by the elimination of postwar labor protections and regulations on capital, the privatization of public goods and services, the export of jobs to countries whose workers can be forced to work under sweatshop conditions and the extension of for-profit market relations into most facets of human life. But like any successful political economy, neoliberalism is also an ideology—a story about who we are and what kind of world we live in, which once ingrained becomes a kind of unexamined common sense. The neoliberals preached that, as Margaret Thatcher famously remarked, there's no such thing as society, only families and individuals. They believed that citizens and workers should see themselves as self-interested consumers, in politics and culture as much as in shopping malls. And they held that history had been leading us here the whole time, to a world where markets were the final arbiter of all value and human worth.

It's no exaggeration to say these people created the world I was born into and the fairy tales I was told to explain it. In school, on television and at home, the message was the same: Orwell's pigs had been slaughtered and the result was a blessed age. With the defeat of "communism" and the discrediting of the socialist ideal, free societies were sprouting up all over the world where people could finally live as they pleased. With the free market finally "unleashed," they could buy and sell whatever they wanted or needed while trusting their elected representatives to mind the knobs of policy. Some societies might be healthier and more developed than others, to be sure, but we were all headed to the same destination of capitalist democracy. Which happened to look a lot like the suburb where I lived.

Some probably felt the falseness of this fairy tale even then, but eventually the statistics would tell their own story about what had really been happening all through my early life. In the forty years since the end of the postwar compromise, in the United States as in all countries that implemented neoliberal policies, the experiment in an unfettered capitalism had proven disastrous. By 2016, Oxfam estimated that not only did the top one percent of "earners" own more wealth than the rest of the human population put together, but "62 individuals had the same wealth as 3.6 billion people—the bottom half of humanity." Likewise, 147 corporations owned the vast majority of the companies in the world. At the same time, and not surprisingly, wages have stagnated massively compared to productivity, even though they had kept up with it all through the social-democratic period. Union membership plummeted during the same time frame, while the combination of outsourcing and automation has left the landscape littered with the desiccated ruins of what were once our factory cities, and marred with new ghettos and tent cities of the wandering homeless. Conditions were even worse in developing countries around the world, which were saddled with sweatshop labor, massive debts to the IMF and the privatization of even basic resources like water.

Of course, I knew none of that back then. It took time for anyone to fully understand it. Yet all through the end of the last century and the start of this one, the story Americans had been told—which my parents and their neighbors had tried to live—was growing ever more distant from the promised reality. Eventually the gap would become wide enough that I would see, in my own lifetime, another kind of dream explode.

II. PRESENT

When do we move from merely reading about history to having entered it? Each generation has a different event—World War II, Vietnam, 9/11—when it becomes clear to them how much their individual lives, seemingly so private and contained, are part of a larger story. For my generation, that moment was the 2008 financial crash. Even the headlines, with their horrifying images of economic chaos around the planet and their endless talk of "the worst recession since the Great Depression," seemed to confirm what I'd suspected ever since I'd first picked up Orwell: that the hermetically sealed bubble of the suburbs was an illusion; that it concealed the true condition of most people in society; and that the world of bread lines and carpet bombings, of rationing and five year plans, of revolutions and dictatorships was not nearly so far away as everyone imagined.

It didn't get quite that bad, of course—and, in at least one way, the crash seemed at first like good news. There was a feeling in the air that the crisis had discredited all the old dogmas. The same pro-capitalist policies that had made a handful at the top of society so rich in the boom years of my childhood had caused the crisis, pushing ordinary people even deeper into bankruptcy and precarity. Popular magazines were discussing Keynes and even Marx, while politicians were talking, seemingly seriously, about nationalizing the banks. It seemed likely—to me anyway—that the tax cuts and privatizations and union-busting and welfare abolition that had dominated both parties since Reagan would soon become a thing of the past. What would replace them, I assumed, was a renewed commitment to the social-democratic compromise that had created the good decades after the war.

Obama's election in particular was—as the cliché he established goes—a moment of enormous hope. Although I was not yet old enough to vote I fought hard for him, canvassing door to door in hostile neighborhoods, handing out literature I printed out myself at shopping malls, giving potted speeches to the other kids at my reactionary Catholic high school. Like so many people across the country I was inspired by the promise of a black president, and more specifically what that meant: that America was not in some robust sense a white country but rather a country of all colors, where late-comers like my family were just as important a part of the social fabric as anybody who'd come in at Ellis Island or off the *Mayflower*.

But I was also inspired by Obama's message about the economy. All through high school I'd thought of myself very seriously as a "Tony Judt social democrat," and during his campaign it appeared that Obama, in the wake of a world-historical recession, was planning to steer us in that direction.* Instead, immediately upon get-

---

* In an economic manifesto he delivered in Flint, Michigan in 2008 he followed up promises to regulate the banks, expand Social Security and create a system of low-cost universal health care by emphasizing that these "short steps" weren't enough. His government would "rebuild the manufacturing base here in Michigan," "end the addiction to oil" and "invest in innovation . . . rebuilding our crumbling roads and bridges." ("Roads and bridges" was to become the typical mantra Obama invoked whenever he made promises, never fulfilled, for full employment and investment in infrastructure.)

ting elected, Obama appointed a number of neoliberals to key positions in his government, the most prominent of which was his
choice of Wall Street insider Timothy Geithner as secretary of the
treasury. The policies they pursued ultimately extended a recession
that, contrary to the Panglossian reports of the business press, has
never really ended.

I could quote many statistics to prove this: for instance, living
standards and consumer demand have not substantively improved
since the crash, while the jobs that have been created have largely
been low-paying dead ends. But perhaps the most damning and astonishing comment on the period was recently released by the Centers for Disease Control, who announced in a 2018 report that American life expectancy has undergone the deepest and most sustained
decline since the start of the twentieth century—which is to say,
since they began to rise wildly for ordinary people during the postwar compromise.

What resulted was a lost decade. And with it, the beginning of a
generation's loss of political faith.

•

Like a lot of earnest young left-liberals, I experienced the Obama
years as a massive disappointment. If I'd previously believed, based
on my reading, that moderate social democracy was all human beings in our fallen state were capable of, what I witnessed in the wake
of the crash seemed to prove we were incapable even of that. What
then *were* we capable of, and what did we deserve? For all the cracks
that were beginning to show in the social order, nobody could yet see
what lay behind its image—least of all me. All I had to go on were
hints from history, and I began to wonder if these were bringing me
any real insights or if I was just trying to role-play as Orwell or another of my dead socialist heroes.

It turned out that 2011—much like 1848 and 1968—was an auspi-
cious year to be having such thoughts. I'd only just arrived at college
to find the world suddenly rocked by a global revolutionary wave.
The Arab Spring kicked it off, but copycat revolts took place over the

next few years in many different countries: the 15-M movement of self-described *"indignados"* in Spain, the anti-austerity demonstrations in the U.K., the Pots and Pans Revolution in Iceland, the Snow Revolution in Russia, the public-transit protests in Brazil, the Gezi Park movement in Turkey, Euromaidan in Ukraine, the Umbrella Movement in Hong Kong, the Sunflower Movement in Taiwan. Each was grounded in local circumstances, but there were also strong common themes: the public's right to public space, the rejection of neoliberal economic policies and the desire to replace rule by elites with one or the other form of direct rule of the people over themselves, something many of them embodied in their famously "horizontal" forms of organizing. Their propensity to kick off with the occupation of plazas and public squares gave them their name— internationally minded activists have referred to them collectively as the "movements of the squares."

The American iteration of this movement, Occupy Wall Street, began in September of 2011. It was launched by, of all things, an email to subscribers of the Canadian anti-consumerist magazine *Adbusters* calling for America to mount "its own Tahrir." Led by an eccentric conglomeration of avant-garde artists, graduate students, community organizers, unions and representatives of nearly every crevice of left-wing activism, a thousand people arrived on September 17th at a park in downtown Manhattan near Wall Street to protest the rule of what they famously called "the one percent." The occupation of Zuccotti Park and similar spaces across the country lasted until the middle of December, when there was a coordinated crackdown by the national counterterrorism apparatus.*

What everyone remembers about the activists at Occupy was the same thing the mainstream media often emphasized at the time: that the protesters had no specific agenda. This, like so many other things that are "known" about the encampment, is false. "As one

---

*For my money, the best written accounts of Occupy are Nathan Schneider's *Thank You, Anarchy*, David Graeber's *The Democracy Project* and essays by Astra Taylor, Rebecca Solnit, Carla Blumenkranz, Sarah Resnick, Keith Gessen and Alex Vitale in the *n+1* and Verso Books collaboration *Occupy! Scenes from Occupied America*.

people, united," the collectively drafted "Declaration of the Occupation of New York City" announces that "corporations, which place profit over people, self-interest over justice, and oppression over equality, run our governments."

> They have taken our houses through an illegal foreclosure process, despite not having the original mortgage. They have taken bailouts from taxpayers with impunity and continue to give Executives exorbitant bonuses. They have perpetuated inequality and discrimination in the workplace based on age, the color of one's skin, sex, gender identity and sexual orientation. . . . They have continuously sought to strip employees of the right to negotiate for better pay and safer working conditions. They have held students hostage with tens of thousands of dollars of debt on education, which is itself a human right. They have consistently outsourced labor and used that outsourcing as leverage to cut workers' healthcare and pay. . . . They have participated in the torture and murder of innocent civilians overseas.

It goes on and on like that, and even adds a helpful footnote: *These grievances are not all-inclusive*. Perhaps not, but it's remarkable how well the statement can still stand, nearly eight years later, as a digest of the causes uniting this country's radical left.

That said, it is true that Occupy wasn't *all* about its agenda. People sometimes ask me how this short-lived movement could matter so much to people my age. And when I answer them, I don't read them the declaration. If I had to cram the answer into a thesis statement, it would go something like this: Occupy was ultimately an attempt to reclaim public space, and in so doing it reclaimed our ability to create new worlds.

I should admit that I missed Occupy proper, instead monitoring it online from my freshman dorm. I was only able to make it to my first Occupy events on May Day 2012, after the initial Occupiers had been evicted from Zuccotti Park. Even so, I was able to experience some of the occupation's ecstatic, almost carnivalesque character. The air of the camps vibrated with chitchat and soapbox speakers and human microphones and the famous din of the drum circles. One educational event I attended, called the Free University, filled Madison Square Park with little circular groups led by teachers (some amateurs, some college professors) who gave talks on subjects as varied as the history of May Day, deep ecology, a protest songwriting workshop and something called "Occupy Algebra." Occupiers were obsessed with a kind of street-theater performance-as-protest—inspired by the Situationists as well as by conceptual artists like Banksy and Ai Weiwei—to which I was subjected and, to my infinite shame, even once participated in myself. There were the bizarre and vaguely obscene hand gestures they tried to use in the general assemblies. I even had my first kiss there, from a business student I met at Occupy May Day who took me back to his NYU dorm to make out. (A big deal for me, as I was still in the closet.) That, too, was the sort of thing liable to happen among the Occupiers.

It's a commonplace in urban studies that architecture has a way of structuring consciousness: we construct spaces that are the embodiment of an idea, and these in turn shape the people who later find themselves within them. "The ideal city," wrote Rebecca Solnit in her essay collection *Wanderlust*, "is organized around citizenship— around participation in public life." Yet under the neoliberal regime what we find all around us is the opposite: spaces segmented and divided in accord with the dictates of those who own them. The suburbs where I grew up were an extreme example. But even New York, the city I loved and where I now live, is on closer examination a series of vacuum-sealed enclosures. For decades the parks have closed at night out of fear among those in charge that junkies, hobos, criminals and homosexuals would assemble there. Ordinary people's rights to assembly are hardly guaranteed, either, given the widespread privatization of public spaces. Neighborhoods are rigidly (if informally) segregated by race and class, their boundaries enforced by police patrols that harass poor people in the "wrong place." And since the political bribes of the real-estate conglomerates guarantee that rent controls will remain a distant dream, crystal towers full of the empty second or third apartments of hedge-fund managers will continue to be built while sixty thousand people live in the streets and freeze to death in the winter.

Such spaces are not only the symptoms but the creators of our social malaise. To live and work in them is to lead a stunted existence. But what if we forced our ideal city into existence? What if we clawed back our rights to assembly and association from the owning class, the laws drawn up by their hired politicians be damned? This was the prospect of Occupy—strangers who came to regard each other as siblings, shopkeepers who donated free food to the encampment in solidarity, professors at nearby colleges who opened up their lectures to the wide public, people discussing philosophy under the tent of the People's Library full of donated books. The overwhelming feeling was of a whole bustling little world, and indeed that was the point. "We are the 99 percent" was just the slogan that got things started: the real motto, which encompassed what it was all actually about, insisted that "another world is possible."

The genius of the thing was that the crazy bastards figured out how to do it. Sure, they were crushed before they could iron out the kinks. But the basic principle was sound. And not only that, but it addressed a crucial question: How can you build a socialism that avoids falling prey to the Stalinist pigs—a socialism where the people are really in charge? The Occupiers answered: by building a democracy of assemblies.

It wasn't a new idea—it had long been the anarchist answer to the question. But there are truths that every generation has to rediscover for itself. And this truth in particular is one best learned through hands-on experience. I probably couldn't convince you with an argument—at any rate not without difficulty—that assembly democracy is the way we ought to run our workplaces and communities. But a well-ordered assembly is its own best propaganda.

Once in assembly you quickly realize how rarely we ever deliberate directly with others, exchange ideas, come to compromises and collectively make decisions. Think about how few opportunities you've had to do such a thing in your life, if ever. People don't even know how to, really, at first, but it's like riding a bicycle: you learn by doing it. In an assembly no one is the boss, and once the matter is settled everyone agrees to do it. Then, when the thing gets done, you become a fanatic. You start to ask yourself, "Why can't we do everything this way?" Why not run our companies, our cities in assembly? So often, the answer is "It hasn't been done." Which is a filthy lie, when you look at the long history of direct-democratic institutions: tribal and village councils, town-hall meetings, workers' cooperatives, syndicalist trade unions, the Athenian polis, the Haudenosaunee Confederation, anarchist Spain. But we also give the lie to it when we construct such institutions ourselves—as so many people have done in the wake of Occupy, keeping its flame alive by trying to build what they found there into a more lasting reality.

·

I counted myself among them, even if my campus at Princeton was hardly the most hospitable setting for such an experiment. Notoriously conservative even by the standards of the other elite schools, with an undergraduate culture defined predominantly by careerism, the campus would seem to have killed anything like Occupy's spirit on arrival.

Contrary to the image of the bellicose social-justice warrior that's emerged since, the typical Princeton student in that age of drowsy consensus was someone focused on having a great time for four years until they got their piece of paper certifying them for a spot in finance, consulting, Silicon Valley or a top professional school. This was reflected as much among the activists as anywhere else. If most people were apathetic, the activists had pet causes. They hung out at officially sanctioned pseudo-political events, or else their little organizations—the College Dems, the greening campus people, the mental-health awareness club—would attract five to fifteen people at meetings and draft feel-good petitions that ended up in some administrator's drawer.

More daring movements—for divestment from fossil fuels, for prison reform, for working with local townies to block the school's unpopular and anti-democratic development plans—were even smaller. They were also pitifully funded, frequently stonewalled by officials and mocked or reviled by other students. Still, they had their activists, and gradually, through the undergraduate magazine and radio show I worked for, I began to meet them. Even within this group a distinction could be made between those who seemed most interested in résumé padding for a future NGO career and the more radical kids: you could tell who they were because they said "queer" instead of "gay" and added "neoliberalism" and "capitalism" to the litanies of -isms recited at the start and end of a meeting.

It wasn't long before a group of us came together. We were a pretty diverse set as far as Princeton goes—various kinds of immigrant kid as well as whites, several flavors of alternative sexuality, a relatively even gender split and even several people from working-class and first-generation college student backgrounds. As college students are uniquely suited to doing, we were looking for answers to the fundamental questions: How had things gotten this way? Could we build something different? If so, how? Our organization, the Princeton United Left, became infamous for three things: its radical anarchist-inflected socialism, its excellent pre-games and its general assemblies.

We began to develop a critique of past socialisms. The failure of Soviet-style "communist" dictatorships was our basic starting point. But the mid-century Western social democracy most of us initially admired was hardly exempt from critique. Yes, its achievements needed defending from the neoliberal assault, particularly its relative equalization of the classes. But we started to notice that the reassertion of capitalist control hadn't come from nowhere. If anything, elites had become *more* resilient in the postwar period through their influence on economic planning—a centralization of decision-making which made it easier for that same elite to dismantle social democracy when they saw their chance.

The postwar grand bargain had also left many people out: ethnic minorities shut out of the welfare state by discrimination, women and queer people forced into positions of subordination to men, people of colonized nations whose cheap raw materials and luxury goods fed the rich countries' social democracies. Empowered by the new freedoms and bargaining power granted by the postwar order, these groups made their own movements in the sixties, which collectively came to be called the New Left. They taught us a lot. From the critical black tradition and postcolonialism we learned to be suspicious of white saviors and that around the world people of color had created and led emancipatory movements. Feminism taught us not only the history of male domination and female resistance but also how to create spaces where the sexes could meet again and live and work together as equals. And queer liberation reminded us that only a world where people could explore and express their gender and sexual desire as they pleased was one in which they could truly become what they always wanted and needed to be, beautiful and free.

But the history of the New Left also contained more practical and sobering lessons—particularly about the persistence of hierarchy. Here was a left that had begun the sixties with organizations— most prominently the Students for a Democratic Society (SDS)— grounded in nonviolence, free speech and participatory democracy, a left devoted to avoiding the mistakes of "communism" and social democracy alike. And yet by the end of the decade this left had fractured into competing neo-Stalinist sects clustered around charismatic leaders and cults of violence.* How had this happened? Still grappling with such questions in our reading, we were soon to learn some lessons from our own experience as well.

As on many other campuses, Princeton's political revival came in 2014. Quietly, since at least the murder of Trayvon Martin (and in many places before), the first rumblings of a movement led by working-class people of color against police brutality had been stirring. After the cop Darren Wilson shot and killed an unarmed boy named Michael Brown in Ferguson, Missouri, mass protests led by some of the poorest people in America seized the city before being suppressed with military-grade equipment by the National Guard. Allied demonstrations emerged over the next year, in New York over the killing of Eric Garner and in Baltimore over the killing of Freddie

* In a lovely pamphlet called "Listen, Marxist!" written at the time, Murray Bookchin called it "all the old crap of the thirties." In a recent essay for *Jacobin*, the historian Paul Heideman sums it up thusly: "Picture a convention of students, split between two sides, one chanting 'Ho, Ho, Ho Chi Minh!' and the other 'Mao, Mao, Mao Zedong!'"

Gray. When Wilson was acquitted in November, Ferguson erupted again in protest. It also woke Princeton from its stupor.

An ad hoc emergency committee formed and quickly disseminated a call that spread through email lists and group chats across campus: there was going to be a march. Hundreds of students came out, many of them black, nearly all of them previously apolitical. By nightfall, at the vigil, my activist friends and I were ecstatic. Black Lives Matter had been founded by queer black women and it was putting a number of crucial intersecting issues back on the table. People were talking about a black liberation movement that wouldn't throw women and queer people under the bus (as the old one often had), about how the only path out of structural racism required a massive rollback of capitalism, about how radical democracy was the solution to a whole basket of problems.* Here at last, we thought, was the opportunity to create a movement that built on Occupy and moved us beyond it.

The very existence of a group devoted to black liberation in the wake of Ferguson energized the whole campus. This included the racist frat boys calling black students "animals" on the popular anonymous message board Yik Yak, which only further motivated those of us in the activist community to show solidarity. The group's next goal, after the vigil, was a "die-in" protest where people would walk out of classes and play dead in a public space to commemorate the victims of police murder. This sounded pretty cool in my book.

Yet there were also things that troubled me from early on about how the movement was being run and organized. The first was the radio silence surrounding what would come after the initial vigil. There was no organization to join, no coordinated group except that one online chat from the spontaneous march—which required a private invite. Eventually a poster spread announcing "a post-Ferguson movement at Princeton." The meeting room was the one where Einstein used to lecture, or so the tours liked to say. It was

---

* For an overview of the Black Lives Matter moment as well as the long history of black liberation struggles since the civil rights movement, there remains no better introduction than *From #BlackLivesMatter to Black Liberation* by Keeanga-Yamahtta Taylor.

packed with people, many of them black and brown, and at the front were the kids from the group chat. They'd dressed in coordinated leather jackets and black clothes. That wasn't their only difference from the rest of the crowd. There was a very clear distinction between us and them, and it wasn't racial: if you were in the little group of half a dozen people in the front, you were giving the orders; if you were anyone else, you were there to listen and obey.

Early on, the fruits of this new hierarchy on campus manifested itself in examples that sound silly now—such as one acrimonious back-and-forth I was involved in over whether it was okay for activists from outside the inner circle to help create a Facebook page for racial-justice activism. It manifested itself more broadly in the group's refusal to put out educational materials or hold public events, opting instead for a year's worth of private negotiations with school administrators. The clique refused to work with the prison-reform group—which was fighting to remove the box on Princeton's college application that asks about previous felonies, disproportionately affecting working-class applicants of color busted on drug charges—or indeed with any group they didn't themselves direct. And there were also ugly power struggles within the clique itself. At one point the little group met after a long absence and two non-black organizers who'd been there since the beginning—two girls, one Jewish and one Latina—were present as always. After a Nigerian girl said the presence of whites was causing her emotional distress, they were asked to leave and discouraged from attending any future meetings. (Some on campus called this "the Purge.")

Things came to a head when, after a year of near-total inactivity, the group occupied Nassau Hall. Their main demands were for the university to remove Woodrow Wilson's name from the policy school, institute sensitivity training for professors and create "affinity housing" and other safe spaces on campus where only people of color would be allowed to live or hang out. It was an incredibly brave act that made national news—not since the seventies had anything this radical happened on campus. It was also the culmination of their top-down organizing style: a more or less closed group had planned the action and drafted the platform with no input from

people of color in the broader campus community, and their supporters didn't so much argue for its proposals as try to shame people
into accepting them. The last demand for no-whites-allowed spaces
was particularly controversial, even among the activist community.

Desperate to show my support for the movement, I made arguments in the dining hall in defense of affinity housing, as much
to convince myself as others. Then I saw a Chinese student get
screamed at and denounced in what was by now the customary
manner for asking, not particularly confrontationally, what the difference was between affinity housing and segregation—a question
I'd been thinking to ask myself. I felt my last bits of sympathy with
the clique evaporating. What was so dispiriting was not our disagreement about affinity housing—surely we could have agreed to
disagree—but their attitude that the debate over the issue could be
settled by fiat. That even wanting to discuss the matter was proof you
were allied with white supremacy. (As if all black and brown people
on campus were in agreement.) This sort of thing was the sign that
whatever the new reality the group was seeking on campus, it would
be imposed on us just like the old one: from above.

I've described the post-Ferguson racial-justice movement because that's where this approach manifested itself most clearly on
my campus, but such behavior could be found in feminist, queer
and other identity-based spaces as well in those years. It remains a
major problem in academia and the left-wing press. People talk a
lot about the toxic influence of "identity politics," but this is imprecise. The problem isn't the fight against sexism, racism, homo-
and transphobia, and other forms of identity-based repression, but
rather a particular set of assumptions that have become conventional in many of the movements advocating for these issues today. These include the assumption that whole ways of looking at
the world are inherent in particular racial, sexual or gender identities; that only people with an oppressed identity know the truth of
their oppression; and that there are unbridgeable gaps between the
epistemologies of people with different identities. Often described
as identitarianism, this story mandates that moral and even political authority can be conferred to individuals by virtue of group

oppression. Furthermore, since speech can be a form of violence on a spectrum with the physical and sexual kinds, disagreement on identity issues in itself constitutes a form of abuse. Thus, discourse must be regulated in order to ensure the safety and protection of minorities and to impede the spread of ideas and discourses that create discomfort. (No great loss, since "free speech" is always policed anyway, just usually in the interests of the powerful as against that of the oppressed.)

Identitarianism has had a noxious effect on the many spaces where, in recent years, it has become prominent. As autocratically enforced dogmas often do, it's also created currents of backlash and resentment. Certainly this was their effect on me. It was all too easy for me as a brown writer to resent the suffocating atmosphere created by identitarianism, which treats anyone of a minority background who refuses to wear its straitjacket as a pariah. For several years following my campus experience, I was so upset by what I saw as the disingenuous manipulation of identity on campus that I was likely to regard somebody even just using the jargon with suspicion and contempt. I became snide and vicious in mocking their excesses, stewed in resentment at the power they seemed to wield online or in publishing, and even began to feel myself considering them an enemy to be vanquished.

I continue to worry today about the influence of identitarianism on left-wing organizations and spaces. But I've also come to worry about the reaction to identitarianism on the left. I saw in my own case the way that contempt can harden into its own kind of authoritarian intolerance. My anger towards the identitarians was causing me to lose sight of the very real experiences of prejudice and oppression out of which their ideology had sprung—even when I could identify with those experiences myself. Throughout the activist world, in the years that would follow, versions of this battle—often framed nowadays as being between identitarians and "class reductionists," who see only economic issues as being "universal"—would play out, most notably in the 2016 primary season between the followers of Hillary Clinton and those of Bernie Sanders. The problem with the debate is not that it's stupid or irresolvable. (Quite to the contrary, I believe it's both essential and complex.) The problem is that, because of the refusal of either side to engage in good faith, it threatens to create new hierarchies in precisely the spaces that claim to be devoted to the ideal I had seen made flesh at Occupy— the ideal of a radically democratic world, of a world without rulers.

III. FUTURE

Memory, when it isn't merely vague, is temperamental. Memoir is by turns a genre of lies and speculations. The dirty secret of auto-biographical nonfiction is that, having forgotten most of what's ever happened to us, we're left only with what survives in records (journals, publications, other people's stories about us) and the vague sensation of whatever, maybe, it felt like to live a certain life. Nevertheless, there are moments of our lives that remain in high definition. Often they aren't of any importance—the record of some petty triumph or embarrassment. A few, however, remain significant beyond ourselves. This is because they connect our personal experience to the larger transformations of our time. For me, one such experience was the May Day events at Occupy. Another came toward the end of my time at Princeton, when I attended my first meeting of the Democratic Socialists of America.

I'd arrived at a squat brick building of a few stories in Brooklyn. At first I thought I'd come to the wrong place, since this was clearly an Episcopalian church. (I'd learn later it was actually two churches— the Spanish-language parish, which owned the building, also let an English-language congregation of hipster Anglicans led by a female vicar use the space after they got kicked out of the bar in whose back room they'd previously worshiped.) On further examination, I found a sign on printer paper attached to one of the side doors: LOOKING FOR SOCIALISTS? → THIS WAY! It was decorated by what is now a historical artifact: the rather clunky old DSA logo from before Remeike Forbes's 2016 redesign, affectionately known as "the rose and gardeners' gloves."

The whole trip was on something of a whim and mostly a kind of favor to my friend Russell, a soft-voiced Quaker from New England who I met while interviewing him about socialist politics for my college radio station. One night I was subjecting Russ to one of my rants. All the old left-wing distinctions were fading! Why couldn't people just open their eyes! What we've needed since Occupy is a broad-based movement devoted to a shared idea of socialism as radical democracy! That sort of thing. Russell, probably tired of hearing my slogans for the twentieth time, said I might be interested to know such an organization already existed. "The DSA?" I said. "Aren't they the reformists who get people to vote Democrat?"* "They used to be that," he replied in his friendly commonsense way, "but now it's different." Mostly because he insisted, I coughed up the $33 for the train and went to find them.

As I got signed in by a homely bearded fellow at the little registration desk, a surge of emotion distracted me from filling out my forms. I felt almost lightheaded. There was the overwhelming sense that I was somewhere familiar, the repetition not as in déjà vu of a moment in time but of a kind of space. The texture of the table and the uneven wood floor reminded me of places I'd been in before, a particular sort of place with certain features and certain ways of moving through them. It was only when I looked up that I remembered.

I was in a *salón*. That was the word that came to mind, and not its English equivalent. It can be approximated as "hall," as in "meeting hall" or "assembly hall" or "union hall." The word feels less old-fashioned in Spanish, maybe because for Latinos—or at least the ones I grew up with—such halls have a contemporary function. Namely, a religious one.

Despite growing up in the Jersey suburbs, my parents took me

---

* DSA ultimately traces its roots all the way back to the classic Socialist Party of America (SPA)—the party of Eugene Debs, Helen Keller, Mary White Ovington and Big Bill Haywood—whose vibrant culture of pluralism and folksiness it greatly resembles. The SPA renamed itself and then quickly split in the sixties. Out of one of the factions came the Democratic Socialist Organizing Committee (DSOC), a social-democratic group, which to everyone's surprise merged with a group of democracy-minded communists calling themselves the New American Movement (NAM) to form the Democratic Socialists of America (DSA) in 1982. For a full history, consult Joseph M. Schwartz's thorough article "A History of the Democratic Socialists of America 1971–2017" on the DSA website.

every Sunday to attend Mass in a small brick church of Latino Catholics in New Brunswick, a university city and pharmaceutical company town with a heavy immigrant population from around the
world. Such immigrant churches, like so many houses of worship
which double as community hubs, had little meeting halls attached
to the main building in which to house festivals, teen socials and
Alcoholics Anonymous meetings. I grew up calling our version of
this place "*el salón*" because that's what I was taught to call it. But it
exists in many societies under many names. I can remember filing
out from under the square redbrick steeple and through the alley between the church and the house of the priest and heading through
the parking lot—trying not to stare at the junkies and homeless who
sometimes loitered outside the Catholic Charities—then entering a
kind of annex building, climbing its narrow stairs and coming into
the open space of the *salón*. The tile floor tracked enough dirt to become permanently stained after rainy days. Catholics always find an
excuse for a party, and Latinos even more so. There was a festival every month, sometimes two: parties to commemorate every visitation
of the Virgin or hillbilly saint the clergy ever beatified to stave off a
peasant revolt. The most important was el Día de la Hispanidad in
September, when each of the shitty little fold-out plastic tables lining the walls was manned by parishioners of a different nationality,
decorated with their home country's flag and decked out with big
cheap aluminum food warmers stuffed to the brim with homemade
cuisine. Not only as a child but long into my teens I resented the
interminable get-togethers: the grown-ups stuffing their faces and
catching up and invariably by nightfall dancing to music so loud it
often blew out the speakers, while I slinked away to a corner with
my Nintendo, trying to avoid the flirtations of church girls whose
interest I was incapable of reciprocating and of whose discernment
I was deeply afraid. Years would pass before was I able to look back
upon the *salón* with affection and nostalgia, because only then was
I able to understand what it represented.

And now, in distant Brooklyn among what I thought would be
strangers, I found myself in the *salón* once again. The same folding
chairs and tables, the same bad insulation, the same subtle echo

of your voice in the air. It was different, of course. The tablecloths were decorated with variations on the rose logo, and topped not with Latin American home cooking but sign-up sheets and free magazines and posters and socialist-feminist pamphlets. The building was not an annex to the church but run by a radical collective as a leftist events space. The denizens were socialists and, famously, predominantly white (with various exceptions, however, not least myself).

The Occupiers had taught me that space is a thing we construct together, something shaped by our forms of social life which shapes them in turn. The arrangement of an office, a park, an apartment, a garden, an assembly, a *salón* is a choice we make about the kind of world we want to live in. What then exactly is the sort of world that builds a *salón*, the world a *salón* builds?

Previously I'd encountered two kinds of activist spaces with two kinds of people. In academic activist spaces, and particularly "radical" ones, everyone was trying to one-up each other on how subversive and edgy they were, deploying warmed-over yet somehow also hip Foucauldian queer theory to "critique" and "problematize" anything within arm's length. In crusty old Marxist circles—your typical Trotskyite reading group—you'd get some old guru starting a cult of personality around himself and training disciples in the appropriate exegesis of the sacred texts (the *Manifesto*, the *Critique of the Gotha Programme*, *Das Kapital* Volume One, etc.). At the DSA meeting, by contrast, I found people who fit neither into a scene nor a cult: nurses, teachers, students, ex-truckers who'd become union reps, as well as lefty mainstays like journalists and grad students. And they talked about concrete problems. I remember the girl who was worried about her mother's immigration status under then-president Obama's record deportations; recent college grads telling me about the jobs with pitiless hours they'd had to accept to pay off their student loans, or about the yearlong hunt for one that had depleted their savings to nothing; a thirtysomething bisexual adjunct professor suffering from increasing depression as he barely scraped by on his pathetic wage; the middle-aged NGO worker whose sister had been foreclosed upon in the 2008 crash and was still living with him years later. When these people talked about socialism, it wasn't as an eccentric literary pursuit or a parlor game but as a solution to the practical problems created by the structures we all inhabited—a socialism of common sense.

I think, too, about the people who hung around behind the various tables between conference events. There were action-based working groups (Racial Justice, Labor, Bernie 2016) but also identity-based ones (Socialist Feminists, Black Socialists, Religious Socialists)—and, most surprisingly of all, a group called the Left Caucus representing all groups to the left of the social democrats. Russ had told me they existed, but two things about them struck me. One was that they were allowed to table at all alongside everyone else despite being an openly ideological formation. The other was that their own materials explicitly spelled out their commitment to the "multi-tendency" nature of DSA, openly advocating for their shared positions while acknowledging the possibility of disagreement.

That above all was what inspired me. If what I'd found in the *salón* in Brooklyn was a socialist church, it was not the high church of popes and cardinals who lived in palaces and commanded the laymen to kiss their rings, but the low church of ordinary people united in a shared communion—Quakers at their friendly meetings, the campesinos leading their own liberation theology masses in each other's homes—the church that revolted against the clerics. Nor was it a church with a single absolute truth, deviation from which leads to excommunication. There were no bosses here, and no one mastered anyone else. It was what the Zapatistas of southern Mexico—political heroes of mine, as they were of many anarchists—called "*un mundo donde quepan muchos mundos,*" a world where many worlds fit. At some point someone passed around a sign-up sheet, and I paid my dues on the spot.

In short order, tens of thousands of people across the country would do the same. This was only partly due to the Bernie effect. Contrary to popular belief, the Sanders campaign in 2016 led to a respectable but only modest growth in DSA's membership, from 6,500 to about eight thousand on the eve of the election. At a DSA event in New York around that time I heard Bhaskar Sunkara, the ever-savvy editor of *Jacobin*, tell us something like "There are only about five thousand socialists in the U.S. right now. I'm hoping maybe by the time I die we'll reach Debs's hundred thousand." It's easy to laugh at him now, but not for the reason he would have expected.

Above all, it was Trump's victory that woke tens of thousands of progressives out of their dogmatic slumber. It wasn't just the fact that a dangerous charlatan, backed openly by fascists and white supremacists, had ascended to the White House. It was also what this event revealed: that neoliberals like Hillary Clinton, and the decades of Democratic Party consensus that she represented, had become part of the problem. While the country was falling into a political and economic crisis they had blathered about the national debt and worried about soliciting campaign donations from Silicon Valley billionaires.

I have it secondhand that, in the days after the election, the national DSA office was so flooded with membership requests that it had to hire a new staffer on dues money it didn't quite yet have just to keep up. Even if that's not literally true, it captures the spirit of the time: manic, hysterical, chapters sprouting up across the country, battles with fascists and police in almost as many streets, new campaigns, new victories, new defeats, a high point of despair as well as hope, a time when the monsters of the past returned as well as its heroes. By the summer of 2017 there were 25,000 DSAers. Today, we stand at over sixty thousand.

•

What does the DSA want? A common enough idea is that, ignorant of the dark history of the Soviet Union and other "communist" countries, we desire a society where every aspect of the economy and culture is planned from the top down by a single Party. I'll grant there may be some of us, a tiny minority, who envision such a thing. But the organization's own commitment to pluralism in the democratic process—all those working groups and ideological caucuses— speaks to something rather different. DSAers themselves repudiate the centralization and authoritarianism so often discussed by the critics of socialism, and much of what defines the new socialism is an acknowledgment that the tradition we've inherited is one strewn with traps. At the same time, it would be a mistake to think that all DSA wants is a return to Tony Judt-style social democracy of the sort I admired in the pre-Obama years, where a basically capitalist system is leavened by a few socialistic elements like welfare or universal health care. Socialists generally see Bernie Sanders's platform as the springboard for the movement, not its horizon.

The various socialisms within DSA are united in the realization that the world has changed and socialism must change with it. For one thing, previous socialisms coexisted more easily than many would like to admit alongside racism, heteropatriarchy and imperialism; much of the identitarianism debate consists of the movement's attempts to figure out just how it can truly ensure these are things of the past. There's also the ecological crisis. While some past socialist movements played a role in raising awareness of environmental problems, on the whole socialism has tended to put its faith in industrial development as a way to raise living standards and achieve democratic mastery over nature, with pretty devastating consequences: "communist" countries were often even bigger polluters than capitalist ones. In light of the apocalyptic scale of climate change, today's socialists are all effectively eco-socialists, and the need for green economic planning on a scale neoliberalism simply can't provide is among the most important things attracting young people to the left.

Above all, though, is a change in the way socialists think about democracy. In this regard, not only the Soviet-style dictatorships serve as a cautionary tale, but also the paternalism of the social-democratic period. The postwar compromise did show how an industrial economy could serve the needs of the many, distributing the fruits of capitalist production more evenly than ever before. But the manner in which it did so—as a top-down technocracy—ended up, ironically, laying the groundwork for the later neoliberal takeover. I think back to the suburbs where I grew up in the nineties. People said we lived in a democracy, but what was meant by this was that my neighbors and I would show up every two to four years at some lower-school gymnasium filled with booths where we'd push a button to choose a leader from options pre-selected by the country's ruling-class oligarchy. Never were we trusted to deliberate over matters that affected us or participate robustly in civic life. The anarchists had always emphasized that no socialism was possible without citizens being directly in charge of production and investment decisions, and this is no longer exclusively their idea. Not only the redistribution of resources but the redistribution of *decision-making power* is a central concern of the new socialism. That is why we are obsessed with the creation of spaces like cooperatives, worker-run trade or tenants' unions, community-controlled housing and neighborhood councils—spaces where real resources are placed directly in the hands of ordinary people self-organized into democratic assemblies.

At its best, DSA itself is such a space. Regardless of its founders' intention to make it a pressure group on the Democratic Party, "the org"—as DSAers affectionately call it—has become a laboratory for experiments in democratic living. It is best understood as a little society within a society with its own vibrant and independent press, its own celebrities, its own legal and political structure, its own heated controversies and de facto political parties. Its practices emulate the future it wants to create. The autonomy of its local chapters to determine for themselves how they'll run things has led to a proliferation of constitutions and other experiments in how to structure decision-making, many of them putting directly into practice reforms the movement advocates for—such as single-transferable voting, proportionality and quotas in representation, digital democracy and direct democracy (whether by online referendum or confederations of assemblies with mandated and recallable delegates). In cities, towns and rural areas across the country, a DSA chapter is not only a hub of activist activity but often a mini-revival of culture and community in areas largely devoid of communal associations of any sort. They organize not only strikes, rallies, campaigns and mutual aid networks but also festivals, talent shows, movie screenings and comedy nights.

This is why most of DSA's members furiously defend the rights of themselves and others within the organization, with arguments around class, race and gender focused overwhelmingly on what is *more* fair, *more* democratic and *more* pluralistic. Opposing opinions not only exist but thrive; there seem to be more of them every day, and they duel and shout and advertise in a messy, earthy clamor which feels a lot more like what democracy was supposed to have been like than anything that I ever saw in my hometown or on C-SPAN. Besides my little chunk of Occupy, a fleeting and half-remembered dream by comparison, DSA is the only time in my life where anyone has tried to figure out what it would look like for the people themselves to be in charge of anything. Shockingly, to a large extent, it works. And inasmuch as I can, in DSA parlance, "trust the process"—that is, paraphrasing Mill and Dewey with beautiful concision, hold faith that if we're democratic then we'll eventually grope our way to the right answers—it gives me hope that some of the techniques and forms of life being developed within it can heal the wounds festering in our larger culture.

Yet this hope, which helps get me out of bed in the morning instead of giving up and rolling over, is in the end a fragile thing. Often enough it's paired with its opposite. Because I would be lying if I said that I only saw the seeds of socialism—the democratic society of free producers—in DSA. Sometimes I look at our organization and see the beginnings of the Party that Orwell taught me so much to despise. Not just because of the presence of identitarians. They do exist, and they have a way of getting up to their old tricks: demanding people be "canceled" for having "bad politics," trying to frame certain issues such that having the wrong opinion on them means you're an oppressor and thus can't even be engaged or convinced but only ejected, tying everything back to identity in loose ways as a pretense for discrediting somebody they dislike for other reasons.

To my surprise, though, their most extreme elements have largely been driven off, or else defanged and integrated into the larger DSA culture, due to the surprising robustness of our democratic norms. Critiques of identitarianism by Adolph Reed, Angela Nagle, Sarah Schulman and Asad Haider circulate widely and get extensively debated with a surprising degree of nuance (though not without vitriol). When articles in DSA-adjacent media cause a controversy, the norm is not to revoke them but for someone to publish an angry reply—in some cases, even in the same publication. DSA meetings and official online spaces are invariably prefaced by a recitation of "civility norms" that anticipate many of the common identitarian formulas and put them off limits, and members in chapters that have had such problems have created sophisticated guides for ensuring pluralism and civility. All this has made identitarianism less powerful in DSA than just about anywhere on the left, including the little magazines and the radical press.

The bigger problem right now is that the battle against identitarianism has come at a cost. A chunk of the movement, whose thinking on these questions was formed in the 2016 Democratic primary, sees "IDPol" as little more than a neoliberal plot to deflect from economic questions and promote the careers of "woke" minority professionals in media and politics. For these class reductionists, it increasingly seems, anyone who so much as brings up the issue of patriarchy and racism within the movement must be engaging in "purity politics." Seen through this lens socialism becomes entirely a matter of "class struggle," so that making any demands other than purely economic ones is at best a distraction and at worst actively alienates "the workers." Anyone who engages in these "subcultural" behaviors is a "wrecker," and, should softer methods prove inadequate to the task of ridding the organization of "wreckers," authoritarian means are perfectly legitimate. (Chillingly, "wrecker" is a legal category under which Stalin persecuted dissenters.)

Bolstered by such arguments, a small faction in DSA called Momentum*, closely associated with *Jacobin* magazine, has consolidated power around itself through increasingly brazen anti-democratic measures. A recent report for the *New Republic* by journalist Miguel Salazar skimmed the surface of the situation,

---

*Well, sort of. Depending on how one counts, this informal grouping has re-branded three to four times—a source of much humor to rank-and-filers. Momentum is what most DSAers know them by. Lately public pressure has driven them to operate in the open as a tendency anyone can join. Their latest iteration is a national caucus known as Bread and Roses.

mentioning their "dismissive" attitude towards critics and their "top-down structure" where "general meetings are infrequent and subcommittees are limited in their scope." This is the tip of the iceberg. The truth is that Momentum has spent the past two years on something like a crusade, alienating vast swaths of the organization who agree with their politics on paper but object to their behavior. Believing that their analysis is the only correct path to socialism, Momentum have thrown themselves entirely behind Medicare for All and Bernie Sanders, using backhanded schemes in the spaces they control to prevent members from participating in any other initiatives while retaining an iron grip over those projects they do support. In extreme cases, they've blatantly violated DSA's bylaws or misused them to punish lower-ranking critics, turning the handful of chapters they control into the effective equivalent of one-party states. They've been allowed to get away with it because they have a plurality on DSA's National Political Committee—at least until the convention this August, when they're up for reelection.

From Momentum's point of view, all this is supposed to prevent "identitarian wreckers" from steering the organization away from "working-class" interests. But I know brave organizers, many of them far more legitimately working-class than either myself or the Momentum crew, who've been driven to leave DSA due to this treatment, or at least consider it. One woman, a single mom from a low-income rural area whose main DSA work is on health care, spoke out against a proposal for a Medicare for All march on the floor of the last convention—and had a lighter thrown at her by a Momentum chapter leader in the hallway afterwards. Other organizers, some of them black and brown, have tried to organize creatively in Momentum-controlled chapters and committees to speak to issues that affect working-class communities in their area—tenants' unions to fight landlords and gentrification, occupations of ICE offices to protest the creation of concentration camps for migrants, and so on—only to have leadership try to shut their operations down or refuse to lend them any publicity in DSA channels on the grounds that these were "particularist" rather than "universalist" demands. Such behavior has already begun to drive smart and dedicated organizers into the arms of identitarian hardliners, imperiling precisely the multiracial working-class coalition *Jacobin* has been harping on about creating for years.

But the conflict also imperils something else: the commitment to pluralism and democracy at the heart of DSA. Both the identitarians and the class reductionists today gain much of their strength from their projection of total moral certainty that they've reached the single correct line—whether intersectional or universalist—on all political issues, as well as the equal certainty that by following this line we will arrive at our own Sugarcandy Mountain of "fully automated luxury gay space communism." In each of these cases one finds the same implicit assertion: if you have the right interpretation of the sacred texts, you know the occult truth about the universe and the path to earthly paradise; thus, to dissent from these views is to become a heretic. Buying into such a theology is liable to make you a fanatic eager to go hunting for apostates—which is the first step towards the kind of authoritarian turn we've seen all too often in the history of the left.

I have no doubt DSA contains the germ of a better society. But in my heart I know that it has other possible futures. In a way these are even more likely, to judge from history. Every socialist with a moral backbone knows exactly what I'm talking about. You know the sort of people the movement can attract in spite of its noble aims: the ones who see others not as human beings but as resources to be managed, who have no compunctions about means so long as the ends are justified, whose sense of their great personal destiny comes from their conviction that the winds of history are at their back. Today they're an annoyance. Tomorrow . . .

Well that's just the thing, isn't it? You don't know. It may be the infrastructure you're helping to build, the network of committees and groups and constitutions and procedures, is really the beginning of a truly free society. Or it could be that, whatever your intentions, it is nothing more than a machine designed to take over the state. And then what has happened to so many socialist do-gooders before you will happen to you: some schemer will take over your little dream and force you to live inside their nightmare. No more talk of democracy and decency. No real talk anyway; the words will by then have become their opposites. Engines of liberation turned into instruments of slavery. One ruling class replaced by another. And it's not like they didn't warn you. Could the philistines have been right all along? It's an irony, but so predictable by now it seems more like a logical deduction: you set out to save democracy, therefore you ended up killing it for good. Maybe clichés exist to preserve primal truths, like cockroaches in amber. Maybe no better world was ever possible. You're helping to assemble the dictatorship that will censor your poetry. Your favored regime will stick you in a labor camp—maybe your friends will be the ones to do it—or else you'll end up some bitter exile, your friends all dead and abandoned, with nothing left to do but write self-exculpatory novels, or become a neoconservative.

These are moments of hysteria. They come and go. There's a good chance, to say the least, that DSA won't prove so important for good or ill in the end. But don't think it's nothing, either. Whatever's coming will likely have the texture, the flavor of these hallucinations, if not their content.

•

There was a time when I thought I would conclude by saying that in spite of everything, socialism—a true and democratic socialism, one that can live up to the aspirations of those who first dreamed of it—is our greatest hope. That far from being impossible, its individual components have already been brought separately into being. That schemes for the universal provision of health care, education and housing as human rights—which is to say, on a communistic basis—have already been developed in social-democratic countries and proven to work. That we've already begun to build, in places like Occupy and DSA, the systems of assembly democracy that will be both the means and the ends of our liberation. I would have told you this, banishing my doubts by chanting my convictions, and then in a fit of bravado I would have ended the essay with my favorite Orwell quote:

All the considerations that are likely to make one falter—the si-
ren voices of a Pétain or of a Gandhi, the inescapable fact that
in order to fight one has to degrade oneself, the equivocal moral
position of Britain, with its democratic phrases and its coolie
empire, the sinister development of Soviet Russia, the squalid
farce of left-wing politics—all this fades away and one sees only
the struggle of the gradually awakening common people against
the lords of property and their hired liars and bumsuckers. The
question is very simple. Shall people like that Italian soldier be
allowed to live the decent, fully human life which is now technically achievable, or shan't they? Shall the common man be
pushed back into the mud, or shall he not? I myself believe, perhaps on insufficient grounds, that the common man will win his
fight sooner or later, but I want it to be sooner and not later—
some time within the next hundred years, say, and not some time
within the next ten thousand years.

I might have tried to ironize it. "Perhaps on insufficient grounds" is
a subtle, devastating phrase. And one doubts we have anything like
ten years to waste, much less ten thousand. Or maybe I'd have let
the quote stand alone. Either way, that's what I would have told you.
And it would have been true. But it wouldn't have been honest. It's
what I believe. But it isn't all that matters.

It's true enough that the ideology I was raised in—the pretty
story where free markets and capitalist democracy, rugged individ-
ualists and innovative entrepreneurs, would lead us to the end of
history—no longer captivates as many as it once did. Nowadays it's
hard to find anyone under thirty who believes that story at all. (Some
might, in the manner of one losing their religion, continue to recite
the slogans out of habit—if only to reconvince themselves.) But that
hardly means we can be certain of a better future. Our movement,
after all, was formed from the ashes of failed socialisms. And for all
our renewed idealism we are also haunted by a sense of our own
belatedness—the suspicion that the time to act may have passed
us by. As fascist regimes march across a planet that more and more
seems to be dying, it's hard not to wonder: Have we come too late?

The sometimes-grating earnestness and fervor you may pick up in our voices is a result of the fact that, for us, the question is no abstraction. The grim world that is today being made, and not the hopeful one into which we were born, is the one where we will spend the rest of our lives.

That's why we socialists have tried to tell a new story, one that can preserve the things we value from this world—and help to create a new one. We've said: Only a socialism that internalizes the lessons of the twentieth century and puts pluralism front and center can win. We want a socialism where democracy permeates every aspect of our lives. We want this not because it would be a perfect world or even in all respects a nice one, but because collective participation in civic life and the extension of that participation into the economy on the basis of equality and human dignity are the only insurance of our individual and collective freedom—our only way of waging war against the dictatorships of today and those of tomorrow.

Maybe you think our story is dangerous or foolish; I can see why a serious person might. And you may say that plenty of people aren't calling for the heads of the ruling class, which is true for now. But it's not the point. People's life stories must, conceivably, take place within a greater story. And right now that means we're all responsible for choosing a story about what's gone wrong and how to fix it. This means that everything, for better or worse, is back on the table: socialisms, fascisms and forms of social life yet to be given names. I've only waited a few years for this reckoning to arrive. The world has waited much longer. And now that it has, let me be perfectly honest about it: I can hardly say I'm confident the collapse of the old order has proven to be a good thing at all, except perhaps insofar as it opens up a space for the possibility of a better world in our time. Yet only insofar, and no further.

Leaving Herland

UTOPIAN LITERATURE AND THE
FUTURE OF #METOO

by Nora Caplan-Bricker

ISSUE 16 | SPRING 2018

Imagine a world without men. Imagine it occurred as a natural experiment. Imagine, for example, a valley cupped by high mountains, accessible by only a single, narrow pass. Imagine that, thousands of years ago, the people of this valley found themselves at war when an unlucky tremor from a distant volcano sealed the pass shut with a shower of rocks. Most of the people who'd stayed back from battle died fighting among themselves in the weeks after the cataclysm, leaving only a small group of women behind to despair that without men there'd be no children, and without children, no future. This is a fantastical premise requiring a fantastical twist. So say the women's bodies adapted to the absence of mates. They became capable of asexual reproduction, previously the province of invertebrates and plants. From there, the society developed between the cliffs of its petri dish. That this could never happen is beside the point—the important question is: What would come next?

This is the setting for the 1915 novel *Herland*, by the first-wave feminist Charlotte Perkins Gilman, and what comes next in her book is utopia: women solving humanity's problems without men getting in the way. I loved this strange novel when I read it in college, though I couldn't say why. It's earnest, even dopey, and, inevitably, outdated. Yet I found myself thinking about it after the Harvey Weinstein revelations this fall, and during the reckoning that followed.

From the start, the #MeToo moment seemed to rest on a utopianism that no one had named. "Don't harass" is a simple demand, but envisioning a world without sexual harassment—without its many tendrils invading every corner of our lives—is not a simple act of imagination. Many women have suggested they came forward with #MeToo stories because they wanted to offer evidence that such a world is possible. "I speak up to contribute to the end of the conspiracy of silence," the actor, director and producer Lupita Nyong'o wrote. "Now that we are speaking, let us never shut up about this kind of thing." In an essay explaining why she started an anonymous spreadsheet to collect allegations against "Shitty Media Men," the writer Moira Donegan said, "We're being challenged to imagine how we would prefer things to be." The document was her imperfect, incendiary way of contributing to that project, an avenue for women to "wield the power we already have."

I'm embarrassed to say that when the first #MeToo stories broke, I didn't want to read them. This is not the reaction I would have expected from myself, a journalist who writes regularly about sexual violence and feminist politics, and a woman in my twenties who knows what it feels like to be called charming instead of promising, to see an editor's eyes wander toward the V in my shirt. Maybe I kept my distance out of discomfort: absorbing the endless accounts of assault and harassment could feel, as Josephine Livingstone wrote at the *New Republic*, like "being pelted with stones in the name of solidarity. Watch out—here comes another!"

But the individual stories were not the same as the stories in aggregate—and if they were stones, they were geodes, each one a uniquely beautiful map of a single person's emotional survival, each one sharp enough to cut. I remember listening to the actor Katherine Kendall describe being harassed by Harvey Weinstein, the first of the fall's stories I heard out loud. "He didn't actually touch me," she said, after detailing how he'd stripped naked toward the end of a business meeting and blocked her exit from his home, "so, you know, I wasn't sure if people would care." I was walking home from the corner store, shifting the milk from hand to hand when its cold bit my fingers, and I cried listening to her voice, which was thick with emotion but measured and calm. It was the voice of a woman who'd decided that people would care. She was proving true what she'd feared was impossible.

But even after I overcame my instinct for detachment, I remained wary of the movement's language, which was a language of binaries: *women* and *men*. I resisted the pressure I felt, from nowhere and everywhere, to think of myself at all times in terms of *womanhood*; to espouse a solidarity both too narrow and too broad; to foreground my gender, as if it were a paper cutout taped over my face. I shared the anxieties that the writer Heidi Julavits articulated in December, when she recounted misapprehending the news, hearing the names of women when the names of offending men were broadcast. She wrote, "Maybe my brain wanted to hear fake news to complicate a secret message that I could not help worrying other people might be hearing and believing: Men abuse power, and women do not. Men have overbearing sex drives they cannot control, and women do not."

Of course, most people are not consciously "hearing and believing" this message, though some are. A few weeks before, the writer Stephen Marche had argued in the *Times* Sunday Review that the problem "at the heart" of the abuse epidemic was "the often ugly and dangerous nature of the male libido." Marche urges men to do better, but his premise suggests that the space for improvement is limited. A few months later, in *New York* magazine, Andrew Sullivan complained that "in our increasingly heated debate about gender relations and the #MeToo movement," the reality of sex difference "is rarely discussed. It's almost become taboo." Both authors took a stab at defining what it is to be a man, while avoiding the even more inflammatory question of what it means to be a woman, how female biology translates to behavior. Not that their views on the matter felt like much of a mystery. Gender essentialism is a binary game: if you believe in a puzzle with only two pieces, you must imagine corresponding opposites, a perfect pair. If men are predators, women are prey; if men are "brutal," women are gentle; if men are bottomless with hunger, women are creatures of little appetite.

I was less worried about the positions of these well-known polemicists than I was about the attitudes of people close to me—and others like them everywhere—who seemed to develop a bad mental habit from our endless conversations about *the women* and *the men*. Let me acknowledge, right off the bat, that I will not be able to solve the question of nature vs. nurture to anyone's satisfaction, including my own. What I can say for sure is that when a male friend sent me Marche's piece with a glowing note about its contents, my throat closed up with anger as if I'd swallowed an allergen, and after a male relative told me that to deny some biological difference in how the sexes wield power was to treat all of human history as contaminated data, I sat at home with a void in my stomach. It made me sad, knowing these men might think I was a little less capable of something than they were, even if that something was terrible. Surely my loved ones felt themselves, their range of moral possibilities, to be definitionally human. Had they entertained the idea that mine were somehow less so? I believe most gendered behavior is socialized, and I also *want* to believe it. This faith feels inextricable from the central promise made to girls of my era: that we, like boys, could be whatever we wanted.

But I don't really know, because I, like you, don't have access to a controlled experiment—a country like the one Charlotte Perkins Gilman imagined, high in the mountains, where women wouldn't grow up as foils for men. The fantasy of such a place is an old one that had its heyday in the lesbian-separatist movements of the seventies and eighties, and also a regressive one that excludes people who are intersex, transgender, gender nonconforming and gender-queer. I'm not interested in inhabiting the binary dream of *Herland* any more than the versions of reality pronounced by Marche. But I've been wondering why our current revolutionary moment seems so tangled up in the language of binaries—wondering why I keep bumping up against its essentialism, as if the utopian hope of #MeToo were encased in an eggshell.

I started searching my past for the things that made me feel the way I felt this fall and winter: like the possibilities afforded my being were growing and shrinking at the same time. I found myself going back to feminist utopias—the fictional ones I'd read in books, and the closest thing to a real one I'd ever experienced, on a small farm hidden in the hills of New England, a tiny Herland for a handful of women. If this moment rested on a still-incomplete act of imagination, I wanted to learn what I could from the imagined-up worlds

I'd encountered years earlier—the ones that taught me to long for alternatives.

•

The mountain country of Charlotte Perkins Gilman's novel is a utopia because women created it, and, according to Gilman, women are better than men: more peace-loving, altruistic and eminently rational. The residents of Herland "had the evenest tempers, the most perfect patience and good nature—one of the things most impressive about them all was the absence of irritability," notes the narrator, Van, one of a trio of male explorers who stumble upon this strange land and stay to study its superior ways. The women have cultivated every grass, tree and creature for maximum usefulness; even their cats are as sweet and trainable as dogs, and though they still purr, they do not "sing." Van marvels, "the most salient quality in all their institutions was reasonableness." This would have gobsmacked readers of Gilman's era, who considered it common knowledge that women were weak, frivolous and prone to hysteria. "Women cannot cooperate—it's against nature," insists the chauvinist in Van's traveling party. He's quickly overruled by his less biased friends: "I tell you, women are the natural cooperators, not men!"

Gilman's vision of femininity comes with its own constraints, however. Motherhood is the society's dominant ethic, and childcare is the most sought-after job in the nation. If human beings have a few ways to touch immortality—children and art, as the saying goes—then the women of Herland have only one. After watching the women's plays, Van acknowledges that "the drama of the country was—to our taste—rather flat. You see, they lacked the sex motive"—sex is a foreign concept in Herland—"and, with it, jealousy. They had no interplay of warring nations, no aristocracy and its ambitions, no wealth and poverty opposition." The intellectual life of the country is equally anodyne. When Van tells one of his hosts that, back home, some Christians believe in the damnation of unbaptized infants, his interlocutor is undone by the thought and runs to a temple for guidance from a priestess. Later, she apologizes, "You see, we are not accustomed to horrible ideas. We haven't any." The women of Herland have little in the way of art, philosophy or ego—ego not only in the pejorative sense, but in the sense of having a self at all. This appears to be Gilman's intent. "This place is just like an enormous anthill," one of the men says with amazement. "You know an anthill is nothing but a nursery."

Gilman's vision of womanhood is not unfamiliar. In fact, it looks a lot like that of James Damore, the engineer whose infamous "Google memo" used evolutionary biology to explain why women have less success in Silicon Valley. Today's gender-essentialist paradigm, as summarized by Damore, assigns women more "feelings" and men more "ideas." Women are "more cooperative," more self-less, more nurturing. They choose children over art or accomplishment ("work-life balance"), while men "have a higher drive for status on average" and make a more dazzling range of things. In men's hands, power is an instrument that imprints the individual on the world. The nature of women's power, as imagined by Gilman, is to disperse for the good of the species, like a million ants scattering to find shareable crumbs.

And yet I see a luminous sense of possibility hovering around the text of *Herland*. Maybe this is partly because, when I read it at 21, I was having fun taking possession of femininity's trappings, trying on different roles, different boyfriends. The women in the novel were many things I wanted to be: playful, graceful, attractive to men without trying. And yet they weren't like me, because they took it for granted that "woman" was a category encompassing every adjective, not only the softer ones. By being close enough to aspire to and yet deeply strange, they opened a little bubble of freedom in my brain.

•

I learned about freedom in what I remember as my own brush with utopia. At twelve, thirteen and fourteen, my world on weekends was 132 acres of farmland that belonged to a woman I'll call Katherine. "I'm the king of my own hill," she used to say, and it was true. She reshaped the land to match her moods, leveling plains and drawing roads in her skid-steer, hunched over the joystick in the caged cab. She was a big woman, almost as tall as my dad, with broad shoulders and a body that looked soft but could heft almost anything—harvest a whole hayfield, stop a runaway horse or shove free a truck spun deep in the mud. There were delicate freckles on the soft skin around her eyes, a detail that struck me as inexplicably beautiful on a woman who wasted no time on her face.

Katherine bred Norwegian Fjord horses, dun-colored, prehistoric-looking creatures with stiff manes like a zebra's and dorsal stripes down their spines. She became the riding teacher of my best friend, who I'll call Abby, and because I went where Abby went, she became mine too. We were middle schoolers, almost-teenagers, who cantered around like horses during recess. In our real lives, we were sheltered, scheduled children of the middle class. We went to school, we went home, we went nowhere unsupervised. On the weekends, I went to synagogue and Abby went to her Polish grandfather's house to sit on his carpet and watch the Pope on TV.

We lived a different life on the farm. Katherine was happy to have us around. She and her partner, Anne, got bored keeping company with the dogs and ponies, and besides, our extra hands were useful. They lived in a two-room apartment over the barn with a view of the pastures and no indoor plumbing, and they gave us a room beneath it that we called the Cave, piled with boxes of their books and old coats, shrouded in smells both sour and sweet: wafts of coffee from upstairs, the nutty pungency of hay and manure, the musk of our bodies, the bright sting of cedar shavings. In the evenings, Abby and I ate soup cold from the can and stayed up late watching horse shows on tape.

Katherine's horses lived outside, and to feed them we stacked a truck bed with hay, grain and water, and trundled down a steep hill to the pasture. At twelve, Abby and I learned how to drive. As with everything Katherine taught us, Abby picked it up fast and I picked it up slowly. For weeks, I couldn't stop training my eyes just beyond the front bumper, which meant I couldn't drive straight but progressed by a tick-tack of course corrections that made everyone sick. I was afraid to soften my focus, which felt like relinquishing control. "Steer toward that hilltop," Katherine would say, gesturing at a misty peak miles away. "You have to pick a stable point. Look beyond where you're going." I was afraid if I listened I would go off the road. "Just do it," she said. "I promise it'll work." I listened, and it did. I came to love driving: the look of my skinny wrist folded over the steering wheel, my hand casually hanging, like a vision from the future, a glimpse of a woman who could go where she wanted.

Rereading it now, I find *Herland*'s vision of the future uninspiring, but it retains its power as a metaphor for a future we can't yet imagine. Gilman was a flawed figure—she was a strident eugenicist—but she was ahead of her time in knowing that much of what her contemporaries called "femininity" was, as her mouthpiece Van calls it, "reflected masculinity—developed to please us because they had to please us." For her, as for today's social constructionists, to imagine a world where women are free of this binary is to imagine a state of nature of sorts, a womanhood uncorroded by misogyny.

It's an odd but inescapable paradox that this state of nature prompts a search for what is *natural*—which is to say essential, biological, determined. Worse, this search is doomed to occur within the confines of the present. Even Gilman's radical imagination fed on her era's stale ideas in the effort to picture what no one can know: What happens after starting over? What selves will we find on the other side?

•

It would be easy to say that on the farm I became a different kind of girl. At home, I was my mother's perfect physical copy, so alert to her moods that there was no space between her wishes and my own. I brushed my pin-straight hair until it gleamed every morning; I pleased my teachers and brought home good grades. My only rebellion was to sneak a book under the covers at night.

In my other life, with Katherine, I was sweat-filmed and dirt-smudged. I once saw a girl kicked full in the face by a horse, and while Katherine called 911, I lured the loose animal back with a treat, catching his lead rope in my firm hand. I once held a colt's head while the vet came to castrate him. He leaned into me, sedated, and I braced him with my body as we both inhaled the metallic smell of his blood. I fell off more horses than I could count; one landed a glancing blow on my back as I rolled away, leaving a radiating, hoof-shaped bruise that I hid from my mother, first purple-black, then sky-in-a-thunderstorm yellow and green.

The farm was a world of Katherine's creation, and she wrote us girls into it as an odd couple. Abby was tall and loud. She loved the color orange, the jokes in *Borat* and the unusually large size of her own feet. I was small for my age, a prim perfectionist, and I don't know if I attached myself to Abby in spite of the way she embarrassed me, or because of it. Abby's gifts revealed themselves on horseback—her long limbs became elegant and her clowning smoothed into a preternatural calm—while I was stiff and cerebral in the saddle.

The balance between us tilted the other way in the evenings, when we would sprawl on the braided rug in Katherine and Anne's bedroom, slurping Swiss Miss and correcting Abby's English papers. Katherine would chide Abby to focus, just as, in the afternoon's lesson, she'd scolded me for thinking too hard. I loved my friend, but I started to live for the moments when I had an edge on her—when Katherine seemed to want her to be more like me. Katherine was the first person outside my family to tell me I was pretty, would someday be beautiful. She praised my habit of guessing what Abby was saying and jumping in ahead of her, finishing her sentences. "You two are so close, and you're so quick, Nora, that you're better at figuring out what Abby means than she is." I became Abby's tutor, and Abby became the demonstration, during riding lessons, of everything I couldn't do. We appealed to Katherine's imagination as opposites who not only attracted but completed each other. *From each according to her ability, to each according to her needs.*

It's hard for me to explain now what went wrong on the farm. I would like it to be clear that I loved Katherine. I loved her devotion to unwanted animals—a pack of stray dogs from a storm-ravaged island; a horse that held its head out of reach, expecting to be hit—

and the way she trusted us to help in their rehabilitation. Driving to competitions in her battered truck, I loved the yellow light of wayside gas stations—places coughed out of someone else's rugged life—and the view through the window of a nighttime hour I'd never otherwise have seen. She interpreted people as scholars do books, and I fed off the narrative energy of her world, even if I sometimes chafed against the stories she told about me. At first, I liked being written into our small society as Abby's opposite; it made me essential to a person I loved. Maybe it was eagerness to find the ways we fit together that brought me to compare us until my sense of self narrowed to that sole competition—a tick, an obsession, a bad mental groove.

I began to feel like the negative of Abby's image, someone who made no sense without her—and I resented it. I started teasing her for not knowing state capitals, the spelling of "necessary," the point of the story of Adam and Eve. Her schoolwork got worse, and so did my riding. I fell off horses over and over. I fell because I believed I would fall. Before I even lost my balance, I felt the whoosh of the ground rushing toward me.

Eventually, Katherine called me into her upstairs apartment to tell me I was being demoted, taken off the horse I'd been riding and moved to an older, more placid mare. I sat on her couch, under a quilt that smelled of dog and sent up eddies of golden dust. Probably her decision was warranted—as I remember it, I was truly getting worse—but that didn't soothe me. Katherine seemed offended by my tears. "This is part of how I'm going to make you better," she said. "If you don't trust my methods, it's not going to work." Before, she could have convinced me this was a step forward, not backward, on the right and only track. But I found that I suddenly didn't believe her, especially when she told me my disappointment, too, was for my own good: "I need to toughen you up, and I will." On the farm, Katherine had created a world where girls could claim the usual province of boys: could be pain-hardened, dirty and brave. But her world still split my field of vision into two parts, the qualities that were Abby's and the ones that were mine. Hers included toughness, and therefore I was weak. The farm reshuffled the rules of who got to be what without dispelling a feeling I had gotten used to in girlhood: the recognition of a possibility in the same moment I saw that it was lost to me.

•

More than fifty years after Gilman wrote *Herland*, the radical feminist Shulamith Firestone published one of the mother texts of second-wave utopianism, the *Dialectic of Sex*, which is not a novel but a Marxist "case for feminist revolution" with a heavy flavor of science fiction. Writing in 1970, Firestone argued that the oppression of women was rooted in a "biological reality: men and women were created different, and not equally privileged."

> Women throughout history before the advent of birth control were at the continual mercy of their biology—menstruation, menopause, and "female ills," constant painful childbirth, wet-nursing and care of infants, all of which made them dependent on males (whether brother, father, husband, lover, or clan, government, community-at-large) for physical survival.

Firestone thinks our differences are natural, but that doesn't mean she thinks they're indelible, or a necessary limitation on what we can be. "We are no longer just animals," she writes. "The 'natural' is not necessarily a 'human' value." She hoped she stood on the cusp of a future where technology would obviate the tyranny of biology. Pregnancy and childbirth, "the original division of labor," could soon be eradicated. She imagined a generation of test-tube babies, children "born to both sexes equally, or independently of either." In this future, Firestone insisted, there must be no men and no women: "genital differences between human beings would no longer matter culturally."

Firestone accepts the Marxist notion that it's impossible to imagine an equal future from the subordinated position of the present. She resists the idea that offering a "blueprint" for the future is part of the revolutionary's task at all: "Any specific direction must arise organically out of the revolutionary action itself." And yet, she says, "I feel tempted here to make some 'dangerously utopian' concrete proposals," because "there are no precedents in history for feminist revolution." We need a literary image of the future, she suggests, not as a destination but as an inoculation against cowardice, so that we can make the leap into the unknown.

It remains as utopian as ever to imagine a world where sex confers no cultural power. But other sections of Firestone's *Dialectic* were far less clear-sighted, especially her ill-conceived argument that "racism is sexism extended," and that racism and classism were merely incidental to sexism. These views shaped a simplistic dream of feminism's way forward—one that has left an enduring mark on the movement. Around the time Firestone wrote the *Dialectic*, she co-founded the radical group Redstockings, which vowed in its 1969 "Manifesto" to "repudiate all economic, racial, educational or status privileges that divide us from other women." As the historian Robin D. G. Kelley wrote in his book *Freedom Dreams*, "Although the 'Manifesto' acknowledged differences between women, it treated these differences as impediments to overcome"—as distractions from the true cause rather than truths to be reckoned with.

The shortcomings of second-wavers is territory so well-trod as to be tiresome—even if, half a century later, self-awareness hasn't stamped out the temptation to see our struggles in the simplest terms possible: men vs. women, monolith vs. monolith. Over a decade before the word "intersectionality" was coined, a trio of black radical feminists and lesbians, members of the Boston-based Combahee River Collective (named for a river in South Carolina where Harriet Tubman became the first woman to lead an American military campaign in an operation that emancipated more than seven hundred slaves during the Civil War), not only criticized the movement's disregard for poor women and women of color, but also traced a direct line from the binary thinking of radical feminists and lesbian separatists to a biological essentialism that could easily backfire. "We have a great deal of criticism and loathing for what men have been socialized to be in this society: what they support, how they act, and how they oppress," Barbara Smith, Beverly Smith and Demita Frazier wrote in a statement on behalf of their collective. "But we do not have the misguided notion that it is their maleness, per se—i.e. their biological maleness—that makes them what they are." The statement warned: "As Black women we find any type of biological determinism a particularly dangerous and reactionary basis upon which to build a politic."

The Combahee River Collective Statement doesn't offer a utopian "blueprint," but it contains a utopian energy. Elucidating the overlapping sources of their oppression—the way their concerns as black women were ignored by black men in the fight against racism, and by white women in the fight against sexism—the authors assert: "We might use our position at the bottom, however, to make a clear leap into revolutionary action. If Black women were free, it would mean that everyone else would have to be free since our freedom would necessitate the destruction of all the systems of oppression." The subjunctive contains the act of imagining the world it wants, as a seed contains the makings of a bud.

•

Utopia is best like this—as a wish, a metaphor, a tiny bubble of freedom, not a blueprint that locks some out and others in. Consider Monique Wittig's novel *Les Guérillères* (1969), which succeeds by immersing us in its slippery strangeness. Wittig largely eliminated male pronouns (*il–ils*) from her book and eschewed the hegemony of linear structure, instead stitching together fragmented scenes of ritual, myth and enigmatic violence. When the book begins, the overthrow of the old world is already far in the past—so far back that the inhabitants of this new society no longer remember it.

A new order has been built on a new religion—one that exalts the female body. Women have no concept of shame. They expose their genitals to the sun: "They say that they retain its brilliance." They worship "the O, the zero or the circle, the vulval ring." Farewell to the semiotic sovereignty of the phallus: they reread every fragment of history through their new mythology, finding their holy circle in King Arthur's Round Table, a symbolic clitoris in Sleeping Beauty's spindle. They laugh at the art of our classical period, comparing a painting of a girl with demurely concealed genitals to a "knife without a blade that lacks a handle." They laugh all the time; they are profoundly irreverent.

But Wittig's endgame is not the veneration of women's bodies. Like Firestone, she wants a world where sex difference ceases to have cultural significance; unlike Firestone, she rejects the idea that sex was ever a real or natural category. In her book of essays *The Straight Mind*, published in 1992, she argues that "man" and "woman" are "political and economic categories, not eternal ones. . . . Once the class 'men' disappears, 'women' as a class will disappear as well, for there are no slaves without masters." In an earlier book, *Lesbian Peoples: Material for a Dictionary* (1979), Wittig and her co-author, Sande Zeig, imagine a future where the word "woman" is an obsolete term, defined as a noun whose meaning was "one who belongs to another." Wittig, herself a radical lesbian, controversially proclaimed that "lesbians are not women," and it is possible to read *Les Guérillères* as a lesbian-separatist statement. In the most widely circulated English translation of the novel (from which I quote in this essay), translator David Le Vay refers to the inhabitants of this future as "the women" (*elles*). But "the people" would have been a translation closer to Wittig's intent. She hoped, as she later wrote, that "this *elles* could situate the reader in a space beyond the categories of sex for the duration of the book."

The novel was intended to elevate the female plural pronoun to the universal usage of its male counterpart. (In French, a group of women is feminine, *elles*, but a group of women with a single man in it adopts the masculine *ils*.) Wittig believed in the power of language to commit "a plastic action upon the real," as she wrote in another essay. *Les Guérillères* attacks the presumption that the male perspective is universal, capable of encompassing everything, while the female is subsidiary, *non-male*, grammatically limited—lesser from the moment it comes into existence.

Wittig neither excludes nor accounts for the presence of trans and gender nonconforming people in her utopia. To contemporary readers who live in a world of diverse gender identity and expression,

the idea that everyone must manifest an identical androgyny—
"a mutual cancellation," as Firestone writes in the *Dialectic*, "a
matter-antimatter explosion"—sounds like just another form of tyranny. But the experimental form of *Les Guérillères* leaves room for
the progress made by future generations. In one scene, set during
the bloody revolution, a young man joins the women and they arm
him with a rifle. Elsewhere, the reader glimpses men in the wom-
en's army who have grown their hair long and adopted androgynous
dress. It's possible to read this not as a world without men, or a
world without gender, but as one in which those identities no longer constitute political classes. Under loose garments, *elles* could be
anybody. The novel's omniscient, incantatory voice allows for this
interpretation, as does its inclusive, repurposed pronoun.

What appeals to me most about Wittig's novel, rereading it in the
#MeToo era, is that it takes the people in her future many years—she
suggests generations—to shed the last traces of our binary world. In
the beginning, they make an iconography of their anatomy because
they need these symbols "to demonstrate their strength," most of
all to themselves. They need something to believe in: a better world,
dormant, suspended in their beings, their bodies. They are just like
the women I know who drift off wistfully, *"If I had a woman boss . . ."*
"If we had a woman president . . ." These are not serious, or sufficient,
suggestions, just as Wittig does not solemnly see vagina-worship as
the key to revolution. But there's some truth to the idea that we can
only imagine ourselves into the future by harvesting some detritus
from our present. To build a spaceship, we hammer together what
earthly materials we have—even if this means weighing ourselves
down, bringing what we should have left behind.

Slowly, very slowly, the inhabitants of Wittig's world realize that
"they do not want to become prisoners of their own ideology." They
come to see a danger in defining themselves by their bodies, taking
a part for the whole, reading too much into biological accidents:

They say that at the point they have reached they must examine
the principle that has guided them. They say it is not for them to
exhaust their strength in symbols. They say henceforward what

they are is not subject to compromise. They say they must now stop exalting the vulva. They say that they must break the last bond that binds them to a dead culture. They say that any symbol that exalts the fragmented body is transient, must disappear.

Utopia becomes dystopia when people become prisoners of their own ideology. Feminist utopia becomes dystopia when its heroines become prisoners of their self-definitions. Stillness, ossification, suffocation. But for Wittig, utopia is less a static destination than a method of forward motion. The society in *Les Guérillères* has no fixed values except that of iconoclasm. When the people decide to do away with circle runes and holy vulvas, they heap the books of the canon they've worked so hard to reinterpret—they call them "feminaries"—in the town squares and burn them. In their place they put a "great register" that is forever unfinished.

The revolutionaries who broke from the old world in *Les Guérillères* never could have imagined how their successors would eventually leave them behind. Or maybe they could—maybe that's why they taught their children to laugh, especially at whatever professes to be serious. The laughter makes the novel generous. *Les Guérillères* is a vision of having more than one shot; of surviving our errors because we're prepared to burn the feminaries as many times as it takes; of accepting that whatever new world we make will limit us and liberate us, both at the same time. It offers permission to learn the wrong lesson from the revolution.

•

Katherine was big on imagining the future—her own, and also Abby's and mine. She decided she would breed one of her mares and produce a foal that Abby would someday ride in the Olympics. Even at thirteen, I suspected there was nothing about the animal in question to suggest her offspring would be fit for the task, but Katherine was at her most generous during these sessions of dreaming. Benevolence blurred her at the edges, as if she were stretching in the direction of what she described, as if her vision might absorb us bodily.

In the future, Abby would be an Olympian, and I would be a famous writer who chronicled Abby's amazing exploits. In the future, we would have our own hilltop, a short ride through the forest from Katherine's. In the future, I would be a woman who lived a wild life on a farm, far from the rules of my coddled childhood. In the future, I would be beautiful. In the future, I would not be weak. In the future, I would not cry. And yet, in the future as Katherine imagined it, I would be stuck in this same binary, playing second fiddle to my best friend, a platonic, early-adolescent image of a wife.

Katherine wasn't there for one of the last weekends I spent on her farm. She and Anne were traveling, leaving a friend to watch their horses and dogs. It was bitter cold, and the friend barely ventured out of doors all weekend, meaning Abby and I were entirely free. We rode bareback, pressing our legs against the animals for warmth. We blasted music from the truck as we circled the pastures, stopping at every bucket of water, hammering the frozen surfaces with rocks and our boot heels to crack the ice.

Then it snowed. The clench hold of cold loosened its grip a couple degrees. Glittering flakes covered horse shit and dog shit and the snaking scars of tire tracks on fields and roads. Abby and I climbed to the top of the hill and looked down on the pond behind the barn, a blind gray eye shutting slowly under snow. We reasoned it must be frozen solid. We decided to find out. I'm sure I was terrified of falling through, and I'm sure I looked at my friend, snow collecting in the whorls of hair by her face, and wondered if she was frightened too. We agreed to take the first step in unison, so neither one of us would be more the hero. We marched clear across to the other side, leaving two perfect pairs of tracks.

Leaving Katherine's for good proved less climactic. Katherine had entered a group of us into a drill-team competition. On the day of the show, I fell, for no reason. The horse I was riding was trotting around a corner when I simply slipped off. My parents were there, so Katherine pretended not to be furious. Afterward, I thought I would let things blow over. Then I thought, *Just a little longer*. Then I thought, *Maybe I don't have to go back*.

I've been thinking about Katherine since the start of #MeToo—

and about Abby, who I saw less and less after I stopped riding horses, drifting apart until we lost touch. Mostly, I've been feeling grateful. In many ways, I've become the person I would have been in a world where I never found her farm. A small woman with a small voice, as fastidious about typos as I am about shirt stains; a writer who sits in a small apartment all day, nudging words back and forth on a page. But I also feel, dormant in my body, the unlikely awareness of what I can still do, even if I haven't done it in years. Mend a broken leather bridle. Clean a deep cut on a horse's leg. Calm a thousand-pound animal with the steady pressure of my palm.

I'm grateful to have touched these possibilities, to have fallen under the thrall of a woman unafraid of her own power, even or especially because she wielded it recklessly. Her last lesson to me, the lesson in leaving, was one more invaluable gift. Utopia starts with starting over, and so we must, over and over again.

It's All Just Beginning

by Justin E. H. Smith

ONLINE | SPRING 2020

Though mild, I have what I am fairly sure are the symptoms of coronavirus. Three weeks ago I was in extended and close contact with someone who has since tested positive. When I learned this, I spent some time trying to figure out how to get tested myself, but now the last thing I want to do is to go stand in a line in front of a Brooklyn hospital along with others who also have symptoms. My wife and I have not been outside our apartment for close to two weeks. We have opened the door just three times since then, to receive groceries that had been left for us by an unseen deliveryman, as per our instructions, on the other side. We read of others going on walks, but that seems like a selfish extravagance when you have a dry cough and a sore throat. This is the smallest apartment I've ever lived in. I am noticing features of it, and of the trees, the sky and the light outside our windows, that escaped my attention—shamefully, it now seems—over the first several months since we arrived here in August. I know when we finally get out I will be like the protagonist of Halldór Laxness's stunning novel, *World Light*, who, after years of bedridden illness, weeps when he bids farewell to all the knots and grooves in the wood beams of his attic ceiling.

I am not at all certain that my university in Paris will be open for business when it comes time to reinstitute my salary in June, which I had voluntarily suspended in order to take a year-long fellowship in New York. I am not at all sure that a few months from now the world is going to be the sort of place where a citizen of one country can expect to resume his public function in another country's education system. I am not at all sure universities are going to be the sort of place where one can, again, get together with others in a room and deign to speak with them of what is beautiful and true. Meanwhile, my mother is in cancer treatment in California, and I fear I may never see her again. Until a few days ago my sister, a glacial marine geoscientist, was stuck in unexpectedly thick ice, on an icebreaker too small to break it, in the ocean somewhere off the coast of Antarctica; now her international crew is floating again, uncertain how they will get back to the Northern Hemisphere in a world of quarantines, closed borders and canceled flights, but still just happy to be back on the open sea. My wife is here with me on a tourist visa that will soon expire. We do not know what things will be like in New York when that happens, or whether there might be an exemption for foreigners who overstay their visas only because they are unable to leave what might by then be a fully locked-down city. She has an elderly grandmother in Europe. Should she leave now to be with her, while she still can and while her papers are still valid? What would become of me, if she were to go?

These are some of the questions we find ourselves asking right now. They are not exceptional, among the billions of small tragedies this pandemic has churned up. But they are mine. I have often wondered what life would be like for the survivors of a nuclear war, and in these fleeting recollections of the old world—there used to be Starbucks and barber shops, there used to be a subway I'd get on to go to the library, there used to be *embrassades*—I feel like I am gaining a small glimpse of that.

I find that I am generally at peace, and that the balance between happiness and sadness on any given day is little different from what it always has been for me. I find that there is liberation in this suspension of more or less everything. In spite of it all, we are free now. Any fashion, sensibility, ideology, set of priorities, worldview or hobby that you acquired prior to March 2020, and that may have by then started to seem to you cumbersome, dull, inauthentic, a drag: you are no longer beholden to it. You can cast it off entirely and no one will care; likely, no one will notice. Were you doing something out of mere habit, conceiving your life in a way that seemed false to you? You can stop doing that now. We have little idea what the world is going to look like when we get through to the other side of this, but it is already perfectly clear that the "discourses" of our society, such as they had developed up to about March 8 or 9, 2020, in all their frivolity and distractiousness, have been decisively curtailed, like the CO_2 emissions from the closed factories and the vacated highways.

Not to downplay the current tragedy—as I've already acknowledged, it is already affecting me personally in deep and real ways—but I take it that this interruption is a good thing.

The interruption is not total, of course. Normies seem particularly fond of toilet-paper joke memes for the moment, while the extremely online instinctively disdain them. Both the normies and the extremely online are, as they have been since 2016, far too reliant on the language of "apocalypse" and "end times." These are not the end times; even a nuclear war would not be the end times for all the creatures on earth, among which there will always be at least some extremophiles to relish any new arrangement of the ecosystem. What this is, rather, is a critical shift in the way we think about the human, the natural and the overlap between these.

Indeed, if I can offer anything to the world to come, it may be in helping to discern early on the possible forms of a renegotiated pact with nature. From here on out, I take it that we must not, and cannot, ever pretend again that we are alone on this planet. Between 1918 and 2020, we learned so much about what viruses are and how they reproduce and spread, but as to what I might dare to call our metaphysics of viruses, and of ourselves in relation to them, everything we have thought remains as false and inadequate now as it was then.

In our ignorance of nature, we are ill-positioned to consider with suitable wonder how strange it is that human history can still be transformed overnight not just by viruses or bacteria but by the most rare of midsize mammals. In a world in which domestic livestock vastly outweigh all animal wildlife combined—that is, if you put all the cattle on one side of a scale, and all the elephants, wolverines, pangolins and so on on the other, it would be like weighing a boulder against a pea—it is remarkable indeed that such "exotic" species as bats, civets, chimpanzees and pangolins should continue to play such an outsize role in public health, and thus in human history. In the *Politics* Aristotle describes human relations with other animal species, including hunting, as a variety of war. By the time of Greek antiquity, in contrast with, say, the Paleolithic, it could easily have seemed that this war was more or less won. But in truth what we did was totally dominate a few varieties of animals, while still remaining open to mercenary attacks, as it were, using biological agents, from the few that still remain free.

The pangolin cult of the Congolese Lele people, as described by the great social anthropologist Mary Douglas, both celebrates and fears the taxonomic peculiarities of this animal, which has scales, but gives live birth, and, like human beings, births only one offspring at a time. Do they kill it and eat it? Yes, they kill it and eat it, but they know that in so doing they are knocking the cosmos out of joint, and the only way to bring it back into joint is through a fair amount of ritual catharsis. Walter Burkert points out that in ancient Greece there was no meat sold in the public market that was not ritually sacrificed: a recognition that to spill an animal's blood is a violent and transgressive thing, and even if we must do it, we must not allow it to become profane, banal, unexceptional. Such a view lives on vestigially in the halal and kosher rules of slaughter of familiar Abrahamic faiths, but for the most part the metaphysics of meat, like the metaphysics of viruses, remains the same as it was in 1918 and indeed for some centuries before: exotic or domestic, endangered or commonplace, an animal's meat is ours to be eaten, for we are the lords of this planet. I am not saying the current pandemic is retribution for our sin, but I will say that the Lele understood something about the pangolin that we have not, and that we are paying dearly for now: that it cannot be lightly killed for no better reason than our own delectation. That era—the era of wanton delectation—is over now, I hope, for those who had been taken in by the reckless culinary adventurism of an Anthony Bourdain as much as for the customers of the wet markets of Wuhan.

What else is over? I had been saying that we can all just stop doing whatever we were doing before that may have come to ring false
to us, and that that is liberating. In my own case, I was working on a
book (one that developed, curiously, out of an essay of mine, entitled
"It's All Over," a little over a year ago) that was going to articulate how
the internet is destroying the fabric of human community. But for
the life of me I cannot, in the present circumstances, see the internet
as anything other than the force that is holding that fabric together.
I used to bemoan virtue signaling. I look at the newly assembled vanguard of the all-volunteer forces of "Wash Your Hands" Twitter, and
though I can still discern that tone that used to get me so bent out
of shape ("Listen up y'all, today I'm going to break down the virus's
lipid envelope for you"), now I just smile and think: "Good for them.
Good for Dr. Brianna Ph.D., and all her loyal followers."

So I'm going have to rethink that particular book project. But
that follows from the much more general point that we are all going to have to rethink everything. One thing that is certain is that
you are now free to put down whatever cool theorist your peers once
convinced you you had to read. None of that discourse is any more
germane to thinking about the present situation than, say, Robert
Burton, or Galen, or St. Theresa of Ávila. Read whatever you want to
read now, and don't be distracted by those writers who are so set in
their ways that they know no other strategy than to recover formulae
devised back in the old world, and to retry them in the new one, like
stubborn Norsemen struggling to graze cattle in Greenland, when
the world they find themselves in demands they learn to hunt seals.
Thus Slavoj Žižek is now blogging for RT, the Russian state propaganda network, about how the virus puts him in mind of Taran-
tino films, while Giorgio Agamben is pushing a species of Trumpian
doubt-mongering by claiming that the "disproportionate reaction"
to the pandemic is nothing more than an assertion of authoritarian
biopolitics. Honestly, at this point whoever's left of the vanguard of
continental philosophy should probably just start hawking men's
vitamin supplements on late-nite TV.

These are not the end times, I mean, but nor are they business
as usual, and we would do well to understand that not only is there

room for a middle path between these, but indeed there is an absolute necessity that we begin our voyage down that path. To the squealing chiliasts and self-absorbed presentists, indulging themselves with phrases like "the end of the world," I say: "Did it never dawn on you that all of human history has just been one partial apocalypse after another?" And to the business-as-usual mandarins I say: "Thank you for your service in the glorious battles of the past."

Contributors

MELINA ABDULLAH is professor of Pan-African studies at California State University, Los Angeles. She was among the original group of organizers who convened to form Black Lives Matter and continues to serve as a Los Angeles chapter leader and as a member of the national leadership core. Melina is a single mama of three school-age children.

PETER C. BAKER lives in Evanston, Illinois. He is finishing a novel—set in North Carolina and Italy—about daily life in the shadow of torture.

JON BASKIN is a founding editor of *The Point*.

ANASTASIA BERG is an editor of *The Point*. She is an assistant professor in the department of philosophy at the Hebrew University of Jerusalem.

LAUREN BERLANT is the George M. Pullman Distinguished Service Professor of English at the University of Chicago. Her recent books include *The Hundreds*, with the anthropologist Kathleen Stewart (Duke University Press 2019), a book of theoretical poems generated by encounters with and atmospheres of the ordinary, and *Cruel Optimism* (Duke University Press 2011), which addresses precarious publics and the aesthetics of affective adjustment in the contemporary U.S.

NORA CAPLAN-BRICKER is a journalist and essayist whose work also appears in the *New Yorker*, *Harper's* and *Ploughshares*. She lives in Boston.

JOHN MICHAEL COLÓN is a writer of essays, poetry and journalism based in Brooklyn.

JAMES DUESTERBERG is a writer and editor in New York City. He is working on a book about the avant-garde, cybernetics and the political imagination.

JACOB HAMBURGER is a writer and coeditor of *Tocqueville 21*, a Franco-American blog on contemporary democracy.

BEN JEFFERY is a Ph.D. candidate in the Committee on Social Thought at the University of Chicago and a contributing editor of *The Point*. He is the author of *Anti-Matter: Michel Houellebecq and Depressive Realism* (Zero Books 2011). He is currently working on a dissertation about Shakespeare.

URSULA LINDSEY is a writer and reporter who covered the Arab Spring from Cairo. She now lives in Amman, Jordan. She cohosts the *BULAQ* podcast.

KATHRYN LOFTON is professor of religious studies, American studies, history and divinity at Yale University. A historian of religions, she is the author of two books, *Oprah: The Gospel of an Icon* (University of California Press 2011) and *Consuming Religion* (University of Chicago Press 2017), and one coedited (with Laurie Maffly-Kipp) collection, *Women's Work: An Anthology of African-American Women's Historical Writings* (Oxford University Press 2010).

DANIEL LUBAN is a research fellow in politics at the University of Oxford.

BEA MALSKY is a coder, zinemonger and occasional writer based in Chicago. She is a developer at DataMade and the co-owner of

Build Coffee, where she stocks the bookshelves and runs the artist-in-residence program.

JESSE MCCARTHY is assistant professor of English and of African and African American studies at Harvard University and an editor of *The Point*. His writing has also appeared in magazines and journals such as *n+1*, the *Nation*, *Dissent* and the *New York Times Book Review*.

MEGHAN O'GIEBLYN is the author of the essay collection *Interior States* (Anchor 2018), which won the 2018 Believer Book Award for nonfiction. Her essays have received three Pushcart Prizes and have appeared in *Harper's*, the *New Yorker*, *The Point*, *n+1*, the *Believer*, *Bookforum*, the *Guardian*, the *New York Times* and *The Best American Essays 2017*.

JUSTIN E. H. SMITH is professor of history and philosophy of science at the University of Paris. He is the author of *Irrationality: A History of the Dark Side of Reason* (2019), *The Philosopher: A History in Six Types* (2016), *Nature, Human Nature, and Human Difference: Race in Early Modern Philosophy* (2015) and *Divine Machines: Leibniz and the Sciences of Life* (2011), all published by Princeton University Press.

BRANDON M. TERRY is assistant professor of African and African American studies and of social studies at Harvard University. He is the coeditor of *To Shape a New World: Essays on the Political Philosophy of Martin Luther King, Jr.* (Harvard University Press 2018) and *Fifty Years since MLK* (Boston Review and MIT Press 2018), and he is currently completing a book titled *The Tragic Vision of the Civil Rights Movement*.

JONNY THAKKAR is assistant professor of political science at Swarthmore College and one of the founding editors of *The Point*. He is the author of *Plato as Critical Theorist* (Harvard University Press 2018).

RACHEL WISEMAN is the managing editor of *The Point*.

ETAY ZWICK is a founding editor of *The Point*.

Acknowledgments

This book, like *The Point*, has always been a collective endeavor, and it is the result of many people working and thinking together.

Our project would not have been possible without our teachers at the Committee on Social Thought at the University of Chicago, where *The Point* got its start. We'd especially like to express our gratitude to Robert Pippin, Jonathan Lear, David Wellbery, Irad Kimhi, Rosanna Warren and Lorraine Daston for their mentorship and support.

We'd like to thank Kyle Wagner and Dylan Montanari from the University of Chicago Press for taking a chance on this book and their thoughtful, steady guidance at every stage, Adriana Smith for her careful editing of the manuscript and Adrienne Meyers for working with us to ensure it reaches an audience. We're also indebted to Bria Sandford and Alex Star for their early enthusiasm for this collection, and for helping us give shape and coherence to the project when it was little more than an idea.

We would like to give special thanks to Helen Zell for believing in *The Point* and for championing our little magazine and allowing it to flourish. And also to Judy Wise—for supporting and boosting *The Point* in countless ways, not least by allowing her basement to serve as our unofficial warehouse for our first five years.

Most of all, this collection never would have existed without so many of our writers and editors over the years—some of whom have had essays anthologized here, as well as many others who have not. Thank you for putting in the work to make such lasting contributions to the magazine and for always keeping your minds open.